Writing for Publication:
A Practical Guide for Educators

Writing for Publication:
A Practical Guide for Educators

Mary Renck Jalongo

Christopher-Gordon Publishers, Inc.
Norwood, Massachusetts

CREDITS

❦

Every effort has been made to contact copyright holders for permission to reproduce borrowed material when necessary. We apologize for any oversights and would be happy to rectify them in future printings.

Evaluation Criteria for Narratives used with permission of The Learning Communities Network, Inc., Cleveland, Ohio. Reprinted with permission.

On Behalf of Children "How I Learned to Appreciate Opera" by Mary Renck Jalongo from *Early Childhood Education Journal*, 24 (4), 211-212. Reprinted with permission of the Human Sciences Press.

Creating A Caring Community in Classrooms: Advice From an Intervention Specialist by Charlotte Krall and Mary Renck Jalongo, used with permission of the authors.

Writer's Block and Writing and the Care of the Soul written especially for this publication and published with permission of the author Patricia Crawford.

Christopher-Gordon Publishers, Inc.
1502 Providence Highway, Suite #12
Norwood, Massachusetts 02062
800-934-8322
781-762-5577

Printed in the United States of America
10 9 8 7 6 5 4 3 2 1   07 06 05 04 03 02

ISBN: 1-929024-39-8
Library of Congress Catalogue Number: 2001093758

Acknowledgments

———————————— ❧ ————————————

In writing this book, I was fortunate to have four tough, yet fair, readers—Kathleen Rowlands, Kelly Chandler-Olcott, Dr. Sandra Fehr, and Janet McCraveen—who recommended revisions, yet offered words of encouragement.

Some of the comments that challenged me and fortified me to revisit the manuscript were:

- "Do one more ruthless edit."

- "I wish I could have a writing conference with her sometime!"

- "If authors would follow this advice, my work as a volunteer reviewer would be much easier!"

- "The voice is warm and wise."

Improvements to the manuscript are largely the result of their nudgings, while any failings in the book are my responsibility.

I first became familiar with Sue Canavan as an editor when I used a book to which she had contributed a chapter on book publishing. Her forbearance after I had failed, not once but twice, to deliver the manuscript by the deadline due to a series of personal tragedies will forever be appreciated. Although I had begun to despair of ever finishing this book after my father died, her gentle voice and patient understanding bolstered me as I struggled to complete the work.

My in-house editor and husband Frank also deserves recognition and gratitude, for he is the one who will wade through the chapters before they are submitted and poke holes in the logic before someone else does.

Finally, but not least, are my former students. First, the two former students who agreed to publish their work in the book—Charlotte Krall, who bravely permitted a revised draft to be published, and Trish Crawford, who contributed her perspective on the struggles of academic authors. And second, the hundreds of students whose manuscripts I have scribbled on over the years while trying to help them find their voices as writers. In the process of giving all that feedback I began to understand what different writers need and started to think that I just might have something to say about how to publish nonfiction.

DEDICATION

———————— ❧ ————————

For those who have done the most to make me believe I could write, beginning in early childhood. First, my family who modeled the ways of the storyteller and valued them in me; next, my kindergarten teacher, Ms. Klingensmith, who delighted in my drawings and stories; then my 7th-grade teacher, Mrs. Humphreys, who read my essay on democracy aloud to the class. Much later, during my doctoral studies, Dr. James R. Johnson who read, reread, and requested revisions until I balked (but managed to get published). And, later still, as a faculty member, four editors who generously coached me in the ways of publishing: Janet Brown McCracken (who, I was delighted to discover, was a reviewer for this book), Lucy Prete Martin, Ann Davis, and Linda James.

Short Table of Contents

———————— ❧ ————————

Table of Contents

Introduction

❦

My initial experiences with writing and scholarly pursuits did not portend well for the future. I was in 7th grade and had the assignment of writing a research report on Jupiter. Like many other junior high school students throughout history, I had waited until the last minute, panicked, and had just about decided to copy down the encyclopedia entry verbatim before my mother intervened and encouraged me to at least paraphrase the material while she typed. The most vivid memory from that experience was the churning sensation in my stomach as I attempted to generate the requisite number of pages; it is vividly recalled because it still happens when the writing is not going well. I deliberately defaced the book by engraving several pencil marks on the page when I could not understand the turgid prose of the scholar who wrote the article for *Encyclopedia Americana*. Ironically, I am now an author/editor for *World Book Encyclopedia*. I like to think of it as paying back a debt for my thinly-veiled plagiarism back in junior high school.

If you are like me, when you pick up a book on writing for publication, your first question has to do with the qualifications of the writer. "What right does this person have to offer advice?" you legitimately ask. When daring to offer advice to nonfiction authors, there are three relevant qualifications: a) extensive experience with the particular type of writing under discussion (in this case, nonfiction written for audiences of fellow professionals), b) in-depth work with novices who seek to write and publish, and c) an understanding of effective teaching and principles of adult development.

Specificity matters. There are literally thousands of books written about writing but few of them have much to do with the writing of full-time professionals who write about matters of importance and interest to their field or related fields, such as the school counselor who writes for other school counselors or for teachers and administrators.

Working closely with aspiring, struggling, and accomplished authors is another important qualification. When I read what has been published about writing, it seems that some authors are show-offs who prefer to frighten other potential authors away. I believe that the effectiveness of our fields is diminished when the same, tired voices do all of the talking and practitioners are silenced. That is why I undertook the Jossey-Bass book *Teachers' Stories: From Personal Narrative to Professional Insight* (Jalongo & Isenberg, 1995) and worked with approximately 20 first-time authors whose reflections on their lives as teachers were published in the book. Another responsibility that gave me experience with new authors' work was my four-year stint as co-editor of *Narratives* a publication, supported by The Rockefeller Foundation, that publishes accounts of professional development experiences from people affiliated with several large, urban schools. Not only educators but also parents, students, and support staff wrote for the publication. In fact, my favorite article submitted to *Narratives* was a high school janitor's account of his pursuit of the General Education Diploma. Such work with the manuscripts of the inexperienced, line by line, keeps you honest as a teacher of writing.

Since adults are the ones who read books about writing, familiarity with teaching adults, both theoretical and practical, is a third qualification. If a book is intended to help others write, it is not all that instructive to write your memoirs or wallow in writer's angst. At some point, you need to encourage readers to join the ranks of writers and offer helpful suggestions about how to proceed; you need to be a teacher.

Those who can teach you to write, not just for your personal edification but for publication, have a difficult line to tread. Somewhere between the hostile editor who writes in the margins, "Who cares?" and a mere sounding board who asks, "How's the writing going?" is about right. Your instructor ought to be like one of those car navigation systems, capable of directing you, keeping you from losing your way. Your instructor should possess a nearly unerring sense of what is publishable and should not be shy about sharing it. If this book has achieved what nudged me to write it, then it should feel just that way—like no nonsense guidance from afar.

In 1999, I invited 13 of my former and current doctoral students to co-author an edited book for the Association for Childhood Education International (Jalongo, 1999). All of them had been students in a course that I have been teaching for about 15 years now on writing for publication. What was fascinating about this experience was the skill with which these students wrote the chapters. I entered into the project eager to function as a mentor and assuming that, because these students were at a very early stage in their writing careers, extensive editing and perhaps co-authorship might be necessary. To my surprise, the chapters were in great shape—definitely a cut above what I normally get in the mail to review and edit for various publishers. And, this was not just my opinion, but also the opinion of the reviewers and editorial staff, who pronounced the completed draft of the project a "delight." Evidently, these students knew something about writing that many professionals from other institutions frequently did not. My students attribute it to our writing seminar together. It would be gratifying to think that they are right.

Perhaps the strongest testimonial that this book has something to offer readers is that I have literally worn the letters off of at least 6 different computer keyboards. I make no claim to being a "Big W" writer (a Pulitzer Prize-winning author or famous novelist); rather, I am a "little w" writer—someone who, perhaps like you, has a full-time job doing something else and writes as a sideline; not poetry or plays or novels or children's books, but information-driven articles and books written for professionals in your field and related ones.

Scope of the Book

The book's scope is reflected in several key words. First, it focuses on *writing* and how it is approached and accomplished, despite all of the struggles and time constraints. Secondly, it is limited to *nonfiction* for *professional audiences*, those works that are true rather than fabricated, grounded in theory and research, and rooted in the lives of practitioners. Third, the book takes the stance that writing is a *craft*, a set of skills that can be improved with practice, rather than the fortuitous visitation of the Muse to some tortured artist's soul. In the Appendices, readers will find numerous resources to support the development of those skills.

Why Write?

As a professional, your success depends upon your facility with spoken and written language. Professionals who seek to be heard take that language ability to a higher level and share their ideas with a wider audience through publication. They seek the authority that often accompanies authorship. Yet while they are dreaming of communicating with fellow professionals and basking in the satisfactions of a well-wrought piece of writing, writers are also beset by worries and self-doubt.

When a group of graduate students from various fields was asked to describe what gets in the way of writing, they expressed these concerns:

- "I find it very difficult to read my work and move beyond my original concept map. I feel locked into my original piece. I need to develop greater flexibility in understanding my work/topic."

- "I need help cutting the 'junk' out of my writing. . . . I also want to be 'in the know' as far as publication resources are concerned."

- "My concerns about my writing include lack of experience writing professionally, knowing how much resistance to give to criticisms, and lack of revision strategies to use when rewriting."

- "Three Concerns:

  1. Subject: Knowing the material well enough to write about it.

  2. Writing style: Developing the skills necessary to have the material flow.

  3. Editing: Having skills to pick out major and minor flaws."

With all of these perceived impediments to writing for publication, why do some busy professionals dare to try?

The motivation to write for publication falls into two basic categories—feeling impelled to write and feeling compelled to write. Writers feel impelled when they care deeply about their subject and are itching to say something about it. Writers feel compelled to write when external forces impinge upon them, such as the due date for a class assignment, a conference proposal, or a grant application. Good writing can emanate from either type of pressure—intrinsic or extrinsic. Sometimes the motivation is a combination of the two. In the main, writers write for one or more of the following reasons:

- To communicate important ideas

- To tell the stories of their professional lives and share their wisdom of practice

- To connect with a wider audience

- To make a contribution to their chosen field

- To obtain tangible rewards (e.g., promotion, consulting work)

- To enlarge, extend, and organize thinking

- To maintain and enhance learning about a topic of interest

- To establish and participate in professional networks of like-minded individuals

- To be heard and engage in the discourse of the professional community

- To develop expertise and be recognized for specialized competence in their field

- To create a source of positive energy in their professional lives that transcends local concerns

- To engage in self-directed learning and develop professionally (Jalongo & McCracken, 1997)

Purpose and Audience for the Book

Writing Nonfiction for Professional Audiences: An Educator's Practical Guide has three purposes:

1. Examining professional writing from the particular perspective of professionals writing for fellow professionals.

2. Demystifying the process of writing for publication and enabling readers to envision themselves as authors by revealing how the publication process works and providing insider information from the author's, reviewer's, and editor's perspectives.

3. Equipping readers with self-evaluation strategies and helpful resources that will enable them to monitor their personal/professional development as authors.

The audience for this book includes educators and others in helping professions who are interested in writing for publication. The book is intended for three main categories of people seeking to publish: graduate students, practicing professionals in various fields, and college/university faculty.

In working with authors from various disciplines, I find that they have several basic questions that correspond to the chapters of this book:

- What are some typical beginner's mistakes and ways to avoid them? What are the common misconceptions about writing for publication and what constitutes the winning attitude? (Chapter 1, Refuting Persistent Myths about Writing for Publication)

- Do I have what it takes to become a published author of nonfiction? How do I get started? What can be learned from professional writers who have experienced success? (Chapter 2, Imagining Yourself in the Author's Role)

- What makes a manuscript for professional audiences publishable? How can I incorporate these characteristics into what I write and become successful with publishing? (Chapter 3, Internalizing the Characteristics of Publishable Writing)

- What strategies and tools do authors of nonfiction use to gain greater insight into what works for them as individuals? How do they go about becoming better, more confident writers? (Chapter 4, Mastering the Strategies Used by Successful Authors)

- How do I go about writing the journal article? How can I make the most of the work that I've done in other professional contexts and convert that work into publishable manuscripts? What are some ways to locate suitable outlets for journal articles and publish in the journals, on paper or on-line? (Chapter 5, Publishing Articles in Your Field)

- Is there a professional book in me and, if so, what type of book? What is the inside story on book publishing? How do you get a contract, negotiate the terms, get the book done, and get paid? (Chapter 6, Writing Books for Fellow Professionals)

- What do editors and reviewers for nonfiction really want? How can I increase my chances of acceptance? (Chapter 7, Working With Editors and Reviewers)

When will you be a real author? That depends on your criteria. Start with some humble indicators. I knew I was a writer when I received an Express Mail package containing the reviews of my third book. After the new delivery person pulled away and the dog finished barking, convinced that she had scared him off, I noticed a tiny map drawn in ballpoint ink on the carton. There were lines to represent roads and an "X" to mark the spot. Next to the X were the words, "writer's house." Like Santa Claus in *Miracle on 34th Street*, I was real by default, at least according to the staff of the United States Postal Service.

So, from one real writer to another, here's how to begin: Stop fantasizing about publication and resolve to do it. Start reading as if all printed materials were slated to disappear from the earth ten years hence. Keep writing as though your life depended on it.

REFERENCES

Jalongo, M. R. (Ed.) (1999). *Resisting the pendulum swing: Informed perspectives on education controversies*. Olney, MD: Association for Childhood Education International.

Jalongo, M. R., & Isenberg, J. P. (1995). *Teachers' stories: From personal narrative to professional insight*. San Francisco, CA: Jossey-Bass.

Jalongo, M. R., & McCracken, J. B. (1997). *Writing about teaching and learning: A guide for aspiring and experienced authors*. Olney, MD: Association for Childhood Education International.

CHAPTER 1

❧

Refuting Persistent Myths About Writing for Publication

❧

Renowned physicist Werner Heisenberg (1971) once defined an expert as someone who knows the worst mistakes that can be committed in a particular field and how to avoid them. When it comes to writing I am imminently qualified as an expert on writing for publication, not so much because I have published extensively, but because I have committed most writing blunders at one time or another. The purpose of *Writing for Publication: A Practical Guide for Educators* is to help other writers, both aspiring and experienced, to avoid such pitfalls and to discover their unique ways of contributing to the literature.

The dangers of writing about writing are legion. On the one hand, it may be construed as egotistical because the author seems to be a self-proclaimed "writers' writer." The author who dares to write about writing will be evaluated not only by the helpfulness of the advice offered but also by how well that advice is written. Additionally, writing about writing is one step removed from "real" writing because it skirts the difficulty of deciding on a topic by writing about itself. Those who write about writing may be resented in the same way that laborers toiling in the hot sun react to a supervisor in shirt and tie who strolls past the construction site and gives directions. Being an educator, however, I see value in coaching the performance of fellow writers and in reflecting on the craft of writing. I also see value in writing about writing for publication; assuming that the authors who presume to do so are not so foolish to think that their idiosyncrasies ought to be a template for every other writer to follow.

Shortly after an article that I wrote earned the "Best Essay" award from the American Association for Higher Education, an administrator asked me, "How many hours did you put into that article?" My response then, and still is, that it depends on what you count as writing. Is thinking about the manuscript while you are driving writing? Is tracking down an errant reference for over an hour writing? Is talking about what you are writing during a college class writing? Because writing is so much a part of other daily routines, it is sometimes difficult to differentiate writing from other activities and arrive at the total number of hours. If I had to make a guesstimate of the time it took to write the article, I would say that it was the equivalent of about 14 workdays of 10 hours. Often, such estimates are shocking to those who think that "good" writers are those who don't have to work at it. They tend to define writing as drafting, that initial attempt at getting words down on the page. They assume that writing is easy for those who have a mysterious knack for producing first drafts that are practically perfect. Those who seriously underestimate the time it takes to craft a piece of writing do much of their writing in the form of memos or lists. They think that, if they collaborate with a "good" writer, all it will require of them is a few conversations. Then the "good" writer will work her or his magic on the manuscript and bring it in, ready to be published, the next day. Aspiring authors usually are disappointed to learn that writing well is far more complicated than that.

I have reached the point where I do not really count anything short of the gut-wrenching revisions that go on and on and on as writing. Drafting is nothing; final edits are next to nothing. It is that very long and difficult process in between that qualifies as writing.

Bogdan and Biklen (1992) address the false hope of easy writing this way:

> Remember that you are never "ready" to write; writing is something you must make a conscious decision to do and then discipline yourself to follow through. People often tell us that we are lucky; they say "Writing comes so easy to you." Writing comes easy neither to us nor to many others. . . . Some become more proficient at it because they have developed good work patterns, confidence, and skills, but it is never easy. (p. 172)

Think of writing as carefully refined thinking that is captured in words and recorded on disk or on paper. Think of publication as a polished composition that is shared with an audience larger than family, friends, or classmates and then duplicated/disseminated through a means more rigorous than e-mail, or a vanity press (where authors pay to have their books appear in print). These are pieces of writing that have been formally reviewed by peers.

Before beginning the topic-by-topic treatment of writing for publication in education and related fields, I'd like to follow the example of many prominent writers and address some of the persistent myths about writing (Smith, 1992; Zinsser, 1998). It makes sense to start out by debunking these myths that just won't go away.

Myth 1: Writing well is innate and published writers write effortlessly.

This is like saying that natural talent is the only element in a professional athlete's career. Clearly, there is much more to it, including such things as motivation, training, persistence, and so forth. The sports world is replete with examples of squandered talent, as well as examples of people who have succeeded despite serious physical limitations. Likewise, the writing world is full of people who can write well but choose not to and, conversely, people who may have less of a natural flair for writing but manage to produce prose that gets published time after time.

I happen to live near a recreational facility where people walk, run, cycle, or, in the winter, cross-country ski down my road. Nearly all of them appear to be in good physical condition. Imagine their reactions if I rolled down the window of my car on my way to work on a freezing cold day and yelled, "You're so lucky to be in good shape! I wish I had your genes. You really like to exercise, huh?" My sentiments are similar when someone says, "You just like to write" or "Writing is easy for you." To be completely truthful, I do not enjoy revising my work and that is mainly what writers do. Actually, I like the very beginning of the writing process, where you conceptualize the piece and the very end, after it is neatly typeset. Everything in between is tedious, at best. Writing for publication is neither easy nor glamorous. Like the experience of those athletic neighbors described earlier, it does drag you out of bed early. Like physical exercise, it gives you a real workout, yet it offers enough satisfaction to become a regular regimen; so much so that you begin to feel out of sorts when a session is missed.

The most admirable authors have two universal traits. First, they write often and strive for continuous improvement. Second, they genuinely care about the craft of writing well, care so much that they will return to a manuscript again and again, long past the point when others would consider it finished, long past the point where they are entirely sick of it. I can recall first joining the ranks of various professional organizations and seeing the same group of authors published repeatedly in the organization's journals and books. At the time, I assumed these people were the well connected, that it must be a closed club. Then I volunteered to join publications committees and editorial boards. It turns out that these prolific publishers were the people who actually delivered the goods. Out of the thousands of professionals who say they want to be published, only a small percentage actually take the time to produce high-quality work and submit it on time. Over and over again, the members of these editorial boards tried to extend opportunities to other authors and, frequently, they let us down. These would-be authors offered a litany of excuses or assured us that they were working on it. In one memorable case an author falsely promised that the manuscript was in the mail! But with few notable exceptions, the truth was that most people were not willing to work as hard as they had to in order to publish.

Just as a child who watches professional figure skaters or ballet dancers will attempt to imitate them afterwards by sliding around on the kitchen floor or walking on tiptoe, nonwriters may assume that great writing unfurls effortlessly from the folds of a writer's brain. Yet consider how Robert Timberg, author of a best-selling book on the Vietnam War, describes his writer's life: "Back when I started the book, I was working in [the basement of] . . . a house in Bethesda, Maryland, I began to think of myself as the troll of Bethesda. I'd just get up in the morning, go down to the basement"(cited in Lamb 1997, p. 213). I know of no one who writes effortlessly—at least not anyone who writes well. On the contrary, they adopt the determined attitude of children's book author Nikki Grimes (1999):

> Easy doesn't interest me. It never did. I'm a sucker for a challenge. I like to take on a work that frightens me, that I'm not sure I can pull off, that makes me dig deep . . . every time I put pen to paper, I'm also writing to stretch myself. Otherwise, I feel I'm not doing my job. . . . I'm always searching for that idea that will send me to the wall— or send me sprawling! Ultimately, it is in meeting such challenges that I find my greatest satisfaction. (p. 46, 49)

Myth 2: You must be brilliant and have a Ph.D. in order to write for publication.

I was nearly finished with a two-hour session presented to a group of teachers in a writers' workshop sponsored by the National Writing Project. One of the participants commented, "You talked about your students getting their writing published, and all I can think is that they must be so much smarter than me. About the only thing I can see myself publishing is teaching ideas in a newsletter. I can't imagine writing an entire article." This classroom teacher's comment is not atypical. There is an assumption that brilliant scholars are the only ones eligible to write for publication. Yet, in nonfiction writing, the truth is that authors rely extensively on previously published, appropriately cited works to support their arguments. Many editors whose reading audiences consist primarily of practitioners fervently wish that more practitioners would write for their publications. When authors feel that they lack the theoretical or research background to produce an article they have in mind, they have two basic choices. The first is to acquire that background themselves by delving into the literature; the second is to collaborate with someone who has that background already. Although more Ph.D.'s are published because higher education faculty usually are expected to publish and are rewarded for doing so, holding a Ph.D. is not a prerequisite for publishing something of value in your field.

Myth 3: Anyone can write for publication.

Some authors agree with Frank Smith (1992), that the only real difference between people who write and people who do not is that writers write. At the risk of sounding self-congratulatory, I really do think that writers are different from nonwriters, based on over 20 years of reading manuscripts submitted to various publications.

Although it is obviously the case that the first characteristic of writers is actually producing some written work, that is not nearly enough to get it published. Most respected authors in the educational field share several characteristics. First, they are avid learners who read voraciously both in and out of their areas of specialization. Second, they have built sufficient confidence in themselves as thinkers to believe that they actually have something to contribute. Third, they have developed adequate skill to say it, in ways that are compelling, clear, and captivating. Fourth, they are relatively thick-skinned about criticism and use it to improve their work. Fifth, they usually are capable of generating lots of ideas. Sixth, they pay attention to details and precision when writing, even if they are not so detail-oriented and precise in other aspects of their lives. Although some professionals who publish may not fit this profile, most of the best ones do. Figure 1.1 is a list of some traits that prolific authors tend to cultivate.

Originality of ideas

Awareness of future trends

Insight concerning issues

Ability to organize thoughts logically

Knowledge of subject matter and the related disciplines

Appropriate use of reference materials

Ability to synthesize, apply, and evaluate information

Clarity of message

Suitability of message for audience

Selection of a suitable outlet for the work

Effective time management

Familiarity with the publishing process

Task persistence

Attention to details

Pride in craft

Figure 1.1   *General Characteristics of Published Authors*

A college textbook sales representative once explained that, when pursuing the possibility of first-time textbook authorship with a faculty member, they had been advised to look over the professor's office. Presumably, those with neat offices would be better organized and more apt to produce a book. Speaking as someone with an extremely cluttered office, I disagree with this advice; yet there are some habits of mind and ethics of work that are more conducive to writing for publication than others.

Myth 4: Writing for publication is little more than an exercise in spelling, grammar, and punctuation.

If you think of writing as homework, don't be surprised if you don't want to do it. If, on the other hand, you think of writing as entering into the professional conversation and joining in the professional dialogue, the prospect of writing becomes a bit more attractive. Forget what some composition curmudgeon has told you. Writing is more than mechanics. Those who dislike writing don't think they are good at it for some reason. More often than not, that reason has to do with the mechanical aspects. When I worked with college freshmen who had some combination of marginal high school grades, a low score on the reading/writing entrance test, or some other significant language hurdle to overcome, such as having English as their second language, they believed themselves to be poor writers because their errors had been pointed out to them repeatedly in school. Overall, however, they were surprisingly good writers who wrote about things that mattered to them with passion and conviction—quite a departure from the stilted and faintly pompous style encountered in the work of many new faculty seeking to publish. The work of these freshmen, who were reputedly "poor" writers, had a vitality and candor that offered a refreshing break from academic babble. Pulitzer Prize-winning author Richard Rhodes (1995) explains how to deal with these nagging doubts about writing that often are echoes of the past:

> Fear stops most people from writing, not lack of talent, whatever that is . . . The fear that grips someone who wants to write is usually not undifferentiated and monolithic but a composite of smaller fears. With time and thought, some can be resolved; others can be shooed back under their rocks or even coaxed into harness and put to work. (p. 1, 8)

In the real world of book publishing, for example, there are several layers of editing functions. You might work with an acquisitions editor, the person who is responsible for getting new projects started. If your book is considered a hot commodity, you might work with a developmental editor who is the creative consultant on book design, marketing strategies, and so forth. You could work with a production editor who oversees the actual publication of the book. Hierarchically speaking, the lowest function for an editor is copyediting. Copyediting is going through, word by word, and making corrections. These editors make even less money than other poorly compensated editors and have, in most other people's estimation, the most boring editing jobs. As one of them once told me on the telephone when I asked a question about book production, "I wouldn't know. We're just the monkeys down here. We don't get to grind the organ." This is not to diminish the contributions of copy editors because a good one can prevent mortifying mistakes. Yet, contrary to popular opinion, mechanical aspects, important as they may be, are not the end all/be all of writing. They are the finishing touches, not the main event, in writing.

Innovative ideas, clarity, brevity, and organization are far more important in the total scheme of things when writing. As further support for this point of view, consider the fact that many of the more routine corrections can now be performed using spell check and grammar check. If worrying about spelling is keeping you from writing, set your word processing program to correct as you go.

Myth 5: Writing for publication consists of good ideas transcribed onto paper.

Aspiring authors will often say that they think they have a good idea for a manuscript. Yet when you study the manuscripts that you cared enough to copy and file, it is clear that they are far from being "one idea" pieces. Actually, the best manuscripts are littered with good ideas. Good writers do not hold back ideas, hoarding them for some later project. Instead, they incorporate many of their good ideas to write the best piece they possibly can, confident that more will surface later as they continue to read and write and think (Dillard, 1998).

Granted, we cannot all be like celebrated author Jane Yolen who said in an interview, "I have enough ideas that if I never got another idea in my life, I could write for the next 20 years" (cited in Glasheeh, 1998, p. 20). The good news is that we don't need to be nearly as generative as Yolen. She is a prolific writer who devotes all day, every day to writing books for a wide array of audiences, young child through adult.

Good ideas are necessary, but not sufficient. It is how and when the author says it, not just what he or she says. So unless you have discovered a cure for cancer, your good ideas will need to be transformed into well-crafted prose. Speaking as a journal editor, it is not unusual for me to receive several manuscripts on the same subject. What causes one author's work to be selected over another's goes beyond good ideas. Clarity, brevity, organization, documentation, and carefully fashioned writing generally tip the scales in favor of one manuscript over another. Good ideas might get you a second chance (e.g., a recommendation for revision instead of outright rejection), but you need to communicate effectively and have a timely (or, better still, timeless) message.

Writing is also more than transcribing ideas and thoughts. Just as Hollywood romance differs considerably from marital relationships in daily life, the writers we see depicted on television hammering away on a keyboard, churning out reams of publishable text are more fantasy than reality.

Real writers report rewriting dozens of times rather than being satisfied with an early draft. When they are finished, their work reads well as a result of all that effort. As biographer Neil Baldwin has noted, writers understand that "the tributaries of hard work feed into and out of the creative mind, and you cannot just expect to have ideas spring fully formed out of your mind from beginning to end" (cited in Lamb 1997, p.125). Like the accomplished musician who is heralded as an "overnight sensation" but actually spent years on the road perfecting a style, the best authors are those who invest a tremendous amount of effort in finding a style and a voice that suits their audience and material.

Writing is much more than mere keyboarding or word processing and, despite technophiles' arguments to the contrary, word processing programs do not have the power to improve the quality of writing, only the ease with which quality writing can be cranked out or the speed with which some low-level tasks can be performed (e.g., sorting a list of references into alphabetical order). Writing is improved when thinking is improved, because writing is thinking recorded on paper.

Myth 6: Effective writing processes are universal.

Visit elementary classrooms, and you will see stages in the writing process posted somewhere in the room. What these posters imply is that writing is linear, sequential, and characterized by incremental stages, each demanding an equal amount of time. Not true! Drafting should be quick; revising and editing are often very long and involved, at least for publishable pieces.

To compound matters further, writers are idiosyncratic. Some write early in the morning and some burn the night oil. Some can dictate text; others are lost without a pencil and a yellow legal pad. I even have one friend who exercises on her treadmill, then jumps off periodically to type a few lines on her laptop, resuming her workout as soon as she runs out of ideas.

Although there are some basics of writing for publication, part of what makes it difficult to teach writing is helping each author to discover a personal style. Any writer who presents her or his experience as the prototype for success in writing is a fraud, because there are few absolutes where writing is concerned. More often it is like stumbling around in a darkened room. About the most that someone else can do for you is to provide ambient light that will enable you to dimly perceive the walls and contours of the furniture. In writing, that illumination takes the form of thoughtful responses to drafts of your manuscript and supportive guidance as you learn the ropes of publishing.

Some writers mistakenly believe that if a piece of writing begins well, then all subsequent writing will follow suit. But this is like parents who think that if kindergarten goes well for their children, the remainder of the child's academic career will take care of itself. A powerful lead paragraph, while certainly desirable, is far from a guarantee of publication. Writers lose readers if they fail to write well throughout the piece. Judgments of quality in writing consider the work in its entirety and how it "hangs together." A manuscript can be rejected because it bogs down in the middle or has a weak conclusion even though it starts off strong.

Begin writing the part about which you have the most to say and do not worry excessively about getting the first line or paragraph perfect before continuing. Novice authors often tyrannize themselves by insisting that they cannot write without that perfect start. After hours at the computer, they have nothing more to show than reams of paper to be recycled. Part of becoming a writer is learning to go with the flow rather than doing things in a lockstep fashion. The writing process is more like a smorgasbord than a formal, six-course meal. The writer is free to graze, to get a clean plate, or to start with dessert. There is no invariant sequence to the writing process.

A corollary to this myth has to do with outlines. Perhaps you have been tyrannized into believing that detailed outlines are a prerequisite for all high-quality writing.

A presenter at a professional conference, a noted Canadian author, confided that he never produced outlines prior to writing an article or book. I'm certain that he had no idea what a revelation that was for me. I had been struggling in vain to write the perfect outline, convinced by my 4th-grade teacher that it was an essential first step. But outlining down to the finest detail is no guarantee of writing well. In fact, it is more often the case that my outlines are easily written *after* the manuscript is completed and, regrettably, not before.

Of course, different types of writing projects present different organizational challenges. Sometimes, when the path is clear, you really can write from an outline that changes very little from start to finish. Other times, when the route to achieving your writing goal is less obvious, you are still tinkering with organizational patterns on the 12th revision. Sometimes you can write to an outline, sometimes you can't.

Myth 7: Writing that is difficult to understand is profound.

College students always want to know how long a writing assignment is supposed to be. Many of the undergraduates appear to be frightened by longer assignments, evidently feeling that they do not have that much to say. Many graduate students, on the other hand, want to write on and on because they realize that it is much easier to do that than to write clear, crisp prose. Some students at both levels resort to what one of my professors used to advise against—"stringing pearls." He used this phrase to describe graduate students' papers in which their words were little more than the lowly string that lightly bound the shining gems of thought gleaned from other sources.

Real brilliance comes from the quality of the thinking behind a piece of writing. Too many academic authors write to impress others with their fancy footwork as thinkers rather than to share their ideas. As a result, much of what is written remains unread because few people have the inclination or patience to discover what the writer is trying to say. There is a concept borrowed from research that applies here called parsimony. The principle of parsimony means that researchers deliberately choose the simplest statistical analysis that is appropriate for the data. Experts in mathematics and the sciences use another word with a similar sentiment. When a theory is stunningly clear and shows great insight, they refer to it as "elegant." Writing should be parsimonious and elegant.

Although it is fine to challenge readers' assumptions, there are no points given for sending them to the dictionary repeatedly or trying their patience with convoluted sentences.

Myth 8: Getting your work published is simply a matter of knowing the right people.

Few beginning authors understand that anonymous peer review is an integral part of professional publishing. The way it works is that you send an unsolicited manuscript in for review. "Unsolicited" means that nobody asked you to write it and submit it. The manuscript is then sent to professionals who have no idea who you are or where you are from. They simply get a manuscript in the mail and critique it, based on their knowledge and experience. They render a decision and the editor makes the final judgment about whether the piece fits in with publication plans. In this "blind" or anonymous peer review system people know your work before they know you. If you submit quality work, editors seek to get to know you, at least as a potential contributor to their publications. After that, you may be invited to write something because you have proven yourself as a writer.

Peer review is deliberately designed to resist tampering and favoritism based on friendship. It is intended to give everyone a fair opportunity to contribute and have their manuscripts evaluated on the basis of quality rather than on personal connections. Authors who invest time in trying to influence an editor rather than in polishing their manuscripts make a critical error. If the peer review system were operating effectively, acquaintanceships would make little difference in the outcome of the review. Well-established and widely known authors who are best friends with editors continue to have work rejected if it does not suit the audience or earns lackluster reviews.

Myth 9: Persistence always pays.

I grow weary of hearing writers regale us with tales of the novel that was rejected dozens of times before it became a best seller and was made into a movie that grossed millions. Identifying good nonfiction is not as subject to individual taste as fiction. For example, a common reason for rejecting a piece of nonfiction writing is that it contains dated or inaccurate information. That is more a matter of fact than of taste or style. If you are a teacher who writes for other teachers, no one expects you to create a new art form as they might if you were seeking to publish The Great American Novel. This folklore of the doggedly persistent writer who meets with rejection after rejection and never alters a word is a destructive myth for nonfiction writers.

Research suggests that the great majority of manuscripts are revised again and again—even *after* they are accepted for publication (Boice, 1995). Flatly refusing to change any of your golden words will not serve you well in nonfiction writing. Instead of treating the criticisms of others as barbs, think of their comments as suggestions that just might strengthen the work.

Myth 10: Somebody else can eliminate writing problems for you.

When doctoral students meet with extensive criticism of their dissertations, they sometimes seek out the help of English teachers and secretaries. The trouble is that when writing for publication, particularly writing a manuscript that is highly technical, few English teachers or secretaries possess the specialized knowledge required. Most education articles, for example, use American Psychological Association (APA) referencing style. English teachers probably know Modern Language Association (MLA) style. Likewise, when it comes to content, neither a secretary nor an English teacher can be much help. Perhaps most important, there is quite a difference between knowing about the English language or typing papers and knowing how to write for publication. As a particularly candid English teacher who was a student in my class put it, "I teach writing and constantly remind students to stay focused. But when I write and you read it, that's what you tell me to do. It's not so easy."

If you use a word processing program with grammar, spelling, and punctuation checks you have no doubt discovered that these mechanical methods of correction are sometimes wrong. The same thing happens with people. None of us uses language flawlessly. I blush when I think about some of the language gaffes I committed early in my career or even last month. So while it may be useful to ask others to look for the more obvious language blunders, you probably will need a reviewer who writes for publication, preferably one who has been published in the very outlet where you seek to publish your work. This is not to say that other types of review are useless, however. I always ask my husband to read for me, even though he has a business and social services background, because he is an avid reader and looks at the logic of the writing. He is not the world's best speller, so I don't ask him to correct spelling unless he notices an obvious typo. Writing problems are often addressed using a multi-layered editing strategy; the work is subjected to different types of readers at different times to filter out mistakes.

Myth 11: Taking a class in creative writing is the answer.

As a first step in writing for publication in the field of education, you need to recognize that there are different types of writing. You wouldn't go to truck driving school if you wanted to drive a car; and you probably won't learn much about writing for professional journals, magazines, or books from a course in creative writing, newspaper writing, or poetry writing. Such experiences are not without value, it's just that they cannot be expected to address the task of writing for fellow professionals in your field.

Every discipline has its own vocabulary and style. Just think back to when you were in college and all of the new challenges that different disciplines presented. It wasn't just the content of sociology or philosophy or science, it was also that each field had a particular "lens" on the world and particular ways of talking about it.

Professional writing is highly specialized. It is so specialized, in fact, that it usually needs to change when the publisher and outlet changes. What you write for one journal will probably be at least slightly different from what you could get published in another, even though the audience is basically similar. Unless you have time to spare, any writing class in which you enroll should directly addresses the type of writing that you want to produce.

Myth 12: Writing something short is easier than writing something long.

Within every group of aspiring writers, there is always someone attracted to the idea of writing for children. Why? Because they presume that writing something short and cute is the best they could do. But I liken writing for children to painting a masterpiece on a tiny canvas. It too is a real art; it too has numerous constraints. Another sobering fact about writing for children—if you look at a list of the top children's books for the past 50 years, it has not changed all that much. Most of the great books for children have been written already.

Actually, it is easier to write on and on in a "blah, blah, blah" fashion, slapping down sentences one after another as if laying paint on a barn, than to craft a concise manuscript in which every word and sentence is carefully crafted. As Robert Brinsley Sheridan put it, "You write with ease to show your breeding, But easy writing's curst hard reading" (Winokur, 1986, p. 93).

Myth 13: The secret to publication is finding the short cuts.

A business professor made this comment in an 88 degree meeting room one fall afternoon: "I've noticed that some of the big names in my field were people who 'took on' the established authors, challenging their theories and research. Isn't this a faster way to make a name for yourself and get published too?" What he really wanted to know, was, "Are there any short cuts?" "It depends," I replied. "It seems risky to me. First, you have to realize that there is a reason why these people are respected as writers. My guess is that they are good thinkers and do well in an argument. If the author you are refuting is a vastly experienced and respected leader in the field, you may be going into a battle of wits unarmed, as the saying goes. Plus there is the issue of defining yourself as a critic and basing your notoriety on a public feud. Do you want all that controversy swirling around you and your work? My personal preference would be to produce good, honest work and gradually build a reputation over the years." With that, his colleague in the next seat poked him in the ribs with her elbow and said softly, "See, I told you so."

If I knew of a foolproof way to jet start a career, believe me, I would share it. The reality is that those of us who decide to write tolerate considerable wear and tear on our nerves, carpal tunnels, and lumbar spines to make the writing readable. Those who do not write find it difficult to understand why we might subject ourselves to all of this, in much the same way that I have difficulty understanding why a person would take the risks associated with mountain climbing or auto racing. There is no magic formula for fast, easy, accurate, and dazzling writing that will win the accolades of peers.

I don't have any magic formulas, but I do have some general tips, numerous examples, and encouraging words that will guide you in the process of discovering your potential as a writer. As a send-off on that journey, allow me to explain why writers become positively addicted to writing.

WRITING'S REDEEMING QUALITIES

What's so great about writing? Why do so many people aspire to be published authors? I can think of at least ten reasons.

1. Opportunities to Revise
    Writing is, as Frank Smith (1992) puts it, "a plastic art." There are many opportunities to get rid of the mistakes and revise before the quality of your work is judged. You don't have to get it right the first time like nuclear fission or, as novelist Robert Cormier once noted, brain surgery. Writing is also very different from other language arts, even its expressive counterpart in oral language, speaking. Edmund Morris, an author who earned the Pulitzer Prize for his biography of Theodore Roosevelt explains it this way: "the luxury of being a writer is you can edit, you can go back. When I talk, I'm constantly wanting to take that sentence back and change its shape. . . . with writing, you can do that. When you're talking, the fugitive sentence has flown; you can't get it back" (cited in Lamb 1997, p.21).

2. Ownership of Ideas
    Your writing belongs to you and you can exercise control over it. You can cut it down, expand it, or even throw it away and start all over again. Writing well has all the appeal of white water rafting for the enthusiast: you venture forth into dangerous waters, keep your kayak on course and negotiate the rocks that jut out, then you savor the achievement back on shore. Likewise, the writer must "control his own energies so he can work. He must be sufficiently excited to rouse himself to the task at hand, and not so excited he cannot sit down to do it. He must have faith sufficient to impel and renew

the work, yet not so much faith that he fancies he is writing well when he is not" (Dillard, 1998, p. 46).

If you happen to work in a bureaucratic organization, this ownership/ control aspect of writing may be particularly appealing. At the university, I know that interminable meetings are necessary to effect a change and that downplaying ownership of contributions is often necessary to achieve a goal. But what I write belongs to me and I can treat it as I wish, unfettered by agendas, committees, or a sense of duty.

3. Vehicle for Narrative
    Some have argued that all of our work is autobiographical in some way. When you become a writer, you get to tell your stories. You also keep discovering new stories that are drawn from your reservoir of personal experiences and activated by the stories of others. There is a genuine delight that comes from being able to relate a story that matters to you in a way that resonates with your readers' experiences and causes them to say, "Yes, that's exactly how I've felt!"

4. Potential as a Mentoring Tool
    Texts can become the basis for establishing a mentor/protégé relationship. Such relationships begin with reciprocal identification (the protégé aspiring to be like the mentor, the mentor seeing something of herself or himself in the protégé). Grumet (1988) explains writing as mentoring this way:

    > I do not ask my students, "Do you understand me?" Instead I tell them to understand my reading of the text. We pass texts between us. We touch the text instead of each other and make our marks on it rather than each other. The text is material, it has texture, it is woven; we pull and tug at it, it winds around us, we are tangled up in it. (p. 144)

    After some tentative overtures and first steps, mutual trust is built. The writing protégé trusts that the mentor will be forthright about what needs to be done to improve the work, will not gossip about embarrassing mistakes, and will not be exploitative. In exchange, the mentor trusts that the protégé will work hard, follow through on recommendations and make the most of the mentor's ability to introduce the protégé into useful networks and writing opportunities.

    Suppose that you were an accomplished author and had the opportunity to edit a book. How would you identify protégés to work with you? No doubt you would select people who: a) establish a reputation for high-quality work, b) are a pleasure to work with, c) don't whine (at least, not to your face), and d) deliver the manuscript on time without apologies or excuses. Often, those mentor/protégé relationships built around a manuscript mature into a bond of friendship and colleagueship that lasts throughout a professional career.

5. Relative Permanence of Contribution

   The great Greek orator, Socrates, was very suspicious of the written word and believed it would undermine society, as he knew it. To some extent, he was correct. The Socratic dialogues that made his reputation certainly diminished in importance in the new communication environment. In Western culture, the written word has nearly eclipsed the spoken word, at least when we seek a binding agreement. When we make contracts, we write them down so that they can be returned to later as evidence that an agreement was made. You can save examples of good writing whenever and wherever you find them, including your own. Little wonder, then, that when I asked a 1st grader "Why do people write?" he replied solemnly, "You write so you can keep it."

   Writers even use writing as a way to enter back into writing after a hiatus from their desks. Reviewing the words they have already written is a habit of successful writers, beginning in grade school and going all the way through professional authorship. Unlike fame, fortune, and many material possessions, writing is not ephemeral and, at its very best, it is nearly timeless.

6. Responsiveness to Feedback

   While you are writing, others can offer suggestions that are thoughtful, critical, and helpful. While other types of good advice usually are ignored, constructive writing advice is often needed and heeded. Figure 1.2 is a list of my best advice to authors.

   Feedback is to writing like sun, soil, air, and water are to plants; even a small sprout of a beginning can eventually flourish, given the right growing conditions.

7. Basis for Critical Dialogue

   After you have written and perhaps published something, you often get a response. When you read other people's writing, it gives you ideas about how to improve your own. Writing is social and interactive. It gives us something to think and talk about; it invites discussion. It is no mistake that writing uses the same word that musicians use to describe what they do: composition. For just as each musician uses the same musical notes to create a melody, every writer uses words to generate a manuscript that is an original. Our differing perspectives on a topic, forged by training and experience, are what make writing perpetually interesting and capable of eliciting a response. Eventually, after years of writing and publishing, you can enter into this dialogue in a deeper way. Now it is you who will be quoted and included in the reference list; now it is you who has developed and demonstrated expertise.

8. Tool for Professional Development

   As you write more, accept new writing challenges, and become a better writer, you develop as a professional. When I supervised the internship projects of three school principals, they were expected to write a short article for publication about their semester-long endeavors. Although they were too polite to protest much, they discretely inquired about why they had to do this when others did not. My response was, "Too bad, luck of the draw. You got the crazy writer for your internship supervisor and now you'll have to humor her a bit. Think beyond the requirements for the internship and make a contribution to your field of educational administration. You're working on something that could help others. Don't be stingy and keep what you've learned all to yourself." One principal had written about how to get through

---

1. Have something to discover or say and work from motivation, not obligation or trendiness.

2. Be reader-centered rather than author-centered; focus on questions your readers are likely to have.

3. Read widely and well from current and classic sources rather than counting on a few textbooks, a computer search, or the Internet.

4. Invest many ideas and resources into your manuscript rather than hoarding them for some future project.

5. Accept full responsibility for a carefully crafted manuscript rather than expecting others to do your "homework" for you.

6. Recognize the limitations of word processing; just because you can move a paragraph quickly, that doesn't mean it belongs there.

7. Approach reviews and critiques of your manuscripts as opportunities to hone your craft rather than as ego threats.

8. Read articles and books for style instead of always focusing on content.

9. Subject your work to peer review by colleagues before you mail it off for anonymous peer review.

10. After you have said to yourself, "It's done!" let your manuscript get cold, come back to it, and rewrite it at least five more times.

11. Build credibility with the editor and conform to the manuscript submission guidelines rather than ignoring details.

12. Don't trust your memory of referencing styles; master the rules of American Psychological Association (APA) style, and consult the rules often until they are ingrained.

Source: Jalongo, M.R., & McCracken, J.B. (1997). *Writing about teaching and learning: A guide for aspiring and experienced authors.* Olney, MD: Association for Childhood Education International.

Figure 1.2 *Advice to Aspiring Authors*

a major construction project at his school, another had written about rewriting job descriptions to comply with the American Disabilities Act, and the third had written about revamping the curriculum to better meet the developmental needs of adolescents—three interesting and useful projects. All were published. Although none of these administrators is the type that makes excessive use of exclamation points in their writing, they could barely suppress the delight in their correspondence about achieving this milestone.

Without question, having your work reviewed by peers and accepted for publication offers a type of validation that is not possible from those who already know and like you. When others really listen to you, it builds professional self-esteem and opens new avenues for professional growth.

9. Outlet for Emotions
    Even a negative experience can make a positive contribution through writing. As a child, my family moved frequently. I hated being the new kid who didn't know a soul, who worried about eating lunch alone, or who was teased because I had a funny accent. Later on as a teacher, I worked with migrant children and taught in a laboratory school where the children of college students and faculty, often newly immigrated, were enrolled. Many of these preschool children were just learning to speak their native language and were even less familiar with English. One day, I was visiting a classroom to observe my student teacher and saw a child who had come into the class in mid-year being treated so shabbily. Two teachers were talking about him as if he weren't there, complaining about the class being too large, saying that there wasn't a desk available. The child stood in front of the room looking embarrassed while the other children whispered and stared. Little surprise, then, that I ended up writing about geographic relocation and children. I had strong feelings about the topic as a classroom observer, as a teacher, and as a child in that situation.

    Writing about the things that touch us deeply can be therapeutic. Author Michael Rosen (1999) explains how this process works when he writes:

    > An author most often writes in order to discover the unknown outcomes of a predicament as acutely mysterious as the world we are always trying to understand. By revising the words that memory and imagination accumulate on the page, I try not only to improve my writing, but also to revise, and even improve my life. (p. 23)

10. Pursuable Throughout Life
    Writing ability seldom peaks early. Skilled writers tend to improve in old age rather than decline, assuming that their minds remain sharp. Writing has great potential as a lifelong pursuit, partly because it is perpetually challenging, and partly because physical strength, speed, and attractiveness are not necessary.

CONCLUSION

Clearly, writing has much to recommend it. Rather than adopting the tortured artist mentality about writing, think about the potential of authorship as a peak experience. Harvard professor and best-selling author, Mihalyi Csikzentmihalyi (1990), has been studying optimal experiences for over two decades. He uses the term "flow" to describe those moments when high skill and high challenge converge to accomplish a task. Runners are in flow when they are get their "second wind," dancers are in flow when the dance "works," and writers are in flow when the writing is going remarkably well.

Theory states that you enter a flow state when the following requirements are in place:

1. your activity had clear goals and gives you some sort of feedback;

2. you have the sense that your personal skills are well suited to the challenges of the activity, giving you a sense of potential control;

3. you are intensely focused on what you're doing;

4. you lose awareness of yourself, perhaps feeling part of something larger;

5. your sense of time is altered, with time seeming to slow, stop or become irrelevant; and

6. the experience becomes self-rewarding (Perry, 1999, p.9).

As you pursue the goal of becoming a better, clearer writer every time you produce another manuscript, keep these characteristics of flow in mind. Just as a baby learns to give over to sleep rather than fighting it, writers need to set aside all of those negative stereotypes about writers and all of those destructive myths about writing for publication.

When I searched the word "writing" on Internet bookstores in preparation for writing this book, thousands of titles emerged, and it took me the greater part of a day to sift through them all (I ended up purchasing about 40 of them). If the sheer number of books on writing is any indication, writing evidently holds a fascination for many of us. I think it is because it morphs into something new each time we take on a new writing task and reach out to a different audience. Is it any wonder that I chuckled aloud when I asked a kindergarten boy, "Jason, what's the hardest thing about writing?" and he replied with great seriousness, "The hardest thing about writing is being the writer."

REFERENCES

Bogdan, R. C., & Biklen, S. K. (1992). *Qualitative research for education* (2nd ed.). Boston, MA: Allyn & Bacon.

Boice, R. (1995). Developing writing, then teaching amongst new faculty. *Research in Higher Education, 36*(4), 415-456.

Csikzentmihalyi, M. (1990). *Flow: The psychology of optimal experience.* New York: HarperCollins.

Dillard, A. (1998). *The writing life* (2nd ed.). New York: HarperCollins.

Glasheen, L. K. (1998). Dancing with words: The printed page is author Jane Yolen's stage. *AARP Bulletin, 39*(7), p. 17, 20.

Grimes, N. (1999). Reading (and writing) on a dare. *Book Links, 9,* (1) 46-49.

Grumet, M. R. (1988). *Bitter milk: Women and teaching.* Amherst: University of Massachusetts.

Heisenberg, W. (1971). *Physics and beyond: Encounters and conversations.* New York: Harper and Row.

Lamb, B. (1997). *Booknotes: America's finest authors on reading, writing, and the power of ideas.* New York: Times Books/Random House.

Perry, S. K. (1999). *Writing in flow: Keys to enhanced creativity.* Cincinnati, OH: Writer's Digest Books.

Rhodes, R. (1995). *How to write: Advice and reflections.* New York: William Morrow.

Rosen, M. J. (1999). Live it once, revise it a dozen times. *Book Links 8* (6), 22-24.

Smith, F. (1992). *Writing and the writer.* New York: Holt.

Winokur, J. (Ed.) (1986). *Writers on writing.* Philadelphia, PA: Running Press.

Zinsser, W. K. (1998). *On writing well* (5th ed.). New York: Harper and Row.

CHAPTER 2

❧

Imagining Yourself in the Author's Role

❧

Evidently, there are many people who want to become authors, particularly paid authors. One of the perennial best-selling reference books in America is *Writer's Market* (Holm, 2000), a 1,112-page directory, published annually, of places where authors can peddle their wares. It seems as though practically everyone you meet has some writing aspirations. Mention that you are a writer and those stories will venture forth, sometimes on cautious tiptoe, sometimes with a bold stride. My neighbor sees me in the backyard proofreading and tells me about her dream of publishing an autobiography. A surgeon who knows I am an author tells me all about his idea for a book on fishing and travel. An elementary school teacher who finds out that I sometimes teach children's literature assumes that I write children's books (I don't) but she insists that I look at her idea for a picture book anyway, hoping that I can help. A Spanish professor who has been discussing an idea for a textbook with a major publisher calls me for advice on negotiating her contract, and we chat for half an hour. I visit my father in Florida assuming that I will be on vacation from authors and would-be authors, only to discover that Dad wants to write a collection of stories about growing up on a ranch in Colorado. Becoming a writer is like putting a message in a bottle and dropping it into the ocean; ultimately, what prompts us to write is the hope of connecting with at least one other person who will read and respond.

When people think about writing, they often dwell on the more mechanical aspects (e.g., spelling, punctuation, usage/grammar) or the finishing touches of writing (e.g., proofreading for errors). Experienced and accomplished authors take a very different view. Two contemporary experts define writing as: "a challenge to our creativity; an opportunity to know our own mind; and a chance to share our thoughts and feelings with others" (Trimble, 2000, p. 161) and as "a way of arguing with ourselves, a way of keeping ourselves honest by discovering precisely what we believe and finding out whether we are justified in believing it" (Raymond, 1986, p. 2). Unlike the "writing as minutiae" and "writing as drudgery" definitions so often held by students in Composition 101, these definitions of writing from accomplished authors are enriched and enlarged beyond basic skills and linked directly to creative thinking.

THE MEANING OF AUTHORSHIP

Prior to the invention of the printing press, the individual ownership of written work by an ordinary person was a foreign concept. Most "writers" in medieval times were actually human copy machines, like the monks who generated illuminated manuscripts. Yet, any change in the communication environment brings accompanying changes in our definition of authorship. Now that manuscripts are produced electronically, the whole issue of author's rights is the subject of considerable controversy (see *Text and Academic Authors: Declaration on Authors' Rights* http://taa.winona.msus.edu/TAA/Articles/).

Originally, the word "author" meant the originator of just about anything; today, it is used to signify a person who generates a written product, takes responsibility for what has been published, and is recognized or compensated for producing manuscripts.

According to the American Educational Research Association (1994) the concept of authorship includes three dimensions: a) writing the text, b) making other substantive contributions to the work (e.g., conceptualizing the study), and c) bearing primary responsibility for the published work. Disagreements about whether a contribution is "substantive" or "primary" abound. When determining what contributions merit authorship, "Most standards revolve around two issues: knowledge and responsibility" (Luey, 1995, p. 16). An author must be intimately familiar with the content of the entire work as well as willing to stand behind it. Suppose an administrator has had minimal involvement in the development of a major grant proposal. He signs off on the cover page and the faculty responsible for the grant list his name as a "courtesy." Neither the criterion of knowledge nor the criterion of responsibility has been met. It is an unethical practice designed to curry favor with a supervisor. It is not authorship.

Conversely,

> it is grossly unfair to deny authorship to someone who truly deserves it by virtue of his or her intellectual contributions. . . . My own personal policy has been, when the question of authorship is doubtful, to be generous and award it to a student or colleague. I figure that in the grand scheme of things it is better to commit the error of over-inclusiveness that to deny merited recognition to someone. In addition, such a policy helps to attract others to agree to collaborate with you, which is another positive consideration. I don't know of anyone who has gotten into trouble from being overly generous in awarding authorships, but I know of more than a few who earned the reputations of being pretty stingy or, even worse, of exploiting the work of others and not giving them proper credit. (Thyer, 1994, p. 99)

Even when ownership of the work is not an issue, it is sometimes difficult for novices to see themselves as authors. Perhaps you feel as Gabrielle Rico (1991) did during her college studies:

> Writer. I knew the word did not apply to me: Inside my head was a chaos I could not untangle in my own words: I was only a cutter and a paster, a borrower, a fake. While real writers shaped form and content, I felt little more than a hopelessly tangled fullness where ideas should be. (p. 4)

Believing that you are writer is a gradual process that can begin surprisingly late in life. The first inkling, the one that Rico alluded to, is that a writer does more than cut and paste.

Successful authors have learned to bring their formal training, work experience, and personal/professional interests to bear on the subject matter, for it is the intersection of these things that creates a particularly fertile territory for writing. Try filling in the Venn Diagram in Figure 2.1. What sort of manuscript would successfully unite these three elements for you?

Take this book as an example. In terms of formal training, I earned an undergraduate degree in English Literature, a Master of Arts in Teaching Language Arts, and a Ph.D. in Curriculum and Instruction. My work at the university nowadays consists primarily of teaching a doctoral seminar in writing for publication, a qualitative research course, and supervising dissertations. One-quarter of my 12-credit load each semester is as a journal editor. At this stage in my career, I am interested in mentoring graduate students and using writing as a tool for professional development. This book emerged from the confluence of that training, experience, and interest.

After your writing is firmly grounded in your uniqueness and you find a topic you truly care about, you are in a better position to enter into the ongoing professional dialogue through writing. You begin to find your voice as an author.

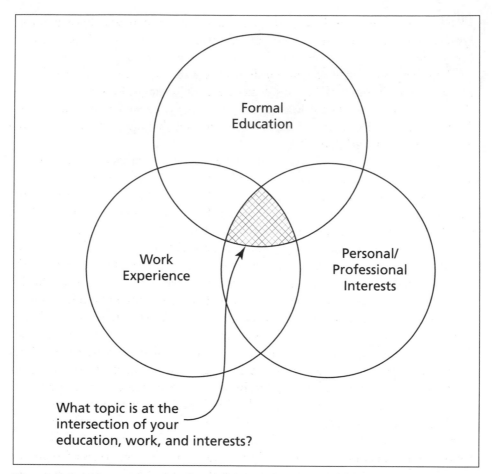

Figure 2.1   *Venn Diagram for Analyzing Writing Strengths*

I like the voice metaphor for several reasons, which I have written about else-where (Jalongo, 1991). First of all, it implies that we are being heard. Second, it has range—that place where your voice neither bottoms out on the low note nor squeaks to hit a high note, that place where your voice does not quaver and rings out loud and strong. A third reason why the analogy of the voice works so well is that, through practice, a person can extend her or his vocal range con-siderably. It is, in fact, the extent of the range and the versatility within it that contribute to a vocalist's talent. Fourth, just as with the singing voice, our writer's voice is developmental. A young child begins with a vocal range of about five notes, and those who first seek to write for publication may also begin with limited repertoires, yet eventually reach the writer's equivalent of a "trained" singing voice. Fifth, a voice is something that you possess, and developing it is an inside-out operation. No one can bequeath a voice to you or improve it for you. Rather, they can listen and encourage, offer suggestions, guide your practice, or function as role models. But you are always the one controlling your own voice. Sixth, and finally, what enables anyone to sing gloriously is a combination of talent, confidence, experience, and persistence. It helps if you have mentors, appreciative audiences, and fellow enthusiasts; it helps if you feel like a member of the choir.

Finding your voice as an author depends on controlling your fear of failure. As Irwin Shaw points out, "An absolutely necessary part of a writer's equipment, almost as necessary as talent, is the ability to stand up under punishment, both the punishment the world hands out and the punishment he inflicts on himself" (in Winokur, 1999, p. 124).

My students struggle mightily to find this resiliency within themselves and to begin writing in an authentic voice. Typically, students who choose a writing intensive course as an elective are reasonably confident of themselves as writers. Those who are required to take the class, however, frequently approach it with all the trepidation of math-anxious students assigned to an advanced statistics course.

Anju used this analogy, "Do you know that beach feeling, that first day when you put on a swimsuit and regret overeating during the winter? Well, that's the way I feel about my writing—exposed, embarrassed, guilty." I hasten to add that this particular student was successful in having her manuscript published in a well-respected journal. But she is right about writing. It does give us the feeling of being vulnerable and having our flaws pointed out. To take her swimsuit analogy further, she must have had a motive for overcoming her embarrassment about looking less than perfect in a swimsuit. Maybe it was the goal of creating happy vacation memories with her family. Maybe she assured herself that she would exercise and blend in better with the beach crowd. And so it is with writing.

You need to have larger issues in mind than your initial discomfort or reluctance to participate. You also need to make some changes in order to join the ranks of published authors. You need to set goals. You'll have to risk feeling out of place at first. If the old saying that a writer's apprenticeship is not over until she or he has written a million words is true, then writing more is the only way to move closer to the goal of becoming a writer.

Perhaps the most adamant about despising writing was Derry, a 6' 5" school superintendent. He had learned to camouflage his writing deficiencies with the help of very efficient secretaries who could "clean up" his writing. Even though Derry protested that he had nothing significant to say at our first individual conference, I pushed a bit and asked him (to paraphrase Lucy Calkins, 1995), "What is it that you know and care about and would like to discuss with other principals?" Still stumped, we scheduled another writing conference in a couple of weeks. I urged him to really look around at what happened at school and think about what he might write that could be helpful to others in similar circumstances. He was expected to arrive at my office with three possibilities for articles.

When we met, he first trotted out the current workshop buzzwords and I asked him, "What else?" Cautiously, he said, "Well, one of the things that concerns me is how foster children are handled when they enter the school system. It is often the case that I have no information, and I'm not just talking about grades or birthdays, but critical information like a food allergy or the fact a child nearly drowned and is terrified of the water when swimming is part of the physical education program. Sometimes, the child is literally dropped off in the office without much more than a first name." "In your conversations with other principals, does this seem like a common problem?" I asked. He nodded, warming to his topic. I said, "Okay, here's the challenge. Imagine an article that would help these children and your colleagues. Pretend you are a first-year principal and write the article that you wish someone had written for you to read. This is a topic that you know and care about. Now *that* would be at the intersection of your training, experience, and interest." I further suggested that he begin without composing sentences at all; first by interviewing his colleagues, just as a journalist might, inviting them to express their concerns and share stories of practice. From there he could avoid the dreaded task of writing even longer by searching the library, reading, and taking notes.

The following week, Derry arrived with good news/bad news. The good news was that every principal he contacted had been enthused about his article idea and each one had contributed in some way to his thinking on the topic. The bad news was that a search of the educational literature on foster children had turned up very little information. When this happens, the best thing to do is to go interdisciplinary. If a particular field fails to provide the needed information, it is up to the author to construct an information base drawn from diverse fields—in this case, psychology, sociology, administration, family studies, and so forth. We continued to work on the manuscript together, and he continued to feel sufficiently daunted at various times to rebel at my editorial suggestions.

About a year after the writing seminar was over, I had a call from Derry. It was a frantically overscheduled day with new faculty interviews and doctoral exams, and I tried to persuade him to choose a different day to meet. But he insisted that, even if I could find just 15 minutes, he really only wanted to stop by. I looked up from my desk when he appeared in the doorway. He had a leather folio in hand and said, "I want to show you something." With that he produced a certificate for an "Outstanding Feature Article Award" from EDPRESS, the coalition of educational publishers that includes everything from *Ranger Rick* to *Educational Leadership*. Derry's first article, "Kids in Limbo" had been published in *Principal* magazine and had earned a prestigious award for writing. I treasure my photocopy of Derry's award more than any I have earned for my writing. This was quite a transformation for a person who was convinced that he could not write, much less publish. But through Derry's story, you can see how selecting the right topic was crucial to his success. What about you? What do you know and care about and what is getting in the way of writing about it?

WRITING OBSTACLES

A popular psychologist explains how we argue for our own limitations and talk ourselves out of being writers (Carlson, 1997).

> When we decide that something is true or beyond our reach, it's very difficult to pierce through this self-created hurdle. . . . suppose, for example, that you tell yourself, "I can't write." You'll look for examples to prove your position. . . . You'll fill your head with limitations that will frighten you from trying. In order to become a writer or anything else, the first step is to silence your greatest critic—you. (p. 119)

Part of becoming an author, then, is replacing negative self-talk with positive self-talk and silencing that critic until you generate a good, working draft and need to enlist that critic's help. Figure 2.2 provides some examples of how that might occur.

What does that critical voice inside you have to say about writing? Possibly, something like this: Who cares what you think? Why would anyone want to read this? What if you do all that work and it is rejected? Why not do something else instead? What makes you think you're so smart? And so on.

Level I   Negative Acceptance

Example of Level I Self-talk: I doubt that I can become a writer. Who cares what I think? Yet I must admit that it would be nice to be a published author.

Level II   Recognition of the Need to Change

Example of Level II Self-talk: I know that I need to develop my writing skills. I want to make improvements but I'm not sure how to go about it. It seems like a daunting task.

Level III   Decision to Change

Example of Level III Self-talk: I want to experience the satisfactions of authorship and publication. Maybe I can do this if I really try.

Level IV   The Better You

Example of Level IV Self-talk: Even though I have not published much yet, I can see a direct relationship between the effort I put into writing and the results. If I make this a professional goal, I can experience success as a writer.

Level V   Universal Affirmation

Example of Level V Self-talk: It is important for any professional to master written communication. I see value in writing for publication for leaders and scholars in all fields.

Adapted from Manning, B. H. (1991). *Cognitive self-instruction for classroom processes.* Albany, NY: State University of New York Press.

Figure 2.2 *The Role of Positive Self-Talk in Writing*

According to Robert Boice's (1990) research on 40 blocked writers, there are five major obstacles to writing for publication. Figure 2.3 suggests a strategy for bringing each impediment under control.

When it comes to writing, I am put in mind of the often-reprinted cartoon in which a student stands in front of the chalkboard looking at a very complicated statistical formula. The beginning of the formula is there and the answer is there. What is missing is the solution in the middle. Rather than filling in the middle of the solution, the student has written the words, "and then a miracle happens." A professor is pointing to those words, while saying, "I think you need to be a little more specific right here." In order to become a writer, you need to begin working out the problem rather that waiting for a miracle. Perry (1999) categorizes would-be and novice writers into three groups:

- Group 1: Those who perpetually wait for a flash of inspiration that will make them famous

---

Obstacle to Overcome: Perfectionism

Typical Comment: "If I can't have a major impact on my field through writing, then why even try?"

Recommended Strategy: Establish momentum by using free writing.

Obstacle to Overcome: Procrastination

Typical Comment: "As soon as I have _____ (leisure time, a brilliant idea, a new computer, etc.) I'll begin to write."

Recommended Strategy: Establish a regimen of regular writing.

Obstacle to Overcome: Aversion to Writing

Typical Comment: "I've always had trouble with writing. I hated it in school and still hate it now."

Recommended Strategy: Avoid negative self-talk

Obstacle to Overcome: Impatience

Typical Comment: "I'll just send it out and let the editor fix it up for me."

Recommended Strategy: Establish comfort (chair, light, take a break)

Obstacle to Overcome: Fear of Rejection

Typical Comment: "What if I do all of this work and it is rejected? I'll be worse off than when I started."

Recommended Strategy: Use a real, live audience

Figure 2.3   *Obstacles to Writing for Publication*

- Group 2: Those who use preparation (reading one more article, talking about their idea) as a way to avoid actually writing

- Group 3: Those who vainly hope that they can exercise total control over their writing output through grim determination

In contrast, real writers are much more likely to adopt the attitude of "Just get up and do the work." They accept that pieces of it will be good almost from the start, some of it will be good after extensive revision, and some of it will need to be thrown away. Yet, like the medical school professor and physician who told a group of future doctors, "Half of what you learn in medical school will be wrong or outdated by the time you graduate. The problem is, we don't know which half." The problem for beginning writers is that they don't know which instincts to follow at first. They aren't sure which parts are really good, which parts are worthy of revision, and which parts will ultimately be tossed.

This is where a thoughtful reader and skilled editor can help. Readers can let us know when we are communicating well and when we are not. They can scrawl in the margin, "I'd like to hear more about this" or "Now I'm confused. Are you saying _____ or are you saying _____?" or even, "I'm not sure that I agree with you. What about . . . ?" When such guidance is offered, it is up to the author to generate the ideas, draw upon experience, and produce the text unless the reader/editor is an active collaborator and co-author. As an editor, I may write in the margin, "Can you provide a specific example here?" but it is not up to me as an editor to supply that example.

When composing text, I often begin with handwritten scrawls, a throwback from the pre-word processing days, then edit as I type, then edit on hard copy, and edit as I type some more—usually about 15 times. That's the "miracle" part. My students are disappointed to find out that I don't know how to sail over the messy part of writing and produce clear prose from the start. In many ways, I see myself like that scene from *The Wizard of Oz* where the little dog Toto pulls back the curtain to reveal an ordinary person frantically working the buttons and levers to create the illusion of power and confidence. What they see in my published writing is the result of that frenzied behind-the-scenes activity that I call writing. It isn't any easier to make my writing flow than it was for the Wizard to put on his performance. But whether we are talking about publishing or wizards, a good outcome in both cases exacts a price. Both demand determination, an investment of energy and time, and a focused, well-concerted effort under the pressure of deadlines.

I am an optimist when it comes to writing for publication. Most professional people are capable of writing for publication when provided with appropriate opportunities and support. Those who find writing aversive often have been mistreated by teachers who are not writers themselves. Such miseducated students have learned to think about writing as bad news messages about their intelligence, ability, or even their character (e.g., "sloppy" writing).

Those who remain at the "exercise" level of writing where it is a chore, a bore, and something done only because somebody else demands it are missing out on the satisfactions of writing. Among those pleasures is the satisfaction of knowing that somebody else read it and enjoyed it. The word "enjoy" literally means to partake in the joy of someone (or something) else. Let me offer an example. It is an editorial that I wrote for *Early Childhood Education Journal* called "How I Learned to Appreciate Opera" that yielded a flurry of notes and e-mails, commenting on how much various readers enjoyed it. Before I published the piece, my husband read it and loved it, even though I think of him as my "tough read," the one who will not fail to tell me if my writing misses the mark. After it was published, it was condensed and reprinted in *Our Children*, the magazine of the National Parent Teacher Association. Next, it was posted on the Internet. I submitted it, along with other editorials I had written to the Educational Press Association, as an entry in a contest for the best set of editorials among all those published during the previous year. Although the editorials did not win the national award, I appreciated a comment written by the evaluators: "The opera piece was especially good." Read the editorial in Figure 2.4 and see if you can decide why other readers were able enjoy it.

Editorial: On Behalf of Children
"How I Learned To Appreciate Opera"

When I was four and my sister was six, we did something really awful. My grouchy grandfather who lived with us was babysitting and had sent us to bed early so that he could watch his favorite television program, the Metropolitan Opera. Margie, my big sister who was in first grade, had learned to tell time on the hour and was able to confirm our suspicions that the bedtime contract had been violated. With evidence to fuel the indignation that only a newly emerging sense of justice can summon, my sister convinced me to be her confederate in an act of protest. We sneaked out of the bedroom, through the kitchen, and under the dining room table where we looked on as grandpa sat completely transfixed by the music blaring from the broadcast, his face nearly pressed against the small black-and-white screen. When *we* sat that close, we were always reminded that it would ruin our eyes. Grandpa Gemmellaro was breaking the rules over that stupid opera singing!

Although I was satisfied that I had been sufficiently rebellious for one evening, my sister decided to escalate by pitching crayons into the living room, first at a distance, then daring to aim closer to grandpa's chair. He began to notice, first looking around, then standing up and cursing in Italian. I begged her to stop and we scurried back to our bedroom, jumped into bed, and pretended to be asleep when grandpa opened the door to check up on us. It appeared that our crime would go undiscovered.

The next morning, my mother confronted us and demanded to know what had happened. At four, I was convinced that my mother could read my mind, so I quickly confessed. My mother made it clear that we had, through miserable example, succeeded in arriving at a definitive answer to two persistent questions in a young child's mind, "What is *really* bad?" and "What

---

Figure 2.4   *Editorial: "How I Learned to Appreciate Opera"*

Figure 2.4 *continued*

would happen if *I* did something really bad?" We were punished with early bedtimes for an entire month. That night, as we whispered arguments back and forth about who was the most culpable, we arrived at a truce by blaming it all on grandpa's opera.

Years later when I was a college sophomore, my grandfather came to our home for a visit. He was nearly ninety and had a significant hearing loss. I had been saving for months to purchase a small stereo and had the brainstorm that grandpa might be able to hear his beloved opera again if he put on the headphones and the volume was turned up. We gathered albums from my mother's collection as well as the public library. I put a record on the turntable and experimented with the volume, treble, and bass, all the while watching intently for his reaction. My grandfather's face lit up when he could hear the first strains of Verdi and, as a favorite aria began to play, tears of joy streamed down his cheeks. He apologized for crying, saying that it was the first time in many years that he had been able to listen to the music that he loved so much. To this day, my immediate visual image of my grandfather depicts him sitting on the white chenille bedspread in my bedroom with puffy, plastic, first-generation headphones adorning his sparse white hair.

Interestingly, when I visited my sisters this summer I had been playing Pavarotti's *My Favorite Showstoppers* in the car on the trip there, Margie had a CD of opera "for people who hate opera," and my younger sister (who was not a part of the crayon crime but who also grew up with opera playing in the house) had tickets to see *Aida*. We all developed an appreciation for opera, I think, because we were immersed in it during early childhood.

When adults are not "officially" teaching them, children learn, as Frank Smith (1992) argues, from the company they keep. Many of us who have been in the field of education for a while were mistakenly trained to think that education is mostly about covering information when in fact, it is mainly about human relationships. Children don't learn by pushing a crayon or shuffling papers or parroting back rules. They learn through thoughtful observation, active participation, spontaneous play, heartfelt laughter, stimulating talk, intense interest, and genuine enthusiasm. One of my education professors used to say that many things were "better caught than taught," meaning that who we are and what we stand for is what teaches children the lessons that last a lifetime. My sisters and I "caught" an enduring appreciation for opera, even though we rejected it at first, because grandpa was our constant companion and opera was his passion.

As a beginning teacher, I can remember having it drummed into my head that "appreciation" was far too vague to be a learning goal, that educators should focus exclusively on observable, measurable behaviors. I doubted this then and I openly challenge it now. I am opposed to abandoning appreciation as a goal just because it is difficult to assess. Albert Einstein reputedly had a sign on his office wall that helps to explain why. The sign read, "Not everything that matters can be counted and not everything that can be counted matters." The fact that a goal like appreciation is difficult to measure does not diminish its importance. Instead, it should challenge all of us who have the audacity to

continued on next page

Figure 2.4   *continued*

call ourselves educators to understand appreciation better, find ways of building it, and devise strategies for documenting its growth.

Although we have scarcely begun to understand the role of emotions in learning, recent books on the mind such as *Emotional Intelligence* (Goleman, 1996) provide a research base for something that early childhood educators have known intuitively all along—that emotion has profound significance for the learning process. In other words, powerful emotions, both good and bad, make the most indelible mark on young children. In *A Celebration of Neurons: An Educator's Guide to the Human Brain* (Sylwester, 1995) observes:

> Our profession pays lip service to educating the whole student, but school activities tend to focus on the development of measurable, rational qualities. . . . We know emotion is very important to the educative process because it drives attention, which drives learning and memory. We've never really understood emotion, however, and so don't know how to regulate it in school—beyond defining too much or too little of it as misbehavior and relegating most of it to the arts, PE, recess, and the extracurricular program. Thus, we've never incorporated emotion comfortably into the curriculum and classroom. (p.72)

It is particularly important for early childhood educators to succeed in educating the whole child and nurturing emotional intelligence because the early years are "prime time" in brain development. An under stimulating or negative environment isn't simply a "disadvantage" (to use the benign language of the 1970s) it can adversely affect the physical structure and development of the brain throughout life. A study from the Carnegie Corporation (1994) states it this way: "The quality of young children's environment and social experience has a decisive, long-lasting impact on their well-being and ability to learn" (p.4). Perhaps my sisters and I were eventually captivated by opera because it was so much a part of our early environment and social experience. It certainly had a decisive, long-lasting impact, although that impact was delayed until adulthood. In my case, two recent incidents awakened my long dormant fascination with opera's power to evoke an emotional response. The first was watching a scene from the film *Philadelphia* in which Tom Hanks shares his passion for an aria from *Madame Butterfly* with his lawyer, played by Denzel Washington. Although opera is completely foreign to the lawyer, he leaves his client's home feeling curiously affected. The second event that revived my curiosity about opera was the Italian National Opera's performance of *Rigoletto* on our college campus two years ago. Afterward, a colleague and I agreed that the very reason why some people do not care for opera is the reason we do. We are attracted to its flair for the dramatic. Much like the red, white, and pink peonies that burst forth in my June garden and bow under the weight of their own blossoms, opera is not timid about being flamboyant and displaying its range of intensity. Both the live performance of *Rigoletto* and the movie *Philadelphia* prompted me to search for recordings of that style of music that was an integral part of my early earliest experience. An appreciation for opera was one of the things that my grandfather assumed he could never teach us. Yet because his appreciation for opera was so deeply and genuinely felt, it became the lesson of a lifetime.

Figure 2.4   *continued*

References

Carnegie Corporation of New York (1994). *Starting points: Meeting the needs of our youngest children*. New York: Author.

Goleman, D. (1996). *Emotional intelligence*. New York: Bantam.

Smith, F. (1992). Learning to read: The never-ending debate. *Phi Delta Kappan*, *73*(6), 432-441.

Sylwester, R. (1995). *A celebration of neurons: An educator's guide to the human brain*. Alexandria, VA: Association for Supervision and Curriculum Development.

MARY RENCK JALONGO
Editor

Here are my hunches. First, I took the time-honored advice given to authors: I wrote about something that I knew very well and cared deeply about. Second, I was honest about things. I didn't try to canonize my grandfather or portray myself as the perfect little child in a perfect family. Third, I had a point to make beyond just telling my story. It is more than a charming trip down memory lane. There is relevance for today. Now, having said all this, I also admit that I am struggling to write another one equally good. I just don't have an unlimited supply of stories that are that compelling and so much a part of the fabric of my life.

HOW REAL WRITERS BEHAVE

As noted educator Mina Shaughnessy (1979) observed in her classic book on composition, *Errors and Expectations*, beginning writers do not know how writers behave. Part of daring to imagine yourself as an author, then, is finding out what writers do. Bloom's (1991) composition students made some observations about how writers learn their craft, a list that I have adapted and included here. Writers learn from

- reading extensively and picking up vocabulary and sentence patterns, a sense of style, as they read;

- reading aloud, from paying attention to the sound of the words;

- writing and revising work that really means something to them;

- soliciting opinions from trusted, truthful colleagues;

- getting feedback from teachers who write; and

- belonging to a learning community of writers.

It is a basic principle of human psychology that people tend to become what they practice the most; therefore, a writer is a person who writes. Like most adult learners, we approach our learning goals as projects and capitalize on the multi-source nature of learning. If you want to learn to cook, for example, you might begin with some simple recipes and later advance to more challenging food preparation tasks. You might seek informal learning experiences such as asking an accomplished cook to show you how she or he prepares a particular dish or watching a chef on television. You probably would take advantage of more structured, formal opportunities as well, such as enrolling in a cooking class. You would look at cookbooks. You would prepare food and try it out on appreciative audiences. In fact, these are the same strategies that writers use.

Professionals who seek to publish write their way into becoming writers. As Roorbach (1998) explains, "if you work on a steady (preferably daily) basis, you'll soon find what you're looking for: access to memory, access to material, access to ideas, access to the unconscious, and finally, access to meaning" (p. 4).

Writers also understand that "One of the most crucial ways in which a culture provides aid to intellectual growth is through dialogue between the more experienced and the less experienced" (Bruner, 1971, p. 107). They might invite a more experienced author to talk about writing or locate a book of advice on writing by a noted author. They would also try their writing out on other writers they respect, writers they trust to be fair and honest. In short, they make writing a project and invest hundreds of hours in getting better at it.

When it comes to being a writer, one thing is certain. At some point, whether you are working alone, with a partner, or on a team, somebody has to generate text—a newsletter, manual, a grant proposal, or article—and polish the manuscript until it fairly shines. Anyone who succeeds as an author recognizes that writing well requires time, patience, and thoughtfulness. Writers have many strategies in place for maximizing their opportunities to write. Figure 2.5 identifies behaviors that are typical of successful writers.

As Temple and Gillet (1989) point out, there are many misleading media images about the writing life:

> Inevitably, the writer is shown tapping away busily at the typewriter or word processor keyboard, often leaning avidly over the keys as the lines roll forth. . . . Such images reinforce the naïve but popular notion that for "real" writers words spring forth almost unbidden, especially when the writer is "inspired." . . . In this way we come to think of writing, composing, as an all-or-nothing process: either the words are there, pouring out in orderly paragraphs as fast as the writer can type or dictate, or the words are completely gone, leaving the writer in despair with his head in his hands. (p.43)

If, to borrow a phrase from the inventor Thomas Edison, writing well relies less on inspiration and more on perspiration, then successful writers must know something about how to get the work accomplished.

- Read voraciously and venture across disciplinary boundaries
- Always keep writing paper or dictation equipment handy
- Plan quiet time
- Use the Internet to find out about publishing opportunities
- Use e-mail to correspond with editors and authors
- Carry a voice-activated tape recorder to use while traveling in the car
- Make files or piles of material for a project
- Listen to books on tape related to your topic as you exercise or drive
- Learn to read for style rather than just content
- Leave yourself a reminder to write on your answering machine or on e-mail
- Give yourself some instant gratification and accomplish a relatively easy writing task
- Find a walking or exercising partner who can respond to writing ideas
- Take advantage of every opportunity to "talk writing"

Figure 2.5   *Behaving Like a Real Writer*

MEETING THE CHALLENGES OF WRITING

It happens all of the time. A copy of the latest educational publication arrives in the mail, you skim the table of contents, flip through until you find an article to read, read it, then say to yourself, "This isn't *that* great. I could have written it." What's stopping you from becoming a writer? When I talk with educators who are preparing to retire, they invariably say that they want to write a book, now that they have the time. But was it the time that they needed or was it the passion for a topic and the confidence and skills equal to the task of producing a book? Based on the publication track records of these retirees, time was not the issue.

The very fact that you are reading this book suggests that you have some writing goals in mind. What is it that you hope to achieve? Twenty years ago, a friend gave me a blank book in which to write my professional goals. At that time, my goals seemed extravagant. I wanted to publish in two of the leading professional journals in my field. There was no mention of writing books because it seemed too far-fetched. Yet here I sit, eighteen books (if you count subsequent editions) and nearly sixty articles later, writing to share what I have learned in the interim.

There is nothing wrong with starting out modestly where writing goals are concerned. Select something achievable rather than choosing something daunting and intimidating. Several times I have heard the nonwriters say that they never wrote for publication because their standards were too high. Unless they could achieve national acclaim and revolutionize the field, they preferred not to write and contribute to all of the second-rate material out there in print. I suspect that this is sheer bravado, that what they really fear is having their ideas scrutinized by others and the resultant threats to fragile egos. As long as there is no peer review, nonwriters can afford to be smug about others' efforts and convince themselves that theirs would have been much better. As the novelist Erica Jong points out, "I went for years not finishing anything. Because, of course, when you finish something, you can be judged. . . ." (in Winokur, 1986, p. 104). When setting your writing goals, use the same rule of thumb as when remodeling a house: take whatever you think might be invested (time or money) and double, or even triple it. Using the list in Figure 2.6, rate your ability to meet each professional writing challenge

---

Rate your ability to perform each task as high (H), moderate (M), or low (L).

____ Selecting topics and issues that are relevant for the journal's readership

____ Remaining focused on the article's main goals. Finding relevant references

____ Creating an attention-getting, communicative title

____ For those whose first language is not English, overcoming the language barrier

____ Successfully summarizing the institutional, cultural, and national context of the project

____ Deciding which findings and other information to present, and how to present them

____ Using a consistent writing style, particularly if there is more than one author

____ Removing ambiguity from the manuscript

____ Presenting clear, persuasive arguments

____ Achieving conciseness and avoiding verbosity

____ Remaining appropriately impartial, when necessary

____ Overcoming anxiety about meeting the journal's standards and those of colleagues

---

Source: Jason, H., Majoor, G., & Westberg, J. (1999). Writing for publication: Outcomes of the Albuquerque workshop. *Education for Health: Change in Training & Practice* *12*(1), 108–110.

Figure 2.6 *Challenges Professional Writers Face*

as low, moderate, or high. Then reflect on who or what might enable you to move up—is it a class or workshop? A book on a particular facet of writing? A tough-minded reader? Figuring out who or what you need and how to get it is part of becoming a writer.

UNDERSTANDING ROLES AND RESPONSIBILITIES

As the highly successful novelist James Michener has noted, "Many people who want to be writers don't really want to be writers. They want *to have* been writers. They wish they had a book in print" (Winokur, 1986, p. 9). The research on higher education faculty seems to bear this out. On average, new faculty spent 30 minutes per week on writing and produced .3 manuscripts per year, although they predicted that they would spend 10 hours per week and complete 1-2 journal articles per year (Boice, 1997). And, although some faculty seem to love repeating that phrase, "publish or perish," it appears that not all that much publishing is necessary to stay alive. Boice (1997) found that the norm for meeting tenure/promotion criteria was just 1.5 refereed journal articles per year. New faculty tended to become productive writers when they had the following habits:

- They actively sought advice about teaching and scholarly writing from colleagues.

- They tended to write across more weeks than less productive peers and rarely complained of busyness or stress. They rarely engaged in binge writing (except for grants).

- They showed high self-esteem that was reflected in their willingness to share their work in formative stages prior to submitting it for publication.

- They set limits on lecture preparation time and emphasized involving students as active learners, thereby excelling in student and peer ratings of their teaching.

Living the writing life is difficult. To begin, you must first accept several responsibilities associated with authorship. Perhaps the most basic of these author's responsibilities are the following:

Get right to the point

Authors owe it to readers to write a statement of purpose that appears almost immediately in the work, preferably within the first three paragraphs. Authors sometimes don't know what their purpose is until they get to the conclusion. More times than you might imagine, the concluding comments actually fit better on the first page because the author has finally figured out what she or he has to say. Today's readers have less patience with longwinded warm-ups. They are accustomed to surfing the net and pausing only when something captures their attention. If you postpone stating the purpose until you are well into the manuscript, you will lose many readers along the way. Remember that more publications are going electronic every day and that the computer screen makes even a short amount of text look imposing. Be succinct and let your readers know, almost immediately, why they should go on reading.

Report information accurately

Authors are obligated to attest to the accuracy of what they have written. Aspiring authors who consider themselves to be sticklers for details have never really been tested until their work has been scrutinized by professional copy editors who make a living by attending to minutiae. A good copy editor can rescue you from mortifying mistakes (like a sentence that is missing the word "not"), ask you questions you cannot answer ("You cite Einstein. Is that Albert E. or his brother?"), and find so many discrepancies between an article and a list of references that you begin to wonder if gremlins crept into your computer at night. Remember to check, check, and check again.

Communicate effectively with a particular audience

Writers are responsible for bringing their readers and their material closer together. Do not approach the writing of a manuscript generically with the thought in mind that, "Everyone will want to read it!" Try to identify a particular audience. Writing first and then searching for a suitable audience and outlet is about as effective as the custom tailor who designs a suit of clothes and then searches for someone to fit them. It is far better to clearly identify your specific audience and two or three outlets at the very beginning. Why? Because it helps you to decide on what Adelstein and Pival (1997) call the ABCs of audience: a) appeal—why bring this material and audience together?, b) breadth—how much ground should be covered in a short article for this group?, and c) complexity—how much background are readers likely to have and how much explanation is necessary?

Revise the prose until it flows

Authors are responsible for skillfully written, carefully proofread manuscripts. Beginning authors frequently mistake a third or fourth draft for a publishable work. I have heard many reviewers and editors who subscribe to the "three strikes and you're out" approach. This means that if they encounter three or more errors within the first couple of pages, they simply stop reading and reject the work. Bear in mind that you cannot expect readers to reread or divine your meaning. Clarity is your responsibility, not your editor's.

Benefit from reviewer feedback

Authors bear responsibility for learning from their mistakes. One writer described the losing attitude this way, "My work keeps getting rejected when it is sent out for peer review. I think it is just too innovative for the referees to evaluate fairly. They say that a truly creative person has no peers so it might be the case that they simply aren't accepting of my work because it is so original!" This author refused to consider any criticism of his work and dismissed it as personal jealousy. But, let's switch roles for a minute, now focusing on the role of the reader. As a reader, you are entitled to scan through the table of contents of the latest issue of a professional journal and decide what you want to read. Would you call that *personal* taste or professional interest? In the philosophical field of logic, there is a type of argument referred to as "ad hominem." Put simply, it means that when we can't get anywhere with other types of argument, we begin to attack the person by saying he or she is unintelligent, closed-minded, unattractive, and so forth. This author seems to be saying that he is so far above the reviewers that their tiny brains cannot comprehend his brilliance. Although incompetence can exist in reviewers just as surely as it does in other walks of life, it would be hard to convince me that no one was this writer's equal. Try to keep an open mind whether you are in the writer's or the reviewer's role. Once, while co-authoring a scholarly book, we received a single-spaced, four-page review. "What did you think of Reviewer 2's comments?" I asked my co-author. She replied, "I think Reviewer 2 knows even more about this subject than we do." We found out later that our reviewer was, indeed, the leading expert in the field and, rather than disagreeing, we used those insightful comments to strengthen the work.

Adhere to the outlet's guidelines

Writers are responsible for following the rules. They are not exempt from such low-level considerations by virtue of their brilliance. One publication wants book and journal titles underlined; another specifically states that they are to be italicized. One publication requires a copyright release before they will review the manuscript, another waits until it has been reviewed and issues a publication agreement. Each editor and publication has slightly different requirements and, if you seek to publish with them, you need to conform to what is expected.

BEGINNING TO SEE YOURSELF AS AN AUTHOR

Pulitzer Prize-winning author Richard Rhodes observed, "I think that writing is something that people find hard to start, primarily because they are afraid—afraid they don't have the right to speak, afraid no one should care about what they have to say. I certainly went through that" (cited in Lamb 1997, p. 264). Part of growing into any role is an act of creative visualization, for unless we dare to imagine ourselves in the desired role it will be hard to fulfill it. Mental imagery is such a powerful technique that coaches of various sports now use it. They urge the Olympic divers, pole-vaulters, or figure skaters to picture themselves executing the perfect dive, breaking the pole vaulting record, or skating a program that earns a nearly perfect score. There also appears to be a developmental sequence to these professional images that we carry around in our heads like video clips. Based on research with educators, they follow a progression like this:

Self → Task → Impact (Loucks-Horsely, 1987)

At first, we are in the "self" stage. We tend to be egocentric, wondering if this role is a possibility for us. We refer to "my paper" and forget that we are writing for an audience instead of ourselves. We want to hear from our readers, "Don't change a word—it's perfect!" Ironically, it is just the opposite perspective we need to take: "The right to fail is of the essence of creativity. The creative act must be uninhibited and marked by supreme confidence; there can be no fear of failure—nothing inhibits so fiercely, or shrinks a vision so drastically, or pulls a dream to earth so swiftly, as fear of failure" (Sullivan, 1963, p. 191).

When I was in my doctoral program, one of my professors used to encourage us to approach high-risk professional ventures with the question, "What is the worst thing that could happen?" Usually, about the worst is that I send my article in and this particular outlet rejects it. The worst thing that could happen is that it is never published at all and, even if that happens, I am not much worse off than before. To the extent that I keep working and improving, my chances of finding a publication outlet increase. In writing about the risks associated with writing, graduate student Pamela Richards (1986) concluded:

> As I write more and more, I begin to understand that it's not all-or-nothing. If I actually write something down, I'm liable to win a bit and lose a bit. For a long time I worked under the burden of thinking that it was an all-or-nothing proposition. What got written had to be priceless literary pearls or unmitigated garbage.
>
> Not so. It's just a bunch of stuff, more or less sorted into an argument. Some of it's good, some of it isn't. (p. 120)

Our preoccupation with self eventually matures into something like, "How, exactly, am I going to grow into the writer's role?" It is during the "self" stage that you gain insight into the strategies that enable you to generate text. Because this is a highly individual matter, it depends on metacognition—your ability to think about your own thinking. At first, your efforts might feel more like some of the metaphors commonly used to describe writing—giving birth, plowing earth, or blasting rock. Eventually, as Rico (1991) found, you become aware of moments when writing flows rather than feeling so forced:

> The flow seemed to be triggered only when I gave myself over to that disconcerting chaotic fullness inside my head, acknowledged the untidy, sideways leaps of thought, let go of logic and prescriptions. I liked the feeling, though it came all too rarely, like dreams of flying that cannot be forced. (pp. 4–5)

The "self" stage of writing can be particularly troublesome for non-native speakers of English who seek to master academic writing in a Western context (Fox, 1994). There is a feeling of being at a disadvantage even before beginning that must be surmounted in order to build self-esteem as a writer. Specific suggestions for writers whose first language is not English are found in Figure 2.7.

For more information on the special circumstances of the writer whose first language is not English, see Barnes (1982) and Byrd and Benson (1994). The "task" stage for writers typically consists of struggling to get enough manuscripts published that you cease to think it was simply a matter of good fortune. I remember a colleague who said, after publishing three articles, "But I'm not a *real* writer—I've just been lucky." My response was, "So, you've won the raffle three times in a row. What is the critical mass? How many articles will it take before you can begin to consider yourself a writer?" This question gave her pause. Maybe five articles? Maybe it would depend on where they were published. An extremely competitive outlet would offer a bigger vote of confidence than a relatively unknown publication, such as one former student who earned the writing award for *Atlantic Monthly* and another who signed a book contract with Cambridge University Press. Interestingly, a prolific author I know told

---

- **Begin writing early**—Seek feedback during the planning stage before investing hours on writing a long draft that is not in the style sought for publication in your field or a particular country.

- **Find outstanding examples**—Study models of other students' writing and samples of academic writing in the discipline to get a sense of the particular style and voice that is preferred.

- **Use a "test audience"**—Establish a network of supportive peers and colleagues who can provide insight about content, organization, audiences, and outlets for a publication. Use the feedback of this less threatening audience to revise repeatedly until the manuscript is ready for critique from a leading expert.

- **Enter into discussions about writing**—Actively participate in opportunities to share ideas verbally in a variety of settings (with one peer, with a small group, with a larger group).

Adapted from Koffolt & Holt, 1997

Figure 2.7 *Suggestions for Non-Native Users of English*

me he would not consider himself to be a "real" writer until he had something published in *The New York Times*. Evidently, the criteria vary from one person to the next. Ideas about authorship are also developmental because writers continually seek new challenges. They seem to embrace the advice of Ronald E. Osborn: "Undertake something that is difficult; it will do you good. Unless you try to do something beyond what you have already mastered, you will never grow" (quoted in Safire & Safir, 1994, p. 106).

Finally, after we amass some experience with the task and decide that we truly are authors based on our own criteria at the time, we consider the consequences of what we have produced. It is no longer acceptable to manage to get something published; we want to know that someone is reading it and that our work is exerting a positive influence on the field. These days that validation comes to me in three basic ways. The first is in helping novices to write and sharing in their excitement when their work is published; the second is watching a book go into subsequent editions; and the third is reading someone else's work, encountering something familiar, and feeling humble, yet proud to realize that someone else is referring to my work.

As you navigate the progression from a focus on "self" to "task" to "impact," several supports will need to be in place. Nancy Atwell (1999) arrived at this list of the writer's minimum daily requirements: a) regular chunks of time, b) freedom to choose topics, c) appropriate responses to their work, d) mechanics of language learned in context, e) opportunities to interact with others who write, and f) a wide range of reading material.

DEVOTING TIME TO WRITING

What is your usual way of working at writing? Do you begrudge every moment and keep an eye on the clock, thinking about other things you might be doing? Are you easily distracted by anything in your environment? Do you engage in unproductive avoidance rituals—reading e-mail, doing the dishes, or sharpening pencils even when you always write in ink? Do you have to force yourself to concentrate and find your attention drifting to "what ifs"—What if I am wasting this time? What if I work all morning and end up trashing it away tomorrow? What if no one likes it or will publish it? Poet Peter Davison describes how time spent writing "is measured on a different scale, a different continuum from the rest of the world. Five minutes of pure attention . . . is longer than a week of clocks and hours" (cited in Perry 1999, p.19).

It is a common misconception that writers "find" time to write. Actually, anyone who writes has to commit time, to carve it out of the 24 hours allotted to every human being. My theory is that you will not do this until you believe you have at least a 50/50 chance of success and that after you have experienced success with writing, you will make time for it. Here is what three admirable writers had to say about time:

- "I just constructed another way of doing it, which would be, oh just sit down and get it done, and get it done in the time it takes a baby to take a nap" (Carolyn See, cited in Perry, 1999, p.149).

- "As I became better at it and writing became more important in my life, I realized I would have to set some time apart for writing. I just started setting time apart every day" (Chitra Banerjee Divakaruni cited in Perry, 1999, p.127).

- "If it doesn't go well, I'll be there an hour or two and just leave in disgust. If it does go well, I can go six hours. When it comes toward the end of something, I can go indefinitely" (Henry Miller cited in Perry 1999, p.111).

A big breakthrough for me was writing a policy paper for a professional organization. I had worked with the group for years and had many respected colleagues and friends on the Publications Committee. I had also waited until the last minute to begin working seriously on the project. Up until that point, I composed only when a) the house was absolutely quiet in the wee hours of the morning, and b) after I proceeded directly from sleeping to writing, still in robe and slippers, with a large mug of coffee. When I was in my graduate program, I believed so strongly that I could write only when I was coming directly out of sleep that I used to set my alarm clock, sleep for about 3 hours, and wake up in the middle of the night to create another "morning!" Sociologist Howard Becker (1986) talks about how, when we feel we have no control over something, we engage in bizarre rituals, and my bed-to-desk routine is right up there with superstition about broken mirrors or fear of stepping on a crack in the sidewalk. What happened in this case was that there weren't enough mornings to get the job done. I had to write around the clock any time I had the chance in order to avoid disappointing my colleagues by failing to produce a paper or, what would be even worse, submitting a substandard paper after they had believed in me. The story has a happy ending, for I did produce the paper on time (just barely—using overnight mail) and it was well received. It also forced me to re-examine my beliefs about when I could write—evidently, it was not exclusively first thing in the morning, although that remains my preference. Only you can decide, through trial-and-error which routines beget writing and which are counterproductive.

So, when it comes to time spent on writing, follow the advice of the Zen masters and "be there." This means that, instead of fretting about other things you could be doing, tell yourself that this is writing time and that writing is the only thing you can be doing during the designated time anyway. If you feel that you really cannot generate text on the task at hand, do something else related to writing—checking references, taking notes from a new book related to your topic, or writing something totally different (I find, for example, that writing editorials is a useful break from other types of writing). The one immutable law is that you must be working on writing. Eventually you will reach a point where you look up to see that much more time has elapsed than you realized while writing. Until you devote time to nurturing your writing in the same unbegrudging way that you would minister to an ailing friend or family member, finding the time to write will seem insurmountable.

Some ways to make time include: a) making (and keeping) a one-hour writing appointment on your calendar; b) using otherwise wasted time to write (e.g., while in a doctor's office waiting room or sitting motionless in a traffic jam); c) writing while doing something else (e.g., writing while on an exercise machine, dictating while walking); d) writing on the weekends; or e) carving out large blocks of time (e.g., while on a long airplane ride).

OVERCOMING WRITING BLOCKS

I have a cartoon that depicts a writer, head in his hands, seated at a desk on a mountain peak with wadded-up pieces of paper all around him. The sign on the mountain reads, "Inspiration Point." Surely, this is the image we have of blocked writers who wait in vain for flashes of brilliance or the visitation of their Muse. Authors' attitudes about writer's block vary, and I suspect it might have something to do with the writing task. I believe in writer's blocks for poets and novelists. I don't believe in writer's block for nonfiction writers because no one is expecting you to create a new artistic breakthrough. A blockage means that nothing can get through—like a completely clogged kitchen drain or an intestinal blockage. You know that writer's block is an all-too-convenient excuse when a college freshman responsible for summarizing three journal articles on a topic claims to be afflicted. To me, protestations about writer's block are akin to the stuffy American professor's tendency to sound faintly British, for both are affectations intended to elevate the status of the user.

As an initial step in considering what might be getting in the way of writing, evaluate your physical environment. Observe your writing behavior with an eye toward trying to discover the times, locations, and circumstances that are associated with your best writing.

- Time—When do you tend to be most alert, energetic, and clear-headed? Reflective and imaginative? Calm and capable of concentration? Patient with detail work? When are you least likely to be distracted or interrupted?

- Location—Analyze the design of your workspace. Are the lighting, comfort level, amount of space, and background sounds working for you? Are there times in the writing when a change of location is helpful, for instance, when you are checking the reference list rather than actively generating text?

- Position—Are there some parts of writing that are best accomplished seated at a desk while others lend themselves to being stretched out on the floor or in a recliner? What about the ergonomics of your workspace?

- Tools and Equipment—Is your workspace equipped with what you need so that you aren't constantly leaving to go and get it? Is your equipment—computer, printer, and software—equal to the task? Have you provided the materials for different stages of the writing—drafting, revising, editing?

- Other Preferences—Do you work best with the family dog curled up under your chair or the cat draped over the monitor? Are there interesting objects or inspiring words that you might display? Are there smells that make your work environment more appealing? What types of food or drink give you energy or relax you without making you "wired, cranky, sleepy, or fat" (Edelstein, 1999, p. 40). Are there some warm-up exercises or productive routines that put you into the writing frame of mind? (adapted from Edelstein, 1999, pp. 39-41).

Strive to make the physical environment as conducive to writing as possible. Another strategy for coping with writer's block is to accept it with equanimity and think of writing as periods of input followed by periods of output. If the output phase falters, assume the pump needs to be primed again. Seek more input—go back to the library, ask someone to read it, or share ideas with students or colleagues verbally and see how they respond. Some tried and true ways of getting the writing going are summarized in Figure 2.8.

CONCLUSION

The German philosopher, Goethe, offers what could be a mantra for anyone seeking to write and publish: "Whatever you can do, or dream you can, begin it. Boldness has genius, power, and magic in it." (from http://members.tripod.com/~kenfran/quotlist.htm) Be bold. Find your voice. Silence your critic, at least long enough to get a good, working draft. Don't wait to write someday, start writing your way into the author's role now.

REFERENCES

Adelstein, M. E., & Pival, J. G. (1997). *The writing commitment* (5th ed.). New York: Harcourt Brace Jovanovich College and School Division.

Atwell, N. (1999). *In the middle* (2nd ed.). Portsmouth, NH: Heinemann.

Barnes, G. A. (1982). *Communication skills for the foreign-born professional*. Philadelphia, PA: ISI Press.

Becker, H. (1986). *Writing for social scientists*. Chicago: University of Illinois Press.

Bloom, L. Z. (1991). Finding a family, finding a voice: A writing teacher teaches writing teachers. In M. Schwartz (Ed.), *Writer's craft, teacher's art: Teaching what we know* (pp. 55-67). Portsmouth, NH: Boynton/Cook.

- Lower expectations—Tell yourself that you are not going to write at all; you're just going to play around at the computer for a while. Remember that first drafts don't matter and no one has to see it until you say so.

- Make a workspace—Create a space for yourself that matches your work style; neat if you require an orderly workspace, messy if you need to have all of your resources spread out and visible. Equip it with everything you need. Minimize distractions, even if that means pulling down the window shade or sitting out in the garage with a laptop.

- Discover your workstyle—Figure out if you are a morning person or a night person when it comes to writing; realize that four times as many writers choose early morning because interruptions are minimized and because their minds are refreshed from a night's sleep (Perry, 1999).

- Confront your internal critic—Bring your internal critic down to size by describing him or her in words or a sketch; try arguing back and give yourself the last word.

- Reread to get back into writing—Put your finished work away for a short while before looking at it again; when you return, get back into the work by reading what you already have written.

- Use the cliffhanger technique—Stop before you are exhausted and at an interesting place; that way you will be more inclined to return to your desk the next day.

- Write around the edges—Try a rhythmic, habitual, routine activity such as walking or spell checking to make your mind more relaxed and receptive to creative ideas.

- Switch gears—Purposely change your audience; see how this affects what you write and how you explain things. Work on a different writing project to give yourself a break; often when you return to the "blocked" project, new ideas will emerge.

- Find a real audience—Get someone whose opinion matters greatly to read for you and give you a quick turnaround time; don't read the comments until you return to your desk and can respond to them through revision.

- Take a break—If all else fails, stop composing and do other writing-related tasks; go back to the library, take notes, or proofread.

Figure 2.8   *Overcoming Writer's Block*

Boice, R. (1990). *Professors as writers: A self-help guide to productive writing.* Stillwater, OK: New Forums Press.

Boice, R. (1997). Strategies for enhancing scholarly productivity. In J. M. Moxley & T. Taylor (Eds.), *Writing and publishing for academic authors* (2nd ed.) (pp. 19-34). Lanham, MD: Rowman & Littlefield.

Bruner, J. S. (1971). *The relevance of education.* New York: Norton.

Byrd, P., & Benson, B. (1994). *Problem/solution: A reference for ESL writers.* Boston: Heinle & Heinle.

Calkins, L. M. (1995). *The art of teaching writing.* New York: Reed Elsevier.

Carlson, R. (1997). *Don't sweat the small stuff . . . and it's all small stuff.* New York: Hyperion.

Edelstein, S. (1999). *100 things every writer needs to know.* Bellvue, WA: Perigee

Fox, H. (1994). *Listening to the world: Cultural issues in academic writing.* Urbana, IL: National Council of Teachers of English.

Holm, K. (Ed.) (2000). *2001 Writer's Market: The Internet edition.* Cincinnati, OH: Writers Digest Books.

Jalongo, M. R. (1991). *Creating learning communities: The role of the teacher in the 21st century.* Bloomington, IN: National Educational Service.

Jalongo, M. R., & McCracken, J. B. (1997). *Writing about teaching and learning: A guide for aspiring and experienced authors.* Olney, MD: Association for Childhood Education International.

Jason, H., Majoor, G., & Westberg, J. (1999). Writing for publication: Outcomes of the Albuquerque workshop. *Education for Health: Change in Training & Practice, 12*(1), 108-110.

Koffolt, K., & Holt, S. L. (1997). Using the "writing process" with non-native users of English. In D. L. Sigsbee, B. W. Speck, & B. Maylath (Eds.), *Approaches to teaching nonnative English speakers across the curriculum* (pp. 53-60). San Francisco, CA: Jossey-Bass.

Lamb, B. (1997). *Booknotes: America's finest authors on reading, writing, and the power of ideas.* New York: Times Books/Random House.

Loucks-Horsely, S. (1987). *Continuing to learn: A guidebook for teacher development.* Regional Laboratory for Education.

Luey, B. (1995). *Handbook for academic authors* (3rd ed.). New York: Cambridge University Press.

Murray, D. M. (1990). *Shoptalk: Learning to write with writers.* Portsmouth, NH: Boynton/ Cook Heinemann.

Perry, S. K. (1999). *Writing in flow: Keys to enhanced creativity*. Cincinnati, OH: Writer's Digest Books.

Raymond, J. (1986). *Writing (is an unnatural act)*. New York: Harper & Row.

Richards, P. (1986). Risk. In H. Becker *Writing for social scientists* (pp. 108-120). Chicago: University of Illinois Press.

Rhodes, R. (1995). *How to write: Advice and reflections*. New York: William Morrow.

Rico, G. (1991). Writer: Personal patterns in chaos. In M. Schwartz (Ed.*), Writer's craft, teacher's art: Teaching what we know* (pp. 3-20). Portsmouth, NH: Boynton/Cook.

Roorbach, B. (1998). *Writing life stories*. Cincinnati, OH: F & W Publications/Story Press.

Safire W., & Safir L. (Eds.) (1994). *Good advice on writing*. New York: Simon & Schuster.

Shaughnessy, M. P. (1979). *Errors and expectations*. New York: Oxford University Press.

Sullivan, A. J. (1963). The right to fail: Creativity versus conservatism. *Journal of Higher Education, 34*(4), 191.

Temple, C., & Gillet, J. W. (1989). *Language arts: Learning processes and teaching practices*. Glenview, IL: Scott Foresman.

Thyer, B. A. (1994). *Successful publishing in scholarly journals*. Thousand Oaks, CA: Sage.

Trimble, J. R. (2000). *Writing with style*. Upper Saddle River, NJ: Prentice Hall.

Winokur, J. (Ed.). (1986). *Writers on writing*. Philadelphia, PA: Running Press.

Winokur, J. (Ed.). (1999). *Advice to writers*. New York: Vintage/Random House.

CHAPTER 3

❦

Internalizing the Characteristics of Publishable Writing

❦
---

*C*arrie, a college freshman, earned the Music Department's award for the top student musician at our university. It was a particularly noteworthy achievement, given the fact that sophomore, junior, and senior class Music majors were included in the competition. Because she is a friend's daughter, I attended Carrie's recital. The freshman stood on stage, violin in hand, and confidently played intricate solos at the precise moment that they were called for by the conductor. Those in attendance marveled at her intelligence, poise, and level of accomplishment. Yet, not long after that stunning performance, my friend told me that her daughter planned to abandon music study. When I expressed dismay, my colleague said that Carrie had been firm about her decision and had said, "Mom, I'm just not good enough." Carrie had concluded that her talent had taken her about as far as she could go and that even hours of additional practice each day could not bring her to first-chair symphony level. Nothing less would do.

A question that is the undercurrent of many authors' questions has to do with this "good enough" issue. Like the people who line up to have their wares evaluated by an expert on antiques, aspiring writers often seek someone else's opinion and hope that what appears ordinary will turn out to be a prized and coveted possession. Frequently, authors solicit these judgments before ever putting pen to paper. They want to talk about their idea for a manuscript and be given assurances, in advance, that their work definitely will be published. But those who attempt to help others to write are more like coaches than teachers. Although they can recognize raw talent, they still need to see samples of performance before making any predictions and, even then, they are sometimes wrong.

Even an Olympic swimming coach cannot say who has swimming talent early on unless somebody gets into the water. Likewise, no one can predict your success with writing until some respectable sample of writing is produced. To extend this swimming analogy a bit further, our local pool has a policy in which the last ten minutes of every hour are times when only adults can be in the water, and the children hate it. The children grouse and pace and watch the clock. When the ten minutes are nearly up, they stand with their toes curled over the edge of the pool practically bursting to get wet at the first possible second. Too often, those who want to write lack that sort of passion to take the plunge. They want to lounge at poolside until an editor "discovers" them and coaxes them in, all the while buoying them up.

Even after a writing sample is reviewed and somebody (usually a college faculty member) gives the flattering feedback that the author should pursue publication, it is important to consider the source. Unless the evaluator has experience with writing and editing for publication, it may be the case that the student followed directions well and that her or his paper merely stood out from other students' papers. That alone is not enough to merit publication. Even if a class paper has potential as a publication, chances are that it will need to be rewritten extensively for a particular audience and outlet prior to submission. When I teach writing for publication, I allow students to begin with a paper written for another class. I can see their faces relax as they think, "Hey, I got an A on that paper in the other class. This should be easy." Then they get my first set of comments and they are ready to change their topic because so much more is needed.

In fact, this transition from a class assignment with an audience of one and a manuscript suitable for a wider audience is a tricky one, so much so that numerous articles have been written about it, particularly with regard to gleaning a publication from a thesis or dissertation (Harman & Montagnes, 1976). Figure 3.1 highlights some of the useful distinctions between a class paper and a publishable article. Fox (1985) has referred to dissertations as "the ultimate homework" because they are mainly done as exercises that inaugurate a student's independent scholarship. Such documents are hardly ever published in their entirety or in their original form, as so many student writers assume or secretly dream about. Sometimes, after careful rewriting, pruning, and shaping they become an article or a book, but even this occurs far less often than one might expect.

Disappointing as it may be to learn this, it really is not that surprising. Just as a celebrated potter probably did not do his or her best work the first time at the wheel, authors' first serious efforts at scholarship are unlikely to be representative of their best work during an entire career. Actually, I don't think that I know

Writing	Student Writing	Published Writing
Purpose	To dutifully document hours logged at the library and computer	To make an innovative contribution to the field
Audience	Usually a small, known audience of one faculty member who is likely to be interested in and knowledgeable about the topic and obligated to read it	A large, unknown audience of professional colleagues who have varying levels of interest in and familiarity with the subject matter and who are free to read something else
Style	More telling than showing, often relying extensively on previously published, quoted material	More showing than telling, with personal insights and concrete examples integrated into the text
Voice	Student paying homage to the big names and remaining relatively silent	Author entering into the professional dialogue and speaking authoritatively
Expectations	To demonstrate familiarity with the leaders in the field, to collect a sufficient number of resources for the bibliography, to fulfill course requirements	To inform, entertain, enlighten, persuade, or some combination of these so that readers will choose to read, duplicate, and cite the work
Format	Page after page of unbroken text, often loosely organized	Carefully developed visual material (e.g., headings, figures, tables, examples, illustrations) and precise organization tailored to the particular purposes of the work
Focus	Superficial treatment of broad topics deemed suitable by the instructor	Sharp focus on one facet of a topic carefully selected by the author

Figure 3.1 *Making the Transition From Student Writing to Published Writing*

anyone personally who has published a thesis or dissertation as a book, although I continue to urge colleagues and students to consider publication potential from the start of their dissertations and now have two former students with book contracts based on their dissertations. If the longest paper that a graduate student has written frequently is not publishable, what is?

WHAT MAKES WRITING PUBLISHABLE?

Publishable writing has to be good enough to make it through some publisher's filtering system. For a journal, this could mean an editor-in-chief, three peer reviewers, and a copy editor. For a major textbook, this might mean an acquisitions editor, nine reviewers from around the country, and a series of production and copy editors. Although not everything that makes its way into print is good, there are some attributes of writing that render it more likely to earn the privilege of publication. Good writing is powerful writing. According to a leading authority on the writing process, writers write powerfully when:

1. They do not waste words.

2. They speak in an authentic voice.

3. They put readers there, make them believe.

4. They cause things to happen for readers as they happened for the writer (or narrator).

5. They create oppositions which pay off in surprise.

6. They build.

7. They ask something of readers.

8. They reward readers with meaning.

9. They present ideas, actions, or details that are solid, like an apple, with its core and flesh, and however small or momentary, are rounded and complete in themselves (Macrorie, 1984, p. 29).

The word "publication" comes from the Latin *publicus* meaning "of the people" and, "open to all." When you write for publication, your writing is open to anyone who cares to read it. According to James Moffat (1983), publication is the least personal of the communicative acts, that is, it places the greatest distance between the sender and the receiver. He arranges communication hierarchically, from most personal to least personal as follows:

- Reflection—communication within the self, between two parts of one nervous system

- Conversation—interpersonal communication between two people within vocal range

- Correspondence—interpersonal communication between remote individuals or groups

- Publication—impersonal communication to a large, anonymous group extended over time and/or space (p. 33)

When professionals write for publication, they face the biggest communication gap. Why struggle to bridge this gap? Why not just write for yourself, keeping it at the reflection stage of diaries and journals? While writing for a reader of one has its place, it also has limitations. Writing for yourself is like singing in the shower or being alone in a car, free to sing along with the radio—you can belt out a tune with abandon because no one else can hear you. Writing for publication is more like a recital; any mistakes that are made are painfully public, and it will be up to the audience to decide if the performance merits enthusiastic applause. Yet, as author Mary Kay Blakely contends, "it's terrifically important to be published, because the act of publishing makes you say it harder, better, deeper, more than if you're just writing for yourself" (quoted in Wald, 1998, p. 42).

Additionally, nonfiction written by professionals in various fields often incorporates the goals of scholarship. Scholarly work

- Requires a high level of discipline-related expertise

- Breaks new ground, is innovative

- Can be replicated or elaborated

- Provides documentation of results

- Is subjected to peer review

- Has significance or impact (Diamond, 1994)

Pursuing these goals of scholarship and publication all begins with reading.

PUBLISHABLE WRITING BEGINS WITH READING

Suppose that you were responsible for preparing a special dinner for family and friends. You go to your pantry with some dish in mind, yet at every turn, you are missing one or more key ingredient. Unless you make a trip to the grocery store, your dinner making efforts will never be realized. And so it is with writing. Over and over again, writers are reminded that first, they must read "widely and well" (Zinsser, 1998). Authors aim for what Elizabeth Hardwick called a "well-stocked mind" (cited in Roorbach, 1998, p. 14). Equipping your mental pantry depends on three main types of reading:

- Subject matter resources—publications that are read because they focus on the topic of interest

- Models of style—publications that offer examples of remarkably effective writing, both nonfiction and fiction, for authors to emulate

- Sage advice publications—materials that are read because they inspire the author to write, provide a glimpse into the writing life, and/or offer concrete suggestions on writing and publishing

Any writer of real distinction is, first and foremost, an avid reader who reads for style and structure as well as for content (Campbell, 1945). After this long apprenticeship with words, writers acquire a virtual x-ray vision that allows them to glimpse the underlying structures of what they read, much like an x-ray reveals the body's skeletal structure concealed by the flesh. If you read voraciously you will eventually acquire this ability to glimpse the inner workings of the article or book. Be aware, however, that it is a long process. Most writers need considerable practice analyzing and critiquing the writing of others before the infrastructure of written work becomes obvious. And they need even more practice before they can go about incorporating the techniques they admire in others' writing by applying them to their own prose.

In truth, we are what we read as surely as we are what we eat. We soak in the styles of what we read and, after years of such subtle absorption, we write in ways that reflect our reading tastes. People who routinely read *Soap Opera Digest* tend to write in ways that differ from those who regularly read *USA Today* or *Atlantic Monthly.* The connection between writing well and being well read is so strong that veteran CBS News reporter Charles Kuralt said in an interview, "I don't know if I know how to write. I think writing is derivative. I think it comes from reading" (Kuralt cited in Lamb 1997, p.157). Reading extensively enables you to identify more strongly with readers and learn how to write to be read.

PUBLISHABLE WRITING IS OFTEN BAD—AT FIRST

One of the foremost impediments to writing is that feeling of needing to write something wonderful. The more auspicious the occasion, the more overpowering it can become. The writer's dilemma is comparable to that of the award recipient on a nationally televised program who is expected to be charming and witty. In both cases, it is easy to become overwhelmed by the enormity of what is expected. Awards programs are notorious for being slow, boring, and riddled with clichés. Likewise, writers frequently succumb to "pretentious jargon; galumphing sentences and paragraphs; excessive abstractness; impersonality; passive verbs; humorlessness" (Trimble, 2000, p. 110).

If you hope to become a published author, you will need to give yourself permission to write badly at first in what historian Nell Irvin Painter refers to as "zero minus drafts" (cited in Lamb 1997, p. 142). The good news is that you will have ample opportunity to make it better.

Novice authors tend to err at extremes. They either write in haste and mail it off, hoping for a happy outcome, or they fret over it so much that they cannot bear to put the manuscript in an envelope. At least at first, many writers counteract such tendencies by writing quickly and revising slowly. This means that they generate a first draft rapidly without bothering to edit, then revisit the piece over and over again, each time examining it with a slightly different perspective. One time through might focus on the removal of unnecessary material. Another might focus on how each paragraph hangs together and the transitions from one point to the next. Another read might critique the effectiveness of the examples, and so on.

Like the severely nearsighted patient undergoing an eye examination, who cannot read those fuzzy images down the Snelling Chart, we writers keep on trying new lenses until the differences between them are so fine that they are difficult to detect. Where glasses are concerned, it becomes the right prescription; where writing is concerned, it becomes the point at which the manuscript is as refined as we can make it.

Once, when I was working with a co-author, she remarked, "You're just a better writer than me." Later in the conversation, I asked my co-author for an estimate of how many times she had substantially rewritten her portion of the manuscript and she said (as if it were a lot) "Oh, at least five or six times." Meanwhile, I had thirteen revisions stacked up on the floor and they did not reflect the numerous revisions done on screen at the computer, just the times when it was different enough to bother to print it out. So, was I the "better" writer or the one who worked harder at it?

Ernest Hemingway reported rewriting the conclusion to the great American novel, *A Farewell to Arms*, 39 times. When asked what took him so long during an interview, he said, "getting the words right." Fortunately, no editor of a professional journal expects this level of dedication to craft from the typical author. As Luey (1995) points out,

> Good academic writing is clear and succinct. If you can move beyond
> clarity to grace and elegance, you are to be congratulated. Editors will
> happily settle for clarity, however. . . . You can write well by being clear,
> direct, precise, and accurate. If you can accomplish this apparently
> modest goal—and if you have something new and important to say—
> you will be on your way to publication. (p. 9, 12)

PUBLISHABLE WRITING IS SUITED FOR THE AUDIENCE

In my small town it is customary for grieving families to publish a photograph and an accompanying poem to honor a deceased family member. On a literary criticism level, the poems are doggerel. The meter is off, the rhyme of the couplets is often forced, and the deceased person is completely idealized. Despite these flaws, I take the time to look at the photos—typically a grainy snapshot made grainier by the newsprint—and read the verse. Even though years of editing have made me intolerant of poor writing, I set aside my editor's hat and try to imagine how the writers went about producing these poems that always try to rhyme. I picture families seated at a kitchen table reminiscing about their lost family member or perhaps one person taking the lead and sharing what he or she has already written aloud while others read or listen with tear-filled eyes. It is easy to be forgiving about language flaws in these poems of bereavement because the writing has a different purpose. The poems make no pretense of being great literature, only of being a tribute to the deceased and of having been somehow therapeutic for the writer.

What counts as "good enough" in writing is relative rather than absolute; what is publishable in one context is terribly out of place in another. Imagine, for instance, how the published bereavement poems I've just described would be treated by the editors of a prestigious poetry journal. Therefore, the first requirement of publishable writing is that it be suitable for the audience.

As a new college faculty member I attended a writing workshop for women and minorities sponsored by Ohio State University, I had the opportunity to meet briefly with a writing teacher and editor to discuss my work. She asked, "Who is your audience for this piece?" My response, in betrayal of my inexperience as a writer was, "I'm not sure what you mean." "Well, is it written for teachers, administrators, parents? That isn't clear to me." Funny, it wasn't clear to me, either. I hoped, as most rank beginners at writing do, that all educators would be interested in my article and had failed to write with a particular group of readers in mind.

Until you can really picture your audience and imagine how they might respond to your work, your nonfiction writing efforts will be unfocused and unproductive. Frank McCourt, teacher and author of the Pulitzer Prize-winning memoir, *Angela's Ashes*, said in an interview that writing the book was even more challenging than teaching because it is difficult to know how you are doing. To address this problem, he thought of his high school students, who had always been interested in his life in Ireland, as an audience for his book.

When writing for fellow professionals, try imagining yourself at a conference conversing with an intelligent, well read, and interested new colleague, or imagine yourself being interviewed for a professional journal. That should simulate your reading audience rather well and answer many beginner's questions, such as "How much do I have to explain this?" or "Can I assume that my readers would know about _____?"

Still, when you are writing, you know that some readers will know all about your topic while others may not. For the nonfiction author, there are two solutions: the citation and the parenthetical explanation. The citation can be used to lead your reader to other sources, ones that are more basic and will provide the necessary background. The parenthetical explanation can be used to quickly explain or to "remind" readers of something they know, but may have forgotten. Example: In book publishing, acquisitions editors (the ones who identify new authors and offer contracts) and copy editors (the ones who do a line-by-line correction of your text) perform completely different functions. Ask yourself,

- Who really reads this publication?

- How much are they likely to already know about this topic?

- What assumptions, beliefs, and misconceptions are they apt to bring to this topic and the surrounding issues?

- What is my real purpose in bringing this audience and topic together? (Casewit, 1985)

And, as a final way of anchoring your material to an audience, think about the two tasks confronting the nonfiction writer; making what is unfamiliar seem familiar or making what is familiar seem fresh.

Author and Librarian of Congress James Billington describes how his poverty and experience with used books affected his sense of audience:

> It was very interesting reading these used books growing up because they had underlining in them. They were worn. And so, very early, my curiosity was stimulated as to, you know, why did they underline this passage and not that one. What kind of a person is this, that read the book? Not simply, who wrote this book and what were they trying to say, but who's read this book and what were they trying to say about it? (cited in Lamb 1997, p.130)

Figure 3.2 highlights some ways to win over your audience.

Finally, as *Wall Street Journal* editor and author of several noteworthy books, James B. Stewart (1998) asserts, curiosity is the tie that binds writers to readers:

> These days, when there is increasing competition for people's time, writers cannot count on anyone to read their work out of a sense of obligation, moral duty, or abstract dedication to "being informed." They will not read because someone else deems a subject to be important. They will read because they want to, and they will want to because they are curious. (p. 17)

PUBLISHABLE WRITING HAS A CLEAR FOCUS

The following is from a discussion with one of my graduate students:

STUDENT: "I want to write something on child development."

WRITING TEACHER: "Okay, now you are at the encylopedic level."

STUDENT: "Well, child development in the area of self-esteem."

WRITING TEACHER: "Good. You've narrowed it down to a book."

STUDENT: "All right. My article would be about what teachers can do to promote self-esteem in preschoolers."

WRITING TEACHER: "Great! It's beginning to sound like something that you might be able to treat adequately in about 15 double-spaced pages."

- **Identify with your audience**—Imagine that you are engaged in a sparkling dinner conversation with an intelligent person who represents the particular audience you have in mind. Avoid sounding like a bad textbook and speak clearly and directly to this human being.

  Assume that your reader is as busy as you are and could think of many other things to do with her or his time. Imagine that the reader is going to be reading rapidly and will turn to another article or book at the first sign of confusion or verbosity.

- **Strive to be helpful**—Serve readers courteously and offer them something of value that will aid them in their work and lives. Avoid sounding pompous, insincere, or omniscient. Instead, strive to sound like a real human being who is genuine and honest about your limitations, yet willing to take a stand.

- **Settle on a well-focused topic**—Choose a topic to which you have a firm commitment. You need not be the world's leading expert *already*, but you do need to do the work necessary to *become* expert. Have something to say that is worth readers' attention and tailor it to the needs of that particular audience.

- **Proceed logically**—Define your terms and make it clear at the outset what you will be talking about. Organize your argument and have your main points coincide with the headings of your manuscript. Support your argument with authoritative sources and concrete examples.

  Make a diagram of the main sections and headings of your work. Does it look logical? Does it seem well balanced? Now look at the sections themselves. Are they proportional or is one section much longer (or shorter) than others? If so, perhaps the long section needs to be subdivided and two of the short sections need to be combined.

- **Be a wordsmith and lavish attention on writing until it flows**—Choose vigorous verbs, strong nouns, and assertive phrasing (Trimble, 2000, p. 6). Read the manuscript out loud while

---

Figure 3.2 *How to Win Readers*

Figure 3.2 *continued*

---

listening for places where it bogs down or sounds awkward. Keep revising until the writing sounds effortless and is engaging.
   Let your manuscript get cold, then read it through, one sentence at a time. Pause after each sentence or two and ask: What questions have I raised in the mind of the reader? What has been left unsaid/unanswered? Then read the next sentence or two to see if you deliver the information that the reader is expecting.

- **Add interesting details**—Consider what you can do as an author to make a point clearer and *show* rather than tell why it is significant. Imagine that dinner conversation partner saying, "I'm not sure what you mean. Could you give an example?" What anecdotes might you share? What analogies could you use?

For more on writing to be read, see Trimble (2000) and Casewit (1985).

This narrowing/focusing process is absolutely essential for the author. Vague topics and broad domains of interest cannot be addressed in short, article-length manuscripts. Cleanth Brooks and Robert Penn Warren (in Safire & Safir, 1994) explain focus this way:

> Before you undertake any piece of composition, you should try to frame the real subject, the central concern. You do not write about a house. You write about its appearance, the kind of life it suggests, its style or architecture, or your associations with it. You do not write about chemical research. You write about the methods of chemical research, the achievements of chemical research, or the opportunities for chemical research. You do not write about goodness. You write about the different kinds of goodness which have been held by different societies or religions at different times. . . . You must search your own thoughts and feelings to find your true subject. (p. 241)

How do you go about sharpening a manuscript's focus? First, *see what is already out there.* You often will find that articles have already been written about the more obvious and popular topics. Instead of becoming discouraged when you discover that what you intended to write has already appeared in print, try writing it for a different audience. For instance, if the article you planned on the topic has already been written for an audience of teachers, you many want to consider writing a similar article for parents or administrators or perhaps professionals in another field.

Second, *identify strongly with your particular audience*. If you were writing on the topic of bullying and teasing at school for parents (rather than "everyone"), you could frame your work in ways that meet the needs of that group:

- Who will read it? (Mostly concerned parents who have some personal experience with this issue and who subscribe to the magazine.)

- Why would they take the time to read it? (Probably because they are worried about their child and want to help him or her.)

- How much are they likely to know already or need to know? (The research base should be translated in such a way that it is suited to an audience of laypersons.)

Regardless of which particular audience you are trying to reach you will need to attract and maintain the reader's attention.

Third, *let the publisher suggest a focus*. Journals often have special, thematic issues or at least lists of topics they want to address in the coming publication year. Once when I was writing an article on children's friendships, I found that it had been written already. But then *Childhood Education* announced that it was doing a thematic issue on newly immigrated children and there was my focus, an article entitled "Peer Acceptance and the Newly Immigrated Child." As a teacher who had worked with migrant children and families and in a university lab school, the new focus suited me. That article was selected for inclusion in the best readings from *Childhood Education* over a 25 year period and in an issue of the journal that earned an EDPRESS award.

A fourth way to find your focus is to *identify the very best part*. Occasionally, I receive a manuscript that is rather general but includes one particular section that is much longer than the other sections and that is the most innovative and interesting part. When the manuscript is reviewed, everyone remarks on that part and wants to hear more about that. For instance, in an article on children using computers, there is a section on their peer interactions while writing at the computer that is a stand out. With a bit more effort, the author can rewrite the piece with this sharper focus throughout, making it clearer, fresher, and more publishable in the process.

Before beginning a manuscript, it is helpful to consider what broad category of manuscript you intend to create. Do you want to speak to novices in the field? Then you are probably looking at textbook writing in higher education. Do you want to write exclusively for scholars and researchers? Then you are looking at professional journals that publish original research in the form of articles, monographs, or books. Do you seek to "translate" theory and research in the field, making it accessible to practitioners or perhaps the layperson? Then you are writing for professional magazines or popular press magazines and newspapers. This is only a cursory look at types of writing and each one demands something different from the author.

Above all, once you have selected a focus, stick with it. Provost (1985) refers to this as obeying your own rules. If your title is *Bilingual Education in the Elementary School: What Can Educators Learn from the Quebec Experience?*, then you have established a rule that everything in this article will be about bilingual education, the elementary level, and the valuable lessons Canadian educators have to share with others. You would be violating your own rule of focus if you included material on general curriculum, the situation in secondary schools, or the history and geography of Canada.

PUBLISHABLE WRITING HAS A STYLE APPROPRIATE FOR THE OUTLET

What is style? "Style is form, not content. A reader usually picks up a story because of content but too often puts it down because of style" (Provost, 1985, p. 57). Style is that public persona that we reveal to our readers to varying degrees, depending upon the formality of the writing situation. Some authors disclose much about themselves, causing their readers to feel like confidants while others keep their personal opinions and feelings to themselves, keeping readers at a distance. Contemporary readers tend to have a somewhat keener appetite for knowing about authors on a more personal level. An interesting parallel can be seen in the media. It used to be the case that interviewers were crisp, formal, and prided themselves on never revealing their personal views, much less betraying their emotions concerning the news. Now you can watch the 6 o'clock newscast anywhere in America and see the news anchors engaged in playful banter or watch a talk show host like Oprah speaking with guests as if they were close friends engaged in private conversation. By way of contrast, consider the often-replayed account of the explosion of the Hindenburg when the announcer's voice trembled and belied his emotion as he witnessed the disaster and said, "Oh, the humanity!" At the time, that was about as emotional as broadcasting could get. Just imagine how a broadcaster would narrate that event nowadays, and you'll have a sense of how expectations for reporting have changed.

A similar phenomenon has occurred in education. The American Educational Research Association, a conference that was once dominated by statisticians who presented "just the facts," is now frequent host to emotionally charged sessions that are the very antithesis of its dispassionate data-crunching origins. Whereas it once was accepted practice for researchers to lay claim to objectivity, it is now the case that researchers openly state their assumptions and potential sources of bias. All this is a way of stating that writers in various fields have more opportunities for creative self-expression than previously. Some professionals regard this shift toward more personal styles of writing as an improvement, while others continue to treat it as a threat to the rigor of their field. My opinion is that the best writers have always revealed something of themselves, however subtly, and that laying claim to total objectivity is an affectation designed to make the writer appear more "scientific."

Actually, style is a matter of pragmatics, the appropriateness of particular forms of language in a specific social context. Put plainly, pragmatics refers to who can speak, what they can say, to whom they can say it, and in what contexts a specific type of communication is considered to be socially appropriate. Some things to consider in developing your style are:

1. What is your purpose for writing? If you want to inspire others, chances are that you'll need to get personal and specific. If you want to persuade others to change their practices, you'll need to be credible, support your ideas with convincing information, and draw upon your experiences.

2. How candid do you care to be and how much do you need to reveal about yourself? In an article I co-authored with Charlotte Krall, she talked about the many difficult circumstances that children confront and the need to create caring communities in classrooms (Krall & Jalongo, 1998). In order to make that point, she needed to reveal that she had been an intervention specialist for many years and explain something about her role and experiences.

3. What do you think this audience and outlet can tolerate? Study the outlets where you hope to be published and consider such things as whether or not authors use the personal pronoun "I," how articles are formatted, and how formal they are in tone. The more that you can make your article fit that voice, format, and tone of the desired outlet, the better your chances of being accepted.

4. How much of a storyteller do you care to be? Even the seasoned empirical researcher does not lay claim to "proof" and absolute statements of fact. Rather, she or he owns up to the limitations of the study early on, as well as possible sources of bias. Although it is true that empirical research is generally conceived of as the most authoritative, objective voice, it would appear that, even among researchers, those who do a good job of telling the story behind their study are the ones most likely to be read, cited, and admired. The editors of the scholarly publication *Reviews of Educational Research*, for example, characterize a review of the research as "a good story . . . about a mature body of literature" (Murray & Raths, 1996, p. 417). Figure 3.3 is an example of the specific criteria used to evaluate manuscripts submitted for publication to the journal that I edit.

PUBLISHABLE WRITING IS CONCISE

The number of pages a journal editor has to work with is referred to as the page budget for a good reason. Every word, every line, costs money to print. Over the course of a year, excess verbiage in several articles might mean that

Early Childhood Education Journal uses a peer review system to evaluate manuscripts. The process begins when I receive manuscripts in the mail and screen them to see if they have any potential as an article in the journal. Manuscripts that are obviously inappropriate for the audience or unredeemable are rejected at that point. If, however, a manuscript appears to be at least marginally appropriate it is sent out for review.

—————————— ✤ ——————————

Enclosed is a manuscript that may be suitable as an article for *Early Childhood Education Journal*. Please it read it critically and do the following:

1. **Think about audience.** Read the manuscript critically and consider its appropriateness for an audience of early childhood practitioners and teacher educators throughout the world. Remember that we have many manuscripts awaiting publication and that we now accept only about 8% of what is submitted. Don't be reluctant to reject a manuscript if it would require extensive revision or seems poorly suited for *ECEJ*.

2. **Think about our page budget.** Please be aware that many manuscripts are far too long. Our page limit is 15 double-spaced, 12-point pages, including references and figures. This translates into an article of about 4 journal pages and this is the maximum amount of space we can allocate to a single article.

3. **Write your review as if addressing the author.** Reviews are shared with authors as appropriate. Rather than writing your comments to me, write them to the author as if you were responding to a colleague's work. Try to be specific and offer concrete, helpful suggestions if the manuscript has merit. If you reject a manuscript, provide justification for your decision. Remember that the least useful question in reviewing is "How would I have written this article?" It is far better to focus on the work that is right in front of you, written the way that it was written by that author.

4. **Omit all identifying marks.** We do not share your identity with the authors, so please do not use letterhead or sign your reviews. On a blank sheet of paper, type the title of the article and a 1-2 paragraph critique. You may e-mail your reviews to me at MJALONGO@grove.iup.edu. I will remove any identifying information from the e-mails.

Figure 3.3 *Manuscript Evaluation Criteria for* Early Childhood Education Journal

continued on next page

Figure 3.3 *continued*

5. **Make your decision clear.** Please summarize your review with one of four decisions: 1) accept, 2) accept with minor revisions, 3) revise and review again, or 4) reject.

6. **The manuscript.** Return the marked manuscript only if you are recommending that the paper be accepted or revised and have specific comments written on the manuscript that need to be shared with the author.

7. **Please respond promptly.** Our publisher, Human Sciences Press/Kluwer Academic Publishers, has strict deadlines for delivery of issues of the journal. We depend on you to respond in a timely fashion (**about 3 weeks, maximum**) or to inform us immediately if you cannot review the manuscript.

Some Points to Ponder as You Review
Mary Renck Jalongo, Ph.D.
Editor, *Early Childhood Education Journal*

Does the **title** of the manuscript accurately reflect the content? Could a person read the **abstract** and get a clear sense of what the article will be about? What about the **key words**? Will they be useful for indexing the work so that other researchers can find it?

Is there an opening paragraph that **identifies the topic and a clear focus**? Does the author make her or his stance on the issues clear? Could a reader decide, within the first page, if this article is of interest or is there a long and unnecessary preamble?

Does the opening section **preview** what is to come? Is there a succinct overview of the major parts of the article?

Does the **content** of the article have appeal for the audience of *Early Childhood Education Journal*? Is there material that is timely or innovative? Is the content significant or even timeless in its appeal for early childhood educators and the allied professions?

What about **documentation**? Is the information provided accurate and up-to-date? Does the author seem to be aware of leaders in the field and present a balanced view? Are authoritative sources of support cited?

What is the **quality of thinking** behind the manuscript? Do you have the sense that the author has ploughed deeply into the relevant literature and reflected carefully upon the trends, issues, or controversies associated with this topic?

Figure 3.3 *continued*

What about **style**? Is the language clear and direct so that readers at different levels will understand? Are unfamiliar terms defined?

Does the manuscript have **life**? Are general ideas supported by specific examples that demonstrate the author's concern for young children and commitment to the field? Does the author's voice convey the message that she or he has really lived with these ideas and experienced them personally, rather than just writing about them?

What about overall **organization**? Does every paragraph really belong where it is placed? Does one section of the manuscript flow into the next seamlessly? Is each paragraph cohesive?

Does the author make effective use of **headings and subheadings** to guide the reader through the content?

Are **tables, figures, and other illustrative material** carefully chosen and worth the added expense of publishing them? Has the author included material that others in the field will find helpful? Are there examples of young children's words and work, as appropriate?

Is the article **carefully prepared**? Does it adhere to the style requirements of the American Psychological Association's style manual (5th edition)? Are all of the references in the proper format? Is it free of spelling and typing errors or does it show signs of haste in preparation?

Is the manuscript **succinct**? Does it get to the point and stay on the subject? Are there some obvious places where it could be improved by skillful pruning?

What about the **conclusion**? Does the manuscript give a sense of revisiting the main ideas briefly? Does it give the reader a feeling that all of the ideas have been tied together?

What about the **reprint/republication potential** of the article? Would you recommend it to a colleague as course material? Can you envision the article as a reprint in a book of readings?

there is not sufficient space to publish a few other very worthwhile pieces. Additionally, because the page count has to come out so that all pages are filled and no more need to be added, editors are sometimes desperate for shorter pieces that will fit in more readily. For all of these reasons, editors appreciate brevity. The number one place where manuscripts are cut is at the beginning. Far too many authors take readers on a long, winding journey before introducing their thesis. When writing, do what film producers do—cut to the chase. It should not take more than a short paragraph or two to present your take on the issue and to preview for readers what the entire article will be about. Remember that "Intelligent readers are impressed by ideas and clear expression, not by elaborate constructions and excess words" (Luey, 1995, p. 10). Why don't writers, particularly academic writers, do this more often? One reason might be sheer puffery—trying to sound profound when the underlying idea is unimpressive. Another might be that they have been trained to sling words around rather than choose them carefully. Casanave (1997), a doctoral student, writes of her admiration for *The Writing Life* (Dillard, 1999) and considers its implications for scholarly writing by remarking, "If every academic writer worked as hard as Dillard does to write well, we would all write less. Not a bad idea. I am sure that I would feel more connected to the professional literature that I read if there were less of it, and if it demonstrated the writers' care for their craft and sincere interest in their audience" (p. 195).

One simple way to make your writing more concise is to cut out needless words, such as writing "in the event that" for "if" or writing "at the present time" when you could say "now." Another way to cut the fat in writing is to delete tired phrases and clichés—every editor has a few annoying favorites, such as "the acid test" or "level the playing field." When in doubt, follow the lead of author Elmore Leonard (quoted in Simpson, 1988), who when asked why he had experienced such great success as a writer, replied: "I leave out the parts that people skip" (p. 263).

PUBLISHABLE WRITING HAS BEEN PRETESTED AND PREREVIEWED

During your high school or perhaps your undergraduate days, it was not uncommon to write a paper only once, then turn it in for a grade. These papers were rarely revisited, other than scanning the corrections made by teachers. Unless you were fortunate enough to have teachers who used the process approach to writing, where written work was reviewed and refined on the basis of peer and instructor responses, then you may still think that writing for publication is like writing a paper for class. In fact, you may despise revision because it reminds you of those red (or green or whatever) marks on your papers that point out every flaw.

Far too often, novice educator/authors write in solitude and do not allow anyone else to read their work before submitting it to a publisher. They fail to test their work on a small, known audience before subjecting it to that most impersonal and critical of audiences, the anonymous peer reviewers. I frequently imagine the least experienced author furtively dropping a manuscript into large manila envelope before the work is really finished, then driving by a mailbox and depositing their manuscripts under cover of darkness. The first problem with this practice is that manuscripts are mailed in the heat of the moment before they are sufficiently polished. Like a carpenter who says, "I'll skip those last few light sandings and coats of polyurethane and go ahead and install these bookshelves," the shoddy workmanship tells on itself when subjected to the light of day. Good writing is rarely dashed off to schedule and, even when it is, inexperienced authors would be the least likely to get away with it.

Hurrying with revising is nearly always a mistake, unless you are the type of writer who mulls things over and over in your mind until they are practically written before you start to type. Even the simpler writing tasks, like a brief memo or letter, cannot be accelerated beyond a certain point unless you care little about misunderstandings.

Field-testing is even more important for bigger writing projects. The college-level instructor who fails to let real, live undergraduates respond candidly to what was written before proposing it as a chapter in a textbook is bound to encounter a raft of criticism from reviewers. Naturally, this takes some real building of trust and careful selection of students who will be confident enough to say what they really think, even though it is the professor's work. When I invited undergrads to be brutally honest about my book chapter on conflict resolution, I was horrified to learn that they came away from the chapter thinking that it advocated a *laissez-faire* approach. Evidently, much more direct and explicit conflict resolution examples and strategies were needed to make my point with the uninitiated.

The same need for feedback through field-testing applies to the researcher/conference presenter who has ten minutes to present the highlights of a study and is required to submit a three-page summary. These materials need to be developed far enough in advance that others can read them. Learn to see procrastination in these matters for what it is; not a badge of honor reserved for the extremely busy, but a way of avoiding criticism and circumventing those last few rounds of sanding and polishing that are the difference between rough-hewn and smooth appearance.

Sometimes, the promise of anonymity will encourage writers to submit their work to scrutiny before it is formally submitted to a journal. Anonymity also allows peer reviewers to be a bit more candid about what a manuscript needs. Consider what you and your fellow aspiring authors might need to create a support system. Figure 3.4 is a sample brochure that I developed to provide anonymous peer review services to faculty and students in my department.

PUBLISHABLE WRITING IS CAREFULLY CRAFTED

Whenever I commence working with a new group of writers and tell them that they will be using American Psychological Association (APA) style, I hear comments like the following:

- "I haven't written a paper in years. Does APA style use numbered endnotes?" (No, it doesn't.)

- "Does this book use APA? Is this what it looks like?" (Yes, this book does use APA.)

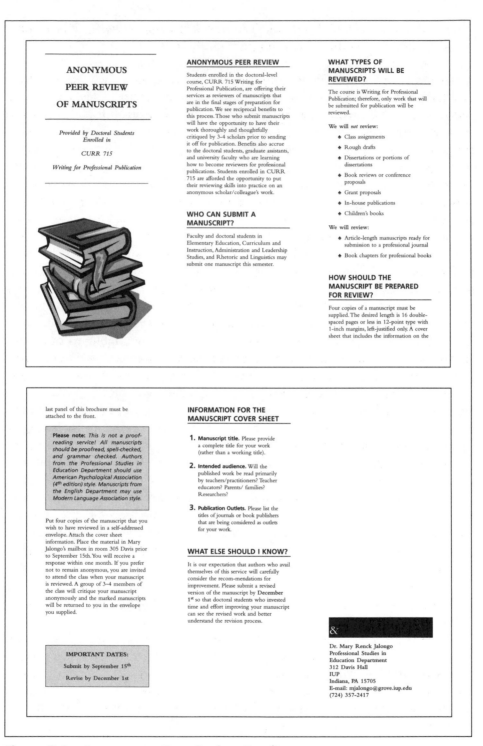

Figure 3.4   *Anonymous Peer Review Brochure*

- "I'm so confused. I just can't seem to learn this. What do you recommend?" (Learn the basics and look up the rest.)

Aside from those in the English department who sometimes use the Modern Language Association (MLA) referencing style, most publishers in the social sciences use American Psychological Association (APA) referencing style. Rather than treating a referencing style as the bane of your existence, the smart thing to do is to study it systematically, master it early, and get maximum pay off for having mastered the rules. The first step is to notice some of the basic patterns. The rules of APA can be clustered in to three main categories: those that govern a) in-text citations in the body of the paper; b) the reference list or bibliography at the end of the paper; and c) the other manuscript preparation issues such as the title page, the headings, tables, or figures. Try not to get overwhelmed by all the unusual situations, such as how to reference a telephone conversation with an author. Instead, learn the fundamentals and refer to resources such as the APA Manual or online sources (Writer's Handbook/APA style, http://www.wisc.edu/writing/Handbook/DocAPA.html). They include not only information on the style, but also helpful hints on typing your paper, spelling, punctuation, and grammar. There are also computer software programs that format the information in APA style, such as *EndNote Plus* or the American Psychological Association's APA-Style Helper 2.0 (for a free demonstration, go to http://www.apa.org/apa-style/).

Another indicator of careful crafting is word choice. You need not sprinkle your manuscript with Latin or French phrases nor reach for words that are found in less than one percent of the population's active vocabulary. When writing nonfiction, your erudition and mastery of vocabulary is evident in the precision of your words rather than the number of syllables.

Imprecision can get you in trouble. I was incensed when someone referred to our house fire as a "mishap." A mishap is diminutive—a fender bender in a parking lot or a splinter in your finger, not over $100,000 worth of damage and almost a year to put it back together again. In another instance of imprecision, an author submitted a manuscript about "poor parents," and the reviewers immediately questioned it. Did she mean to say low-income? Was the author making a value judgment about their parenting skills or, worse yet, was she stereotyping low-income parents as having less care for and commitment to their children? Be cautious, also, about overgeneralizing your personal experience. When a professor from New York City said that "nearly everyone" in the United States has a therapist, members of the audience took issue with it. Although it was true of her circle of friends, it was far from accurate portrayal of the nation. Choose your words carefully and learn to troubleshoot for misunderstandings.

PUBLISHABLE WRITING EARNS PEER ACCEPTANCE

Contrary to popular opinion, publishable manuscripts are well edited before they are submitted to the editor. With rare exception, editors are more like the jeweler who places polished gems into their appropriate settings than they are like the jewelry designer who may actually cut or polish stones, as well as create the settings. The great majority of editors have neither time nor the inclination to "finish" a manuscript for you. If they edit a widely circulated and prestigious journal, they probably will accept less than 10 percent of the unsolicited manuscripts submitted. This happens for a variety of reasons. First of all, the instant name recognition journals are deluged by submissions. Secondly, at least some of the manuscripts are solicited, meaning that the leaders in the field were invited to write them. Third, editors strive to get as much of the best material possible for their audiences into print.

Occasionally, you will encounter an editor who will take the time to really revise your manuscript. This may happen for several reasons, but the most common would be:

- The topic is very timely and in demand by the audience, but no other manuscripts on the topic have been submitted.

- The editor has a publication that is new or less well known and has fewer manuscripts from which to choose.

- The editor feels that an author shows promise and is willing to invest time in developing him or her.

The typical editor reads hundreds of manuscripts a year and publishes only a fraction of what is submitted. Why do they read on, despite the fact that acceptance rates for many professional publications are in the single digits? (Henson, 1998). Assuming that editors I know or have heard present at conferences are representative of the larger population of editors, it is because they have a commitment to the publisher, the audience, the publication, and the profession. Finding good manuscripts amongst the many inferior ones that are submitted is the editor's everlasting quest.

WHO CAN HELP YOU TO GET PUBLISHED?

As writers, we learn from the company we keep; "readers and writers do not learn from methods, they learn from people" (Smith, 1992, p. 440). When graduate students in a writing course are told that they will be evaluating one another's work, they are frequently skeptical. Surely, this is a case of the blind leading the blind: How can a person who has not published provide any helpful feedback?

Although none of my students has come out and said so, I suspect that they think I am merely trying to lighten my workload by recommending peer review.

Yet as the semester is about to end, they have very different views about the ability of others, even unpublished authors, to help them gain an understanding of their writing process and ways of communicating. They have learned to appreciate that fresh perspectives on their work often suggest ways to improve it. The people who read your manuscripts need not be wildly successful writers nor the great editors, all of the time; it is sufficient that they be thoughtful readers who will think along with you and let you know when they've lost their way in your argument or stumbled over your prose. Peers are also more accessible than big-time editors or authors and can provide an instant audience for your work that will not send you an official rejection letter. Therefore, one of the most valuable, yet frequently disregarded sources for review of work is your peers. If you want to acquire a good reputation as a peer editor, strive to make your reviews gentle, tough, and wise (Roorbach, 1998). Figure 3.5 is a set of questions that peers might use to evaluate your work and make it more publishable long before it reaches the editor's desk.

---

1. **General reactions**—What did you think? Does the writing make sense? Do you know what the author is talking about?

2. **Telling it all**—Elaboration. Are the ideas fully developed? Are there details (facts, figures, people, places, and events) that make ideas come alive? Are there details that inform, persuade, and move the reader?

3. **Written organization**—Are ideas presented in an interesting, logical order? Is there a beginning that creates interest? Does the body of the paper sustain interest? Is there a conclusion that sums up the ideas?

4. **Paragraphs**—Do they hang together? Look at each paragraph. Does each idea or detail relate to the paragraph?

5. **Sentence sense**—Do all sentences make sense? Are they complete sentences? Do all sentences start the same way? If so, how can the writer change some of them for variety? Could some of the short sentences be combined to make them more interesting? Are some of the sentences overly long? Can it be read aloud with ease?

6. **Exactness of words**—Are the words specific? Is there appropriate use of vocabulary? Are there words that relate to the senses? Is there a use of unusual expressions, word combinations and comparisons that add life to the paper? Did the writer avoid excessive jargon?

Source: DeStefano, P., Dole. J. & Marzano, R. (1984). *Elementary language arts.*, pp.108-110, New York: Wiley.

Figure 3.5   *Questions to Guide the Peer Editing Process*

Writing teachers who are also published authors are another source of feed-back on your work. No one who presumes to teach writing can do so unless she or he is a writer. And, there's more. That person needs to want you to become a writer too. It is not enough for the teacher to share anecdotes about the writing life. It is also insufficient to maintain a "hands off" approach and fail to offer concrete suggestions. A real teacher of writing will be able to diagnose writing difficulties, nudge you a bit, and offer concrete suggestions. It is also important that this writing teacher has done the type of writing you have in mind because, ultimately, the writing teacher's role is to invite you, as a newcomer, into the group of writers to which they already belong.

Another key source of support for writers is active collaboration with other writers. Perhaps this has happened to you. You go to a conference and meet some-one who attended the same session as you based on a mutual interest. You chat and one of you suggests, "Maybe we should write something together!" Should you? It depends on a number of different things. First of all, how do you define "writing together?" You may find that the other person defines it in "The Lit-tle Red Hen" story fashion as "You sow, plant, harvest, and bake, then I'll show up for the bread-eating part." You may discover that this person has been denied tenure at two universities and is a desperate person who has to get something published almost immediately, a nearly impossible task. You might also find that there isn't much advantage to writing with a like-minded individual at a simi-lar level of experience, because it does not add much to the mix. Generally speaking, it has been my experience that the greater the level of accomplish-ment, the more likely the co-author is to be the most generous and reliable. Put plainly, the best predictor of who will write and write well is who has already written and written well. A "misery loves company" approach rarely produces anything other than misery squared.

When we conducted a survey of co-authors several years ago, one of the most striking findings was that when troubles arose, the project was frequently abandoned and all of the work lost. Like marriages, collaborations in writing are great when they work and horrendous when they break down. Things that you once did in the interest of the team are now onerous and cited as further evi-dence of unfair treatment. Every flaw in your co-author(s) becomes amplified until it is impossible to overlook.

Before you consider extending or accepting an offer of co-authorship, real-ize that co-authorship is more than listing two or more authors on a cover page. Actually, it is quite involved and can become mired in ethical issues about own-ership of work. Yet as Thyer (1994) explains, co-authorship can offer reciprocal advantages when it works well:

> Of the last 50 articles I have published or had accepted in scholarly jour-
> nals, 29 were co-written with students of mine. Many of these works
> could not have been attempted without the willing collaboration and
> diligent efforts of these talented persons. To be sure, I have had my share

of incompetent students who failed to follow through on assigned tasks, were sloppy in their data collection, or were simply lazy With proper supervision on my part, however, the large majority of them have proved to be valued collaborators to whom I owe an immense debt of gratitude and from whom I have learned a great deal. (pp. 90-91)

Despite all of these cautionary words, collaboration has much to recommend it. Like any other social relationship, when it works well, it is particularly satisfying.

> For some reason, due no doubt to some personal foible of my own that intensive psychoanalysis would reveal, I have always found it easier to collaborate with my students than with my faculty colleagues. Remember those dreaded group assignments in school? There was always someone on you "team" who fumbled his task or who simply let the others carry him along, leaving you to pick up the slack at the last minute. Perhaps worse was the bossy person who, in a dictatorial manner, assumed managerial responsibility and abrasively directed everyone on what to do. Unfortunately, such individuals have their counterpart in academia, individuals with their own research agendas to prosecute, career timetables to consider, and personal axes to grind, not to mention personal psychopathology. (Thyer, 1994, p. 91)

Yet another source of support for writers is the field of journalism. Although there are some obvious differences between writing for a city newspaper and writing for a scholarly journal, there is much to be learned from people who pay their mortgages by writing. Too many scholars write in a "literary" style designed to impress their readers, and a dash of journalism may be just what is needed to make their writing less pedantic. What sort of guidelines do journalists follow?

In general, they are advised to get directly to the point, to keep sentences short, to write a succinct and powerful first paragraph, to use the active voice, and to prefer a positive approach. To illustrate, journalist James Kilpatrick (1984) got this note from his editor at *The Richmond News Leader:*

> Kilpo:
>
> I have something for you.
>
> . . . .
>
> . . . .
>
> Those interesting objects are called periods. They are formed by the second key from the right on the bottom row. Please put them to good use.
>
> CHH

Peers, writing teachers, co-authors, and the no-nonsense style of the journalist all are helpful resources in producing a publishable manuscript.

CONCLUSION

As you think about writing in the future, try to remember that writing is:

- A means of organizing thinking and discovering what you already knew and have recently learned.

- A way of communicating with various audiences for particular purposes and bringing your material to them in ways suited to their needs.

- An art, a craft, and a set of skills that are used to accomplish important goals.

- A way of making sense out of otherwise chaotic information and connecting it with your experience.

- A vehicle for reaching an audience and encouraging responses from readers.

Athletes talk about being "in the zone" and writers, too, have a zone where they are comfortable. That zone changes, of course, with different writing tasks. Try to situate each writing project at just the right balance point along each continuum in Figure 3.6. Gradually, you will begin to find the fulcrum and the delicate balance that fits the writing situation. Gradually, too, you will learn to be resilient as a writer; to learn from blunders and rebound, eager to try again. There is a considerable body of research now on this transition from novice to expert. It has been gathered from many different pursuits (e.g., playing chess) and occupations (e.g., becoming a medical doctor). Figure 3.7 summarizes how these findings are applicable to the task of writing nonfiction for professional audiences.

Part of this growth from novice to expert is knowing what to keep and what to discard. I have a lateral file drawer that is bulging with notes and articles that I began to write and never finished. In some cases, I lost interest in the topic. In others, I produced a draft of a manuscript but did not like it well enough to finish it. In still other cases, I presented a paper or a research report at a conference and planned to produce an article later but never did follow through. I'm not sure why none of these writing projects ever came to fruition, but they didn't. I have maintained that file for nearly two decades now, always expecting to return at some point and resurrect some of those pieces. It was only recently that I threw nearly all of it away because: a) all the information in there was dated and b) there are so many new writing opportunities that I don't want to backtrack. It was not publishable and had to be let go.

The question that is the basis for this entire chapter, "What makes writing publishable?" can be answered this way: Gradually, after years of reading and

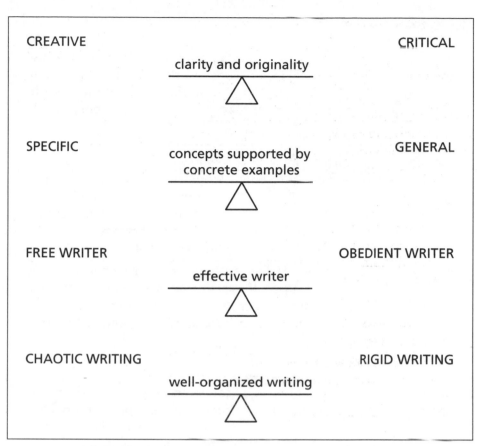

Figure 3.6   *Finding the Balance Point in Writing*

FROM	TO
general knowledge on a variety of topics	highly specialized expertise that enables them to excel mainly in one domain
Implications for Authors: Identify an area of interest and pursue it intensely. Make learning about a particular facet of a topic your project. Make yourself an expert through extensive reading and writing.	
FROM	**TO**
knowledge that is piecemeal and difficult to synthesize	a storehouse of cases, episodes, and accounts of experience that are stored in memory as narratives (stories)

Figure 3.7   *From Novice to Expert*

continued on next page

Figure 3.7   *continued*

Implications for Authors: Outstanding authors have learned to use their personal/professional experiences as a rich resource for writing. They draw upon these narratives to introduce a topic, illustrate a difficult concept, or persuade their readers of an issue's importance.

FROM	TO
focusing on the surface and being overwhelmed or confused	seeing the big picture and recognizing large, meaningful patterns in their domain of expertise as well as representing problems on a deeper, more principled level

Implications for Authors: Skilled authors have developed effective ways of analyzing, applying, synthesizing, and evaluating information from many different sources. They use logic to bring order out of chaos and make interesting connections and juxtapositions that others might miss.

FROM	TO
being confounded by problems and making beginner's mistakes	spending proportionately more time analyzing problems qualitatively and then solving problems efficiently with few errors

Implications for Authors: When work is criticized or rejected, the novice author frequently gives up and assumes that the work is hopeless rather than trying to learn from mistakes, improve the work, and resubmit. After many years of trying, a very high percentage of what the author submits is accepted with only minor revisions.

FROM	TO
reliance on others to gain a sense of their progress and achievements	greater self-direction and strong self-monitoring skills

Implications for Authors: Until an author begins to trust his or her instincts, to know when the writing truly is good, and to sense when he or she is drifting from the focus, that author is dependent upon others to validate and critique. After many experiences with useful feedback, the author gains greater confidence in a personal ability to determine when the writing is going well or when the product is of high quality.

Adapted from Pressley, M. (1995). *Advanced educational psychology for educators, researchers, and policymakers.* New York: Harper Collins College Publishers.

writing, you will acquire an inner sense of when you are writing well and when you are not; what to save and what to cut; and when work is publishable and when it isn't.

REFERENCES

Campbell, W. S. (1945). *Writing non-fiction* (2nd ed.). Boston: The Writer.

Casanave, C. P. (1997). Body-mergings: Searching for connections with academic discourse. In C. P. Casanave & S. R. Schecter (Eds.), *On becoming a language educator: Personal essays on professional development* (pp. 187-200). Mahwah, NJ: Lawrence Erlbaum Associates.

Casewit, C. (1985). *Freelance writing*. New York: Collier.

Diamond, R. M. (1994). *Serving on promotion and tenure committees: A faculty guide*. Boston: Anker.

Fox, M. F. (1985). *Scholarly writing and publishing*. Boulder, CO: Westview.

Harman, E., & Montagnes, I. (1976). *Thesis and the book*. Toronto: University of Toronto Press.

Henson, K. T. (1998). *The art of writing for publication* (2nd ed.). Boston, MA: Allyn & Bacon.

Kilpatrick, J. (1984). *The writer's art*. New York: Andrews, McMeel & Parker.

Krall, C., & Jalongo, M. R. (1998). Creating caring communities in classrooms: Advice from an intervention specialist. *Childhood Education, 75*(2), 83-89.

Lamb, B. (1997). *Booknotes: America's finest authors on reading, writing, and the power of ideas*. New York: Times Books/Random House.

Luey, B. (1995). *Handbook for academic authors* (3rd ed.). New York: Cambridge University Press.

Macrorie, K. (1984). *Writing to be read*. Upper Monclair, NJ: Boynton/Cook.

Moffat, J. (1983). *Teaching the universe of discourse*. Boston: Houghton Mifflin.

Murray, F. B., & J. Raths, (1996). Factors in the peer review of reviews. *Review of Educational Research, 66* (4), 417–421.

Provost, G. (1985). *100 ways to improve your writing*. New York: Mentor/New American Library.

Roorbach, B. (1998). *Writing life stories*. Cincinnati, OH: Story Press.

Safire, W. & Safir, L. (Eds.) (1994). *Good advice on writing*. New York: Simon & Schuster.

Simpson, J. B. (Ed.). *Simpson's contemporary quotations*. Boston: Houghton Mifflin.

Smith, F. (1992). Learning to read: The never-ending debate. *Phi Delta Kappan, 73*(6), 432– 441.

Thyer, B. A. (1994). *Successful publishing in scholarly journals.* Thousand Oaks, CA: Sage.

Trimble, J. R. (2000). *Writing with style.* Upper Saddle River, NJ: Prentice Hall.

Wald, C. (1998). The power of self revelation: A conversation with Mary Kay Blakely. In L. Gutkind (Ed.), *The essayist at work: Profiles of creative nonfiction writers* (pp. 37–43). Portsmouth, NH: Heinemann.

Zinsser, W. (1998). *On writing well* (5th ed.). New York: Harper and Row.

CHAPTER 4

❦

Mastering the Strategies Used by Successful Authors

❦

When accomplished professionals share some marker of success in writing, such as the number of manuscripts published or honors earned for written work, the obvious question from aspiring authors is: How do they do it? Surely they must have some secret that enables them to be so prolific. Based on the high percentage of authors who complain about writing, I suspect that they have learned to put up with the irritating parts of writing long enough to enjoy some of writing's pleasures. Just as the vacation traveler contends with flight delays, lost baggage, physical discomfort, and inclement weather in order to accomplish the goal of a much anticipated beach vacation, the writer has learned to tolerate writing's aggravations in hopes of producing pieces of writing that flow. Renowned historian and author Barbara Tuchman (1981) explains the primary pay-off of writing well this way:

> When it comes to language, nothing is more satisfying than to write a good sentence. It is no fun to write lumpishly, dully, in prose the reader must plod through like wet sand. But it is a pleasure to achieve, if one can, a clear running prose that is simple yet full of surprises.

> This does not just happen. It requires skill, hard work, a good ear, and
> continued practice. . . . The goals, as I have said, are clarity, interest, and
> aesthetic pleasure. (p. 48)

Despite every effort to persuade and demonstrate that writing for publication demands new ways of approaching writing, my students often persist at "Ph.D. illiteracy"—dull reports of others' research and one quotation after another, lightly linked together. They write in a voice that is not their own, imitated from the worst of what they have been assigned to read; "they simply empty their notebooks, moving from one source to the next, ladling quotations directly into their text" (Stewart, 1998, p. 167). As Price (1984) explains,

> Besides being ugly and artificial, Ph.D. illiteracy is also dishonest. The
> intent is to deceive, to make the simple complex, to make the obvious seem brilliantly and even arduously discovered, to make the tautological seem like a giant leap forward for mankind. The writer's first
> priority is to impress or trick you. The more that tricking outweighs
> telling, the more language is deformed—that is the essential dynamic
> of Ph.D. illiteracy. (p. 18)

Understand that my students continue to generate such papers, even *after* examining manuscripts that started out this way and were transformed into published work. Why? Am I that bad as a teacher? I hope not. I think this happens because, when you write for publication, you have to *un*learn much of what you thought you knew about writing. The nature and extent of these changes is evidently so discomforting to aspiring authors that they cling to their old ways in the futile hope that their work will be pronounced publishable. Most of us would prefer to become published in the absence of any stressful adaptive demands on behavior. My students seem faintly surprised when I remind them about what we discussed in class, writing in the margin, for instance: "Write headings that are specific to your topic, not generic ones like 'Recommendations.' You might be able to organize this manuscript around common questions since you can assume that this audience is relatively unfamiliar with autism." They can't quite believe that the advice they remember really does apply to them and will say things like, "You mean I'm allowed to do that? Use questions as headings?" Like young children who attempt to play a game but do not think that the rules pertain to them, my student writers are not serious players—yet. I suspect that many would-be authors are curiously resistant to changing the behaviors that never had much to recommend them in the first place. Until writers can expand their repertoire of writing strategies beyond those learned in grade school, they will continue to struggle mightily with composition.

The purpose of this chapter is to replace or restock your supply of writing strategies. There will be some recommendations that seem odd while others sound familiar. It will be up to you to experiment on your own with the strategies and give them a chance to modify your writing behavior in ways that will eventually yield greater success, skill, and confidence. My overarching goal for this chapter on strategies is consistent with that of a "paper mentor;" it is an effort to offer you the collective benefit of a wide array of writing experts who will enrich and enlarge your concept of writing by sharing some tools of the trade. Perry (1999) uses the task of hanging a picture on the wall as a metaphor for writing advice.

> For instance, how do you hang a picture on the wall? Simple, some one might tell you. "Hammer a nail or picture hook into the wall at the height you want the picture." But it doesn't work that way. Maybe our brains are more like computer programs than we'd like to think. I have to be told *exactly* how to perform physical tasks that are new to me, until I know what I'm doing. What kind of hammer? What size of nail or hook? When I tried it the first time, a chunk of plaster fell out of the wall. I later read that a little bit of tape on the wall might prevent loosening of the plaster. And if you don't mark the spot first, making allowance for the fact that the hook won't usually be quite at the top of the frame, the picture won't end up where you intended it to. (pp. 209-210)

What follows is a collection of strategies, like that bit of tape on the plaster, that are designed to equip your toolkit with better ways of accomplishing a task.

CARING ABOUT WORDS

One day I boarded the elevator at the university and saw a former M.Ed. student who had been enrolled in one of my classes. We greeted one another and I found out that he was now a building principal in an elementary school. Then he said, "I guess you know, Mary Jalongo, that you really have ruined me as a writer. I used to dash off memos and letters and reports. Now I write and rewrite them several times. In some ways I am disappointed that knowing more about writing doesn't make it faster and easier. But I still want to thank you. You taught me to care about writing." As with anything else that you hope to accomplish— be it playing golf or growing a flower garden—caring enough is where it begins. There are thousands of people who wish they were accomplished on the golf greens or who dream of filling a vase with an armload of flowers they have cultivated. But only those who care about it enough and have learned to use the tools properly will realize those dreams. Because words are the author's tools, any self-respecting author has learned to care about them. As editor/author Jacques Barzun (quoted in Safire & Safir, 1994) makes the point raised by my student in the elevator a bit more eloquently:

> The price of learning to use words is the development of an acute self-consciousness. Nor is it enough to pay attention to words only when you face the task of writing—that is like playing the violin only

on the night of the concert. You must attend to words when you read,
when you speak, when others speak. Words must become ever present
in your waking life, an incessant concern, like color and design if the
graphic arts matter to you or pitch and rhythm if it is music, or speed
and form if it is athletics. (p. 265)

American writer Mark Twain used humor to illustrate the importance of
words when he said, "The difference between the right word and the almost
right word is the difference between lightning and the lightning bug" (Winokur,
1986, p. 89). Some writer's behaviors that reflect caring about words include:

- Referring to a dictionary, thesaurus, or other reference tools as necessary.

- Defining specialized terminology and professional jargon using the works
  of leading authorities in the field.

- Reading your manuscripts out loud to listen to the sounds and cadence
  of the language.

- Avoiding obscure words that will distance members of your intended
  audience.

- Using spell check and grammar check, as well as proofreading carefully.

- Editing out clichés and using your own figurative expressions.

- Using concrete details, analogies, and examples based on your experience
  that emphasize key points and bring ideas to life.

- Cutting out excess verbiage, needless repetition, and double-speak.

After you make a commitment to caring about words then you are ready to
choose a topic.

SETTLING ON A TOPIC

One of the questions most often asked of accomplished authors is: "Where do
you get your ideas?" When you really think about that question, the answer is
rather obvious. Where does any good idea come from? Partly from our imagi-
nations, partly from our personal/professional experiences, and partly from
making connections that others may overlook.

One day while standing in line to rent a video, I watched several parents
negotiating with their children about which ones they were permitted to take
home and watch. At that time, videocassettes for children were just becoming
widely available and affordable. I had seen several lists of recommended videos,
but had the idea that it might be more helpful to provide general guidelines that

could be applied to the many new titles that were coming out almost daily. So, I wrote an article on the topic for the National Parent Teacher Association. I asked Louise, a former colleague and parent of a preschooler, to critique it. She raised some additional points concerning monitoring the use of videos that I incorporated into the work. Because the article was timely and built around the questions that parents and families actually had, it earned an EDPRESS Feature Article Award.

What beginners often miss is that, after you have identified an area of interest, the best ideas are more likely to surface *during* writing rather than prior to writing as noted historian and author David McCullough (cited in Lamb, 1997) explains:

> People will sometimes say to me, "Well, what's your theme?" as I start on the new book. "I haven't the faintest idea. That's one of the reasons I'm writing the book." "Well, you don't know much about that subject." "That's exactly right. I don't know anything about the subject— or very little. And, again, that's why I'm writing the book." I think if I knew all about it and I knew exactly what I was going to say, I probably wouldn't want to write the book, because there would be no search, there would be no exploration of a country I've never been to—that's the way one should feel. (p.6)

Good ideas are vastly overrated by newcomers to publication. They frequently fail to realize that, when a topic is "hot," it is not uncommon for an editor to receive numerous manuscripts on the same basic subject. The issue then becomes how expertly each writer treats an idea—the original thesis, persuasive argument, authoritative support, captivating examples—rather than the domain of interest that first attracted the writer's attention.

GATHERING INFORMATION AND DOCUMENTING SOURCES

Works of nonfiction are information-driven. Therefore, it is essential for authors to get the most up-to-date and authoritative information available. When I say authoritative, I do not mean the local newspaper, scandal sheet, or magazine for homemakers. I also do not mean overreliance on material from secondary sources, meaning that it was written by someone else somewhere else before being included in the work. Why avoid secondary sources? Because you are relying on an author's interpretation of another author's work. This makes it difficult to stand behind what you have written. Just like that old game of whispering a sentence from one person to the next around a circle, then checking to see how far the final message deviates from the original, many misconceptions can be introduced when words and ideas pass through the minds, hands, and word processors of others. Go to the source and make your own interpretations.

When I say to up-to-date information, I do not mean the statistic that has been quoted for so many years that no one seems to remember where it came from (such statistics are notoriously incorrect). When you consider that after journal articles are accepted, a year or more may elapse before they actually appear in print, it becomes doubly important to get the latest information.

Part of what makes a manuscript not just timely, but timeless, is the author's ability to take off those disciplinary blinders and view his or her subject from multiple disciplinary perspectives. The importance of cross-disciplinary reading cannot be overemphasized, so here is my recommendation: stop limiting your reading to only those things that appear in the journals to which you subscribe or that come up on a computer search of your topic. Expand your reading interests. Devote at least half of your reading to material *outside* your field.

Figure 4.1 offers useful guidelines on reviewing the literature gleaned from Merriam (1998).

Precision is another habit of mind that writers acquire. Even if they are absent-minded or haphazard about other aspects of their lives, like balancing their checkbooks, respected authors are tremendously attentive to details. It is surprisingly easy to introduce errors when printed sources are transcribed or

---

Definition

- "The literature review is a narrative essay that integrates, synthesizes, and critiques the important thinking and research on a particular topic"(Merriam, 1998, p. 55).

Audience

- Readers want to know "what you think of the literature, its strengths as well as its weaknesses, whether or not it constitutes a major breakthrough in the thinking on the topic, what it adds to the knowledge base, and so on" (Merriam, 1998, p. 55).

What is Included in the Literature?

- "Think pieces"—the theoretical or conceptual writing on a topic, both within the field of education and in other, related fields

- "Data-based pieces"—research investigations published in research journals that report on data collected and analyzed by the researcher

- "Synthesis pieces"—reviews of research written by others in published work

Figure 4.1 *Reviewing the Literature*

Figure 4.1 *continued*

What Can a Literature Review Achieve?

- Establishes a foundation and theoretical framework for the work
- Sets forth a persuasive argument that demonstrates how the current discussion advances, refines, or revises what is already known
- Enables the writer to know exactly how the current work departs from what has gone on before
- Informs the writer about what has been written on the topic previously
- Helps to clarify the thesis and focus
- Provides authoritative definitions of terms and concepts
- Suggests specific directions for future research
- Situates the work in the larger context of the professional literature, thereby making the nature of the contribution clear

How to Go About Conducting the Review

- General Overview—use encyclopedias, handbooks, yearbooks, and indexes
- Computer & Internet Search—search by topic AND approach in bibliographies, abstracts, and other indexes
- Full-text Documents—decide which materials are important to obtain

Which Resources Are Most Appropriate and Relevant?

- Leaders in the field
- Classic and contemporary sources
- Relevance to your topic and approach
- Insight, originality, and usefulness of other sources

Why Is It Important to Review Prior Research?

- To avoid pursuing a trivial problem
- To avoid duplicating work already done
- To avert the mistakes committed by others

Source: Adapted from Merriam, S. B. (1998). *Qualitative research and case study applications in education*. San Francisco: Jossey-Bass.

when words are moved at the touch of a button. Your misspelling of an author's name will not be appreciated. The nonfiction writer's motto must be to check, check, and check again.

Another way in which authors learn to be precise is by saying what they mean and meaning what they say. Look at this example from a student's first draft of a piece on environmental education in which she begins by talking about projects such as Earth Day or picking up litter around the school:

> Traditionally, many school districts called these common, once-a-year activities environmental education. While these activities were helpful and well intentioned, did they really help children develop a strong awareness of environmental issues and problems?

Here was my response: "You seem to be contradicting yourself here. You said they were helpful but now you say that they were not. Also, the word 'traditional' is bothersome. To me, traditional is age-old. I am 50 years old and did not experience these things as a student. Other members of your audience may not have, either. Do you mean to say something like this?"

> Many school districts considered these common, once-a-year activities to be the essence of their environmental education programs. While these activities are well intentioned and apparently enjoyed by students, it is doubtful that such short-term projects result in a lifelong interest in environmental issues and a personal commitment from students to address environmental problems.

So, gathering information accurately, reporting it correctly and saying what you intend to say are essential.

When writing nonfiction for professional audiences, keep in mind that readers rely on published authors as a source of information and support. After you become a published author, others may be quoting you, so accuracy is of paramount importance.

COPING WITH INFORMATION OVERLOAD

Conducting a comprehensive, integrative literature review is like finding yourself waist-deep in quicksand. Even though you are convinced you will drown, struggling only makes it worse. You must resist the urge to panic and begin flailing about. When my graduate students become immersed in the literature, I hear statements like these:

- "At first I didn't find that much, now I have found so much that it is overwhelming. Is it possible to have *too much* information?"

- "I have piles of highlighted articles and books marked with Post-it notes but now I'm not sure about what to do with it all, about where to begin."

- "I'm worried about unintentional plagiarism. After I've read all of this material, how do I know those are my ideas surfacing as I am writing and not something I've read somewhere else bubbling up to the surface?"

When conducting a literature review, nonfiction writers use simple tools to arrive at a high level of information synthesis. Think of it as a jumbled grocery list. It makes for much more efficient shopping if you cluster items by areas of the store—all the dairy products, produce items, bakery products, etc. A similar strategy can be used with the literature review. Begin by clustering items with some conceptual similarity together, realizing that these categories are provisional and may change as the work progresses. I often use boldface, all capital letter headings for the names of these clusters so that I can spot them easily when scrolling through my notes for the manuscript. Use something flexible—a set of index cards, the cut and paste function on your computer, or a mind map. When I want to produce a literature review, I begin by typing my ideas and examples in boldface print. This helps to keep my material separate from any other I might find. Figure 4.2 highlights additional ways to avoid unintentional plagiarism.

Biographer Clare Brandt (cited in Lamb, 1997) explains how she copes with information overload:

> There are difficult moments where you think you're never going to get a handle on it. You end up with a bulging computer with all these little disparate items of information. . . . and you can't figure out where in the world they fit. They look like they belong to a different jigsaw puzzle, and [as if] you shouldn't be bothering with them at all. Until you get a handle on it, it can be very difficult. I always write a first

---

- In your notes, make certain that you have recorded information from your sources completely, carefully, and accurately.

- As you take notes, put all words taken from outside sources inside quotation marks and enclose your own comments in brackets.

- As you write, differentiate your ideas from those of your sources by clearly introducing borrowed material with the author's name(s) and by ending with the appropriate citation.

- In your manuscript, enclose all direct quotations within quotation marks and cite the source or sources of any paraphrased or summarized material.

Figure 4.2 *Ways to Avoid Unintentional Plagiarism*

draft that has everything in it, and it reads about as interesting as a laun-
dry list. . . . Only after dealing with that, and wrestling with that by
just getting it down on the page, which is a chore, do murky shapes
begin to appear. Then you just go with those, and you test them and
make sure that they work before you finally decide to use them. It's
really feeling in the dark for a while, and it can be discouraging. (p.91)

After you have the material roughly sorted into categories, start making decisions about where you might need specific things, such as a direct quotation from
an authoritative source, a current statistic, or a concrete example. Stay loose at
this stage so that you are free to make interesting connections and juxtapositions. This is a time to keep your internal critic quiet.

DEVELOPING A THESIS AND FOCUS

When I was a preschooler, my mother gave me her discarded costume jewelry
to play with. I kept it in a pink jewelry box that had a broken, wind-up plastic
ballerina and usually the junky jewelry, especially the necklaces, would get tan-
gled together as I carted it around. At first, I didn't even attempt to untangle that
Gordian knot. I would try to find some patient adult who had the knack of
pulling the items apart, but when I imitated what I thought I saw them doing,
randomly tugging here and there, it only made the knot tighter. What I could
not detect from my naïve observations was that these adults were solving a problem, not using magical powers. It took much more explanation, demonstration,
and trial-and-error before I started to understand how to approach the unstruc-
tured problem embodied in that jumble of jewelry.

Finding your thesis and focus is like that wad of metal, glass, and plastic that
stumped me as a child. There are times when you despair of ever sorting it out
and there are times when the moves that you make toward discovering the thesis, the main point for your manuscript, only worsen the situation. But with time,
experience, and gentle coaching you learn to follow a promising lead and grab
in the right places. Then the next few moves are the right ones and a pattern
emerges; you see a way to build your argument, as long as you keep that focus
firmly in mind.

Finding your thesis, your stance on the subject, is a major breakthrough. It
produces a feeling of elation comparable to seeing a substantial income tax refund
check in your mailbox. Once you know your point, your fundamental reason
for writing the manuscript in the first place, it is like switching from the page
format setting on the computer to balanced newspaper columns and watching
as everything realigns right before your eyes. After this happens, you will become
determined to find the time to finish the work because the detangler for all of
that material has emerged.

Most readers want to know where authors are "coming from," what assumptions and biases they bring to the topic. Inexperienced authors sometimes think

that, in the interest of being more persuasive, they are supposed to sweep dissent under the carpet. A better approach is to make it clear from the outset why you are taking a particular stand. If others disagree with you, approach their counter-arguments head on rather than waiting for them to appear in a letter to the editor. This is particularly important if you are taking a point of view that deviates from the prevailing opinion. An example is Don Murray's (1998) statement that "Talent doesn't produce writing, but writing *may* produce talent" (p. 1). Now that is a dramatic departure from most what most people assume, from deeply ingrained beliefs that "good" writers are somehow blessed. As a writer, you simply cannot take a stance like this without considerable groundwork to overcome the natural tendency to misinterpret your meaning. So, don't leave your readers wondering if you are unaware of what is going on in the field or if you are actually asserting a different perspective. When you find your thesis and focus, state it early in the manuscript. The mechanism for doing this is the pronouncement paragraph, a succinct overview of what you will treat in the manuscript and from what point of view. Figure 4.3 explains the structure of the pronouncement paragraph.

GENERATING A WORKING DRAFT

You have your list or mind map or clusters, you've thought about a pronouncement paragraph, and now you'll need to begin generating a working draft. Ann Lamott (1994) relates the following story that inspired the title of her book, *Bird by Bird*:

> Thirty years ago my older brother, who was ten years old at the time, was trying to get a report on birds written that he'd had three months to write. [It] was due the next day. We were out at our family cabin in Bolinas, and he was at the kitchen table close to tears, surrounded by binder paper and pencils and unopened books on birds, immobilized by the hugeness of the task ahead. Then my father sat down beside him, put his arm around my brother's shoulder, and said, "Bird by bird, buddy. Just take it bird by bird" (p. V).

Writing a first draft sometimes feels like taking a 100 item multiple-choice test in 60 minutes. You do not linger over confusing items; you simply plow through as much as you can without pausing. Try beginning with freewriting. When you freewrite, you jumpstart your writing by getting your ideas out as quickly as possible. Freewriting consists of

- putting words down on paper without stopping

- not showing your words to anyone (unless you later change your mind)

- not having to stay on one topic—that is, freely digressing

- not thinking about spelling, grammar, and mechanics

- not worrying about how good the writing is—even whether it makes sense or is understandable (Elbow, 1997, p. 35)

Next, try chunking—identifying broad sections of the manuscript rather than struggling with outlines that are down to the 1, 2, 3 and a, b, c levels. If you need an example but cannot think of one, just write EX and keep going. One will come to you later when you least expect it. If you need facts and figures but don't have them yet, don't lose your momentum by stopping to surf the Net,

---

Whenever you attempt to write an article or a book chapter, you will need to focus your ideas around a central statement. This statement, called a thesis statement, usually appears in your first paragraph and performs three very useful functions:

- It identifies your topic.
- It narrows your topic and focuses the reader's attention on the particular aspect you will be discussing.
- It makes a clear statement about the point of view or perspective you will be taking on the topic (Kirszner & Mandell, 1992).

──────────── ❧ ────────────

Developing a Thesis
(Based on Chapter 5 of this book)

select a topic
writing nonfiction for publication

narrow your topic, make it more specific
using conference presentations as the basis for publication

take a perspective on the issue
professionals who are skilled as presenters often fail to take their oral presentations to the next level by preparing a written manuscript and developing it into a publishable article or book chapter.

make an announcement
This book chapter will . . .

Adapted from Kirszner & Mandell (1992), and cited in Jalongo, M. R., Twiest, M. M., & Gerlach, G. (1999). *The college learner: Reading, studying, and attaining academic success* (2nd ed.). Upper Saddle River, NJ: Prentice Hall.

Figure 4.3   *The Pronouncement Paragraph*

just write "F & F" and keep on. After you have generated quite a bit of text in this way, begin to fill in the blanks and re-examine your clustering strategy, always asking the question, "Is this is the best way to present this material to this audience?" Don't let anyone tell you that this process is orderly, sequential, and invariant. Most of the time, it is the way Miles (1990) describes it:

> The writer often organizes, composes, and revises at roughly the same time. Writing does not occur in separate and discrete stages: successful writers work backward and forward through their drafts, picking up and elaborating on undeveloped ideas and condensing or revising others. The more experienced writers become, the more efficiently they perform this process, and the better results they achieve. (p. 40)

Although it may seem like vague advice at first, experienced authors generally allow their material to suggest a shape rather than imposing a rigid structure on the material from the very start. Moreover, the experience of real writers treats writing as a recursive process in which many functions are going on simultaneously—drafting, getting feedback, and continuing to conduct research. When seeking feedback, consider who might serve as a helpful manuscript critic. Edelstein (1999) offers this list of criteria:

- Honest and forthright

- Willing to address both strengths and weaknesses of the manuscript

- Considers the work on its own terms rather than according to a predetermined ideas, preferences, or biases

- Has your growth and best interests at heart and cares about your work and what it attempts to do

As Paul Kennedy (cited in Lamb, 1997), a Yale University professor and author observes, ways of generating first drafts are task specific and idiosyncratic:

> I don't know how other authors do it, but I find I'm reading into this topic; I'm beginning to get the ideas; and they're beginning to tumble around in my head like clothes in a tumbler dryer. Now, I don't want to go on reading, and reading, and reading until I get it perfectly. At a certain stage, I want to get some of the ideas out of the tumbler dryer and get them on paper. Very early on in this process of drafting, I'm very happy to start showing people my work. There are some authors who are very, very private and hardly anybody will see it before they send it off to an editor to comment on. I much prefer to have it circulated . . . just to make sure I'm not getting things too terribly wrong. So I get the feedback, and then I would be getting more information, and amending, and altering. This is a long process-you're snipping, and chipping, and turning it around. (pp. 101-102)

Accept the fact that there is a certain amount of muddle-headed thinking that is an inescapable part of writing. Accept the fact that you probably will generate much more material than you need. When teaching composition, Garrett Keizer (1996) uses the tomato as an example of nature's tendency to be bountiful; cut it open and there are hundreds of seeds inside, yet it takes just a few to produce a bumper crop. To extend his analogy further, even after many seedlings (or ideas) have germinated, the wise gardener (or writer) will thin them out so that the strongest plants (or best resources and parts) can develop more fully. As writing style experts Strunk and White advise, "Vigorous writing is concise. . . . This requires not that the writer make all his sentences short, or that he avoid all detail and treat his subjects only in outline, but that every word tell" (in Winokur, 1999, p. 179).

Nonfiction writers are apt to proceed through four stages:

1. *Summarizing* what other writers or researchers have said about the topic, clearly documenting the sources during notetaking and culling out the less useful sources.

2. *Synthesizing* the ideas of other writers and researchers to discover clusters of ideas, recurring themes, or underlying principles prior to drafting the manuscript.

3. *Presenting a logical argument* by describing and analyzing patterns and finding the best organizational structure for the material.

4. *Asserting a new synthesis* by developing a strong thesis and contributing your views, experiences, and research to the existing literature (adapted from Miles, 1990).

Figure 4.4 provides twelve different tools that writers might use to work through these four phases.

---

1. **Brainstorming**—Generating brief lists of ideas on a topic quickly, then going back to select the best ones.
2. **Clustering**—Developing categories for ideas (much like a shopping list), then clustering ideas around common themes/topics that may later become headings or sections of the manuscript.
3. **Note card shuffle**—Writing ideas and notes taken from readings on index cards, then arranging them into categories/ sections of the manuscript (the same effect can be accomplished with the cut and paste function of a word processor).

Figure 4.4 *A Dozen Writers' Tools to Try*

Figure 4.4 *continued*

4. **Freewriting**—Prewriting that capitalizes on the mind's ten-dency to make connections by designating a time to write and quickly writing down whatever comes into mind. The goal is to overcome "writer's block" or reluctance to write by intention-ally producing a bad draft. The rule is no editing until some text is generated. For word processor users who cannot resist going back over their copy, try "invisible writing" in which the writer turns off the computer screen and alternates between visible and invisible writing in bursts of 2 to 5 minutes.

5. **Nutshelling**—Used to summarize freewriting. Consists of one-sentence summaries that capture the essence of the most use-ful and interesting material generated during freewriting.

6. **Devil's advocate**—Generates writing in two columns (e.g., our case/their case) as a way to anticipate counterarguments, see both sides of an issue, and take a stand that is supported by logical argument.

7. **Rhetorical prompts**—Uses questions to encourage the writer to think about the breadth of the topic (e.g., What was gifted education like in the past? What is it like today? What might it be like in the future?)

8. **The Five Ws**—Uses the journalist's tool of answering Who? What? When? Where? and Why? as a way to begin generating text.

9. **Choose the best sentence**—Ask peers to read your paper and highlight the best sentence in each paragraph. Cull out or revise those sentences that weren't selected.

10. **Conclusions as Introductions**—Moves the conclusion of the paper to the very beginning as a way to cut down lengthy introductions.

11. **Words out loud**—Author or peer reads the material aloud as a check on cadence, punctuation, and sentence length.

12. **Playing with titles and headings**—Uses various titles as a way to "try on" a different thesis or focus. Uses headings (rather than rewriting entire sections of the manuscript) as a way to see how different organizational structures might work out.

Adapted from Strickland, J. (1997). *From disk to hard copy: Teaching writing with com-puters.* Portsmouth, NH: Boynton/ Cook.

USING QUOTATIONS JUDICIOUSLY

When you wrote papers in high school, you probably tried to find as much "filler" as possible in the form of quotations so that you could do less of the actual writing and produce the minimum number of pages required for the assignment. As a professional writer, expectations for the use of quotations change. First of all, you are the expert now. You are the one that has something significant to say about your topic. Ideally, others would find quotable material in your work. Still, there are times when a direct or verbatim quotation from another published source is in order. Choose to use a direct quotation when the author has said it so well and concisely that it would be exceedingly difficult to do it justice any other way, when the statement fits perfectly with the discussion, or when your argument is in need of authoritative support and this person is a well-known authority. Generally speaking, these are the most common errors with quotations:

1. *Failing to document properly*—If you lose track of where a quotation came from and attribute it to the wrong source, this can be a very embarrassing error, particularly if the person who did not get the credit happens to read the piece because it is in her or his area of interest. Strive to keep the quotations and their origins straight so that credit is given where credit is due.

2. *Using quotations too liberally*—Just about anyone can cut and paste together a piece of writing from multiple sources (in fact, this is a growing problem for student writers, thanks to the easy access to downloading of files on the Internet). Even with appropriate documentation, you can overstep the boundaries of drawing from other sources. These copyright rules are difficult to pin down, because they are relative—meaning that they are affected by the total length of the work and whether the material used is the essence of the work. Just a few lines from a short poem, for instance, can constitute copyright infringement. As a general rule of thumb for most educational writing purposes, you can use no more than a couple of short paragraphs total from one article and no more than the equivalent of about a page from a book.

3. *Chopping up quotations*—If you find that you are adding an ellipsis here and another one there, inserting verb inflections like add(ed), or putting your own emphasis on another writer's words (e.g., making the notation "emphasis added"), or splicing together a quotation from different pages, such things indicate to you that the quotation, interesting as it may be, really is not working that well. Under such circumstances, you would probably be better off simply putting the author's point into your own words, or paraphrasing, then making sure that you follow that paraphrase with the author's name and the date, like this: (Smith, 1999).

   When possible, try to cluster together several different sources that make a similar point, then list the last names and the dates of the sources you consulted, like this: (Adams, 1998; Hernandez, 1999; Zelinski, 1999).

DECIDING ON AN ORGANIZATIONAL PATTERN

When I was an undergraduate, I had an English composition book that started each chapter with a diagram of the structure of each type of writing (e.g., comparison/contrast, the classic structure of the essay). Even though I was an English major who volunteered to tutor students who were struggling with writing, I must confess that those diagrams were mystifying to me. I honestly believed that they were there as a decorative feature rather than templates for specific types of writing! It was not until after I had written in several of the styles that I realized they were actually structures for composition.

Now that you have your material gathered and sorted into categories, you can begin experimenting with a more specific structure for the manuscript. An author once remarked that she wished she could write on a sphere so that she would not have to struggle with where to place what or decide on the beginning and the end. Organization has been one of the toughest parts of writing for me; and the cut and paste option in word processing programs has tended to make it easier to do and, therefore, worse. As a first step, try some of the more common organizational patterns. Figure 4.5 highlights some of the organizational principles in Keenan's (1982) *Feel Free to Write*.

We see many predictable organizational patterns in published work (e.g., chronological), but the authors who are a bit more creative with organization are more interesting to read. Novices tend to go for the obvious. They want to put all the theory together, then the research, and then the practical applications. That may work. But what is more apt to be captivating to readers is a blend of those three things, for instance, beginning with a concrete example, examining the underlying theory, and then offering research-based recommendations.

Much of the writing that professionals do consists of presenting a logical argument. Frequently, we are in the role of trying to convince our readers to replace an old habit with a newer, more productive one. When writing a logical argument, consider these pointers from Millward (1980) and Trimble (2000) that I elaborate on here.

1. *Define the argument clearly*—What is your point? In a nutshell, what do you contend? In a perfect world, what would happen after a member of the audience reads your manuscript?

2. *Define all terms used in the argument*—Virtually every word of professional jargon has different interpretations. For the purposes of your article or book, how are you defining this term? Be sure to check other professional sources to see how experts in your field have defined the terminology in question.

3. *Limit the argument to the question at hand*—A logical argument is like an express train running on a track—it should proceed directly to its intended destination without digressions or going off on tangents.

Purpose

Is the primary purpose

- To inform?
- To persuade?
- To describe?

Audience

- Who is the audience?
- How much background is necessary?
- Is the reader likely to agree or disagree?

Format

Select an appropriate format that

- Makes main ideas clear
- Uses external cues like headings, underlining, spacing
- Sets the reader's expectations
- Provides a summary statement

Evidence

Evidence to support your ideas. These data can be obtained through

- Careful observation
- Intelligent field work (e.g., interviews)
- Library research

Organization

Selection of an organizational pattern. Write ideas on index cards, then experiment with different structures

- Chronological (e.g., background, present status, prospects)
- Spatial (e.g., by geographical location)
- Logical (e.g., cause-effects)
- Problem-analysis-solution
- Order of importance

Adapted from: Keenan, John. (1982). *Feel free to write.* New York: John Wiley.

Figure 4.5   *Putting It All Together*

4. *Present adequate evidence to support the argument*—If you are writing for fellow professionals, they will expect you to present current, credible evidence that substantiates your point. Get into the habit of backing up what you say. "Assertions are fine, but unless you prove them with hard evidence, they remain simply assertions. So, assert, then support: assert, then support—and so on, throughout your essay. Remember, examples and facts are the meat of it. They do the actual convincing; they also have their own eloquence" (Trimble, 2000, p. 47).

5. *Reason clearly and logically*—In first drafts, writers often contradict themselves. It is like a heated argument where you wish you had said something else that made your point stronger. Unlike a heated argument, however, you have an opportunity to revise until your argument is convincing. As novelist Kurt Vonnegut would have it, "This is what I find most encouraging about the writing trades: They allow mediocre people who are patient and industrious to revise their stupidity, to edit themselves into something like intelligence" (cited in Trimble, 2000, p. 18).

6. *Anticipate contrary arguments and evidence*—As you are writing, you know that there will be members of the audience who disagree with you. When one of my students was writing an article about the dangers of emphasizing competition in schools, I asked him this: "What about the person who says, 'Hey, it's a tough world out there. I want *my* kid to be a winner.' What would you say to that person?" Don't pretend that these other points of view do not exist, for that only makes you look uninformed or foolish.

Think of organization as

> a structure, a backbone, which unifies even seemingly disparate elements. The presence of the structure reassures the readers that they are in the hands of . . . someone they can trust with their time and interest. They know they are going somewhere, which means they can relax and enjoy the journey. (Stewart, 1998, p. 167)

Organization also applies a smaller scale to each paragraph. Speaking as a person who taught 4th graders paragraph structure, I must confess that I frequently failed to see or to use that advice in my own writing. Figure 4.6 provides a simple structure for paragraphs that will, if followed, reduce the amount of time spent moving sentences around.

Although all of the paragraphs need to hang together, the beginning and ending paragraphs are particularly important. The beginning paragraph of an article often includes one of the following devices:

- A brief anecdote, narrative, analogy or metaphor

- An interesting fact or startling statistic

- A question or series of questions (that will be answered in the sections of the work that follows them)

- A few verbatim quotations from people you have interviewed or observed (with their anonymity preserved)

- A concessive statement in which you recognize an opinion or approach different from your own

- A puzzling issue or paradox

Packaging and mailing a gift to someone is similar to writing a paragraph in a nonfiction manuscript. Both processes involve four basic steps:

1. *Find a suitable container*—If you were packaging a gift, you would first need to locate a carton of suitable size. This is comparable to the selection of an appropriate topic sentence. Begin with a general statement that sets the reader's expectations.

2. *Insert the contents*—Both in writing and in packaging an item you need to carefully arrange and support the contents. A fragile gift might be surrounded by crumpled newspaper, puffs of styrofoam or plastic injected with air bubbles. In writing, details are the equivalent of that packaging material. Add statistical evidence, references from leading authorities or real life experience to support the basic concept. Arrange ideas in a logical sequence, one that supports the premise of the topic sentence.

3. *Wrap it up*—Now comes the closure. As the paragraph comes to a close, the writer should tie everything together. Usually this is accomplished by relating back to the topic sentence.

4. *Give instructions for its destination*—Before leaving a package at the post office, the mailing address must be clearly marked. The equivalent of this in writing is a transitional phrase, words that connect this paragraph with the next.

Now look at this paragraph that follows the "package" pattern:

———————— ✤ ————————

One of the ironies of teaching writing is that most teachers give of their expertise when the student needs it the least. They give a lot of help before the student starts to write and after the student has written, but too little during the process. Once the student has done a rough draft and has freely committed himself to doing a revision, he then truly needs a teacher's help (Clark, 1975, p. 68).

Figure 4.6   *Package Paragraph*

- A statement of long-term effect or effects (cause is stated later) (adapted from Keenan, 1982)

For more on writing introductions and conclusions, see Figure 4.7.

INCORPORATING ORIGINAL SOURCE MATERIAL

As a writer, I find it helpful to gather a variety of material on my topic in addition to the customary library search. While writing for this book, for instance, I found it helpful to talk with authors about their questions and concerns at

---

Look for examples—Begin by collecting 10 outstanding introductions and conclusions from the journals in your field. Analyze them to see what makes them successful and try to "soak in" that style; try to imagine yourself writing those paragraphs as you read them (Trimble, 2000).

Identify with your reader—When writing introductions, do what you seek as a reader and come straight to the point. When writing conclusions, resist the temptation to yield to fatigue and just stop; write the satisfying conclusion that you seek as a reader.

Save the best for first and last—When writing introductions, begin with something captivating (e.g., a surprising statistic, direct quotation from a participant in the research). When writing conclusions, avoid merely repeating in a bland and routine way; revisit your main point but add at least one new twist or phrase to make it memorable and give your conclusion emotional impact (Trimble, 2000).

Understand introductions and conclusions—In the introduction, the sections of the body of the paper are *previewed*; in the conclusion, they are *reviewed*. In both cases, be brief. Introductions and conclusions frequently are mirror images of one another. An article often begins with a more general statement that quickly moves to your point. Articles often end by summing up the main points and then revisit that larger view.

Avoid beginner's mistakes—When writing introductions, don't leave your reader wondering where the argument is headed or why. Spell it out. When writing conclusions, don't introduce an entirely new subject and leave the reader hanging; instead, give the reader a sense of having neatly tied together your argument.

Link introductions to conclusions—As a final check, cut and paste your introduction and conclusion into a file and position them side-by-side to facilitate comparison. Operate on the two of them until they are distinctive, yet conceptually linked.

Figure 4.7 *How to Write a Good Introduction or Conclusion*

conferences. In the seminar on writing for publication, students also have the assignment of documenting their growth as writers. Their presentation on the final day includes their responses to the following:

- How did you first approach the prospect of taking a course on writing for publication? What were your concerns? Why? (They wrote this the first day of class.)

- What signs of progress did you note in your writing? Please select a few concrete before and after examples from your writing in a format that can be shared with the group (e.g., handout, overhead transparency, poster).

- What exerted a positive influence on your efforts to become a better writer? Choose some favorite published advice from your readings and identify examples of helpful feedback.

- What will you need to work on next? How do you plan to go about it?

- Has your view of yourself as a writer or your perspective on writing for publication changed? If so, how?

Additionally, because I am obligated to write four editorials per year, I am constantly gathering material for these short pieces. I may be looking for something specific, as when I already have a topic in mind like an editorial on children's art, or, I may be inspired to write an editorial about a topic by a particular incident, as when a 1st grader looked at the colors on the globe and asked her teacher, "Is Pennsylvania really pink?" When I am writing a textbook, I might take some observational notes that will not only help a student teacher to see a particular child's behavior in greater detail, but also later serve as a vignette in the book. Sometimes the discussion during a conference session that I present suggests possibilities for writing. I will tell the group that I am working on an article or book and invite them to comment on what they yearn to know and ask them to give examples. If I really like a particular example, I will ask their permission to use it. Such exchanges of ideas often lead to forms of collaboration with students, teachers, and faculty. Even if the writing project you have in mind does not lend itself to anecdotal material, such observations and conversations can often help you to uncover the best organizational pattern for your manuscript as you hear the common concerns and questions.

Anecdotes are another way to bring your manuscript to life. We human beings have been referred to as the "storytelling animal" because our brains naturally gravitate toward the narrative mode. When I use the word story here, I am not referring to something fabricated and deliberately false, as in a fairy tale. Rather, I am speaking of real life accounts that gain their authority from their lifelikeness or verisimilitude.

The word anecdote means "things unpublished," so it isn't an anecdote if you read it somewhere else. You have to produce your own examples of these stories in miniature. Like spices and seasoning in cooking, true stories carefully interspersed in nonfiction make it more appealing and satisfying. To get a sense of what a particular outlet will accept and how far you can go with incorporating narrative, study what has been published previously. In all of your writing for publication for professional journals, the journal becomes your textbook and you study it in the same way that a marathon runner would study the course. Anecdotes are the "tiny tales" that writers use to grab the audience's attention at the beginning of the article, or to illustrate a key point that makes the abstract more concrete. Figure 4.8 provides some strategies for writing anecdotes.

Still, there is reluctance on the part of many professionals to be themselves in print. Casanave and Schecter (1997) found that when they invited leading authorities in the field of language to write in a more personal way, it presented a major challenge:

> Little did we surmise how challenging this task would prove for some of us. Some folks bailed out early, stating openly that they did not feel comfortable going into print with personal revelations. Others were intrigued by and committed to the task, but faced great difficulty in realizing it. As editors, we found ourselves sending drafts back to authors with advice to become more personally reflective and less teacherly or researchy, with requests to use a story to demonstrate a point to readers rather than to explicate or preach it. We received revisions, parts of which inspired and moved us with their insight and color, and other parts which distanced us with their objectivist, academic stances and rhetoric. (Casanave & Schecter, 1997, p. 205)

Strive to be yourself when writing.

Dive right in—Do not waste words with long introductions or warm-ups. Take a minimalist approach and describe only what is absolutely essential to get the gist of the story.

Weave it in—Rather than devoting entire sentences to description, incorporate the descriptive material into the story as needed for the reader to understand

Wrap it up—A story needs to build to a satisfying conclusion. Sometimes, it will build suspense or end with a surprise or humor. Writers often save the best for last, and end the story with the line that made it worth telling, using it as a punch line. In other cases, where the story is being used to make a point, it might end with commentary that makes that point clearer.

Figure 4.8　*Writing Anecdotes*

PROVIDING VISUAL APPEAL

In recent years I have been involved as a member of the editorial board for the Dushkin Publishing Company's *Annual Editions* series. For those who are not familiar with the series, it is an edited collection of the best previously published articles on a topic such as psychology, bilingual education, or research that have been published recently. If you obtain one of these collections and merely flip through the pages, you will note that very few of these articles are column after column of uninterrupted text. Rather, they are replete with drawings, diagrams, tables, charts, graphs, and figures. Skillful writers have learned to use such tools to attract readers and keep them reading until the end of the article. One way of achieving this objective is through the use of headings.

While waiting for a taxi in Portland, Oregon, I noticed an elderly woman who was in obvious distress. The woman had an address for the place where her niece's wedding shower would be held and a couple of helpful taxi drivers were checking maps and the computer without success. Eventually they discovered that the woman was nearly a continent away from her destination, for she had intended to fly to Portland, Maine, rather than Portland, Oregon. The woman broke down and cried when she realized how far away she was from her intended destination and, after she left to plead her case at the ticket counter, others marveled aloud at how this mistake could have occurred. Likewise, it is surprisingly easy for readers to lose their way in a manuscript; and one strategy for avoiding destination disasters is the use of headings. Pick up virtually any published book or article and you will notice that professional writers use headings much like guideposts to keep readers on course.

Headings can also suggest different organizational patterns to the writer. Could you organize your material around a series of questions and answers? Would it be better to take what you put at the end and move it up to the beginning? Maybe you want to rewrite (as I did for the beginning of this book) into a list of misconceptions because you want to clear them out of the way. You may want to deliberately break the rules to make a point, for instance, using present/past/future instead of past/present/future. Write these headings yourself. The worst thing that can happen is that they will be changed. If you don't write them at all, several negative outcomes are likely:

- Your readers will get lost or bored without these signposts in place.

- Some editorial assistant may write them for you and you may not like them or agree with their placement.

- The reviewers will instruct you to write them anyway.

And now, because it is such an important point, I'll put it in boldface and italics:

Usually, there is a one-to-one correspondence between your headings, your main points in the argument, and the list of things that you said you were going to do in the pronouncement paragraph.

In fact, it is this match that makes the organization of the piece abundantly clear to your readers. Even if your readers cannot articulate this rule, they have internalized it and learned to expect it.

An additional advantage of headings is that, if you are required to write an abstract, the headings suggest a framework for doing so.

There are other types of visual material that are equally important for the writer. Occasionally, when you are writing, you will find yourself getting bogged down in explaining something, comparing two things, or listing one point after another. Often this is a sign that the usual prose style is failing you and a different method of presenting your ideas might be in order. That list of recommendations might be more helpful to readers as a checklist or more concise as a bulleted list. Perhaps that comparison of two things would be clearer in two columns or that explanation of a process might work better as a flow chart. In making decisions about whether or how to use visual material in a publication, look at the publication. I find it fascinating that people who read *Educational Leadership*, which is replete with examples of tables, charts, and various graphics, often produce manuscripts intended for that journal that have no such features. When I inquire about it, they say, "Oh, I thought the editor did that part" or "I didn't think you were allowed to put that in a formal article." Not so on both counts.

Likewise, when authors are writing for publications that routinely include samples of students' work or photographs, it is appropriate to include them. One caveat would be to submit ordinary copies rather than the originals of any drawings or photos until the manuscript is actually accepted. You are not required to submit photographs and, although some editors may appreciate them, simply including photographs will not significantly improve your chances of publication. If you do include photographs, it will be necessary to get a signed photo release from every person pictured, or, in the case of minor children, a signed release from the parent or guardian.

Select photographs, student work samples, and design graphic aids carefully. Use them judiciously and appropriately, realizing that they are more expensive to produce and publish than ordinary text. Don't overdo it. I frequently receive manuscripts (often those based on a thesis or dissertation) that include 7 or 8 tables of statistical data. This is excessive and the author will be asked to thin them out. Whatever embellishments you choose, make sure that they are really making a significant contribution to the content and clarity of the overall piece. Another common flaw for the linear thinker types is to overuse bulleted lists rather than really writing and crafting an article. This appeals to me about as much as sports figures or movie stars who are determined to make a record but cannot sing, so they speak the lyrics. Talking does not qualify as singing and making lists isn't really writing.

GETTING IT OUT THE DOOR

I remember that back in the days before cholesterol was a concern, my college roommate and I decided that we should buy a big ham that was on sale rather than purchasing lunchmeat that was three times the price per pound. But the taste of ham was so distinctive that we grew tired of it quickly. Later, when reading a cookbook, I ran across this definition of eternity, "A ham and two people," and burst out laughing. A manuscript develops an equally sickening taste when you have revised it so many times and still know that it just won't work and doesn't flow. Although those who do not write for publication assume that "real authors" are in a constant state of euphoria, I doubt that this is true for the sober or the sane. Granted, there are times when the writing is going well that are pleasurable in the truest sense but much of it is drudgery performed while most other people are sleeping.

Despite all of the advice about mailing out manuscripts prematurely there are perfectionist writers who seldom or never manage to get a manuscript out the door. I know one college professor who often refers to the book that he has on his computer. The trouble is that the book remained there forever. There comes a time in every writer's life when you have labored long and hard, when tough and honest readers tell you it is ready to submit, when you are changing sentences today back to the way they were a day or two ago, and when it is simply time to get the manuscript out the door. The manuscript has come of age and hanging onto it any longer will not significantly improve the manuscript's content, organization, style, or format. So, let it go. Of course there is a useful distinction between growing weary of a manuscript and being a perfectionist. But before you conclude that it is perfectionism, be aware that editors have a well deserved reputation for being incredibly picky. Chances are, their definition of perfection is considerably more rigorous than your own.

PROOFREADING THE FINAL COPY

If someone told you that the editor for the very publication in which you hope to publish your manuscript had provided him with detailed, insider's information on how to be published, wouldn't you want to see it? Actually, you can. Virtually every publisher has such material on the Internet and on paper that are referred to variously as instructions to authors, submission guidelines, contributors' guidelines, or some similar title. Reading and adhering to them can save you time and may get you a recommendation for revision rather than an outright rejection. No one wants to be delayed or disqualified on a technicality, yet writers so often fail to follow the guidelines that it happens all of the time. Read these rules as carefully as you would the rules for entering any contest.

If you want to endear yourself to the editorial staff, try mastering the basics of marking the galleys or proofs by learning the proofreader's marks commonly used in publishing. Galleys are the marked-up typewritten copy or the typeset copy that requires you to make a final check on accuracy. When manuscripts are at the final proofs stage, they are nearly ready to publish. This means that the overall number of pages has been budgeted and, in the case of typeset copy, the actual page numbers are set. This is not the time to rewrite! You had your chance long ago to do that. Most editors will tell you only to change "absolute errors of fact or format" because one sentence's worth of difference can repaginate the entire journal or book. If you have to make a change, it may help to literally count the number of words, both letters and spaces, and make your revision fit in the same amount of space as in the original copy. At the very least, pay particular attention to whether the change you propose will fit in at the end of a paragraph or cause it to bump everything down or up a page.

When you proofread, read everything, in a slow, deliberate, word-by-word fashion. This includes the things that you may normally skip over as a reader, such as the chapter headings or the page numbers. I have even heard it recommended that you proofread not only forwards but backwards to keep yourself from overlooking errors in the left-to-right eye sweep. In my experience, it is possible to have several layers of editing and still find an undetected error. Try getting others to read it anyway. You may want to try making two copies and marking one, then reading the second unmarked copy a little while later to see if you overlooked anything the first time around.

Although some editors will invest more "clean-up" time to get the name recognition of the most prominent thinkers into the journals and books that they edit, the truth is that only the geniuses can get away with slipshod work in the details department.

CONCLUSION

It is a basic psychological principle that, all things being equal, people will do what they would rather do. If you would rather be writing than watching television, you will tend to write. If you would rather be writing than lingering over lunch, you will tend to write. You've heard it before: that your daily professional duties are what stand in the way of writing. For professors, it is the teaching vs. research dilemma. For years, researchers have been asking the question "How do college and university faculty spend their time?" In contradiction of the "publish or perish" mantra, many of them are not publishing. What about combining work and life? You have a huge project at work—write about that. You conduct training sessions for fellow professionals—write about that. You have an insight about an issue that colleagues find interesting—write about that. Whatever you write, keep in mind that "All writing is communication. But most writing hopes to go further. It hopes to make the reader react in certain ways—with pleased smiles, nods of assent, stabs of pathos, or whatever. So we can say, generally, that writing is the art of creating desired effects" (Trimble, 2000, p. 6). By mastering the strategies that published authors use, you can do a better job of achieving those desired effects.

REFERENCES

Casanave, C. P. (1997). Body-mergings: Searching for connections with academic discourse. In C. P. Casanave & S. R. Schecter (Eds.), *On becoming a language educator: Personal essays on professional development* (pp. 187-200). Mahwah, NJ: Lawrence Erlbaum Associates.

Clark, W. I. (1975). How to completely individualize a writing program. *English Journal*, 64(4), 66-69.

Edelstein, S. (1999). *100 things every writer needs to know*. New York: Perigree/Putnam.

Elbow, P. (1997). Freewriting and the problem of wheat and taxes. In J.M. Moxley & T. Taylor (Eds.), *Writing and publishing for academic authors* (2nd ed.) (pp. 35-47). Lanham, MD: Rowman & Littlefield.

Jalongo, M. R., Twiest, M. M., & Gerlach, G. J. (1999). *The college learner: Reading, studying, and attaining academic success* (2nd ed.). Upper Saddle River, NJ: Merrill/Prentice Hall.

Keenan, J. (1982). *Feel free to write*. New York: John Wiley.

Keizer, G. (1996). *No place but here: A teacher's vocation in a rural community*. Hanover, NH: University Press of New England.

Kirszner, L. G., & Mandell, S. R. (1992). *The Holt handbook*. Orlando, FL: Holt, Rinehart & Winston.

Lamb, B. (1997). *America's finest authors on reading, writing, and the power of ideas*. New York: Times Books/Random House.

Lamott, A. (1994). *Bird by bird—Some instructions on writing and life*. New York: Pantheon.

Merriam, S. B. (1998). *Qualitative research and case study applications in education*. San Francisco: Jossey-Bass.

Millward, C. (1980). *Handbook for writers*. New York: Holt, Rinehart, and Winston.

Miles, T. H. (1990). *Critical thinking and writing for science and technology*. Philadelphia: Harcourt Brace College and School Division.

Murray, D. M. (1998). Unlearning writing. *Learning Matters* http://www.heinemann.comhbbc/lmv2n6p1.html (Retrieved from the World Wide Web on November 27, 2000).

Perry, S. K. (1999). *Writing in flow: Keep to enhanced creativity*. Cincinnati, OH: Writer's Digest Books.

Price, B. (1984). English and education. *Princeton Alumni Weekly*, May 16, p. 18.

Safire W., & Safir L. (Eds.) (1994). *Good advice on writing*. New York: Simon & Schuster.

Stewart, J. B. (1998). *Follow the story: How to write successful nonfiction*. New York: Tarcher/Simon & Schuster.

Strickland, J. (1997). *From disk to hard copy: Teaching writing with computers*. Portsmouth, NH: Boynton/Cook.

Trimble, J. R. (2000). *Writing with style*. Upper Saddle River, NJ: Prentice Hall.

Tuchman, B. (1981). *Practicing history and selected essays*. New York: Knopf.

Winokur, J. (Ed.) (1999). *Advice to writers*. New York: Vintage/Random House.

CHAPTER 5

❧

Publishing Articles in Your Field

❧

My college students get excited when they see the name of an author they know in a book, journal, or online because, as one student put it, "I never knew a real author before." Undergraduates tend to assume that fame and fortune are what motivates educators to write for publication. My Master's degree students, on the other hand, generally regard writing the journal article as a professional accolade. They may have heard that, usually, there is no payment involved for professional articles and they infer that the reward is for authors to see, as one student described it, "their names in lights." My doctoral students approach publishing the journal article as a coveted survival skill—something that they will need to learn to do with a modicum of success in order to thrive in academia.

Actually, all of my students are wrong about why many prolific authors—at least at this stage in their careers—bother to write journal articles. It certainly is no longer a key to survival, as doctoral students assume. Publishing one more article is relatively inconsequential. Even in terms of the achievement aspect, the prolific no longer thrill at the prospect of seeing their names in print one more time, unless it is in some extraordinarily competitive outlet. As far as fame goes, it is an old saying in academic circles that journal articles establish an author's competence while books establish their reputations. So pure reputation building would be better served by publishing a book. With respect to amassing fortunes, publishing the professional journal article is far from a financially profitable venture since most of these publications have nonprofit status and hardly any of them pay authors.

The typical journal authors' work is donated to the cause of advancing knowledge in the profession. Although it may seem backwards at first, the more prestigious and scholarly the publication, the smaller the audience and the *less* likely it is to pay for manuscripts. Even when authors do get paid for a nonfiction article, it usually is a small token rather than the amounts paid to those who write for widely circulated, popular press magazines with large operating budgets. (If you want to be certain about the publisher's policies with regard to payment for articles, read the guidelines and check *Writer's Market*, an annual directory of publishers that pay for articles and how much.) Stranger still, some of the small market, scholarly publishers charge *authors* to publish their work, a practice referred to as "page charges."

Many authors who plan to write journal articles are disappointed by these facts. Why would anyone expend all of the thought, time, and energy necessary to produce professional journal articles?

REASONS TO WRITE AND PUBLISH JOURNAL ARTICLES

There are at least four general reasons to write journal articles.

1. *Affirmation from peers*—Generally speaking, work that is published in professional periodicals has been critiqued by others who are active and well-read in the field, yet have no vested interest in an author's vita. This makes publishing a form of validation because you have produced a manuscript that was deemed worthy of dissemination. There is certainly something to be said for being held in high regard by respected colleagues and having your work respectfully cited by fellow scholars. If you publish in professional journals, chances are this will happen to you. In fact, there are citation search engines that locate articles in which your name appears.

2. *Potential influence on the field*—Professional journals and magazines continue to be the primary means of getting the word out about advances in the field. Consider, for example, the impact of research findings that are reported in the *New England Journal of Medicine*. A study published in this prestigious publication has credibility because it has been subjected to peer review. If those peers were right about the quality of the article, it is likely to be cited in subsequent studies of the topic, "translated" into an abbreviated popular press account, reported on the Internet, and so forth. Thus, the impact of a professional journal article can be substantial.

3. *Staying current in the field*—Writing an article involves extensive reading and research; therefore, it is a way to keep current in your field. Being on the cutting edge of your discipline is no small achievement, particularly when you consider the knowledge explosion contemporary professionals have to contend with. Writing journal articles can rescue you from becoming less competent over time, and it can help you to participate in a more informed way when groups of professionals gather. Additionally, when you write with others, their experiences and areas of specialized expertise frequently enhance the creativity of your work by providing fresh perspectives, thereby deepening and widening your understanding of complex issues.

4. *Fulfilling the mentoring role*—According to theory and research in adult development, contributing to the professional development of others is a major source of satisfaction for mature professionals. One of the primary ways in which experts experience such satisfactions is by shepherding others through the process and sharing in the less experienced writer's pride at breaking into print.

For all of these reasons, the peer-reviewed journal article generally is considered to be one of the most significant ways of contributing to and advancing the knowledge in your field (Thyer, 1994).

More specifically, writing and publishing journal articles may enable you to:

- Disseminate your ideas to a wider audience than typically is possible through conference presentations.

- Establish a reputation in the field as an expert on a particular topic.

- Master the content at a more sophisticated level, thereby enhancing your teaching.

- Expand your teaching role to include anyone who happens to read your work (e.g., students who are conducting library research, scholars in other countries searching for information on the Internet).

- Provide evidence of your competence as an author and persuade a publisher that you have potential as a book author.

- Convince a performance evaluation committee that you are making an effort to contribute to your field and have been successful in earning the respect and recognition of peers.

- Write about different facets of the same basic topic for several different audiences, thus maximizing investment of time and energy (if you wish).

- Conduct workshops and training sessions, or deliver speeches and scholarly papers based on your published work.

- Possibly provide you with republications of your work, such as when a previously published article is included in an edited book, used by a newspaper or magazine reporter in an article, or condensed for a professional audience (e.g., *Education Digest*).

THE AUDIENCE FOR JOURNAL ARTICLES

The nonfiction article has important purposes that begin with your audience. As Hans Selye (1984), a leading expert and best-selling author on stress management advises,

> Whenever you decide to write anything, whether it is a letter or an entire encyclopedia, the first thing to ask is: Who should and will read this? There is no such thing as a perfectly written piece; at best it can be perfect only for a certain type of reader. It is a common mistake for beginners to send articles to the wrong journals or to adjust the general tone of their communication to a level quite different from that of the probable reader. The usual errors are to talk down to the audience; to be too far above their heads; to use a chatty narrative tone when dry conciseness is desirable, or vice versa. (pp. 334–335)

If you manage to get your particular audience firmly in mind, many nagging questions are answered, such as: How much are they likely to know about this already? How are they likely to respond to this point of view, generally speaking? Do I need an example here?

Many newcomers to the task of writing articles would produce a formula like this to explain success in writing and publishing professional journal articles:

Brilliant Ideas + Good Luck + Knowing the Right People
= Publication

This is an "all about me" approach derived from fantasies about novelists who linger outside posh editorial offices and are discovered. It seldom succeeds.

A better approach is to tap into your readers' expectations. Some of the expectations your audience is apt to bring include the following:

1. If you raise a question, readers will expect an (almost immediate) answer; therefore, do not write rhetorical questions or a series of questions that you fail to directly answer in the manuscript.

2. If you assert that "many studies" support a contention, readers will expect you to cite a few; therefore, get in the habit of backing up what you say with authoritative support, cited in the text and in the reference list.

3. If you expound on what theory and research suggest, readers will expect you to show how this applies to practice; therefore, get into the habit of discussing practical implications.

4. If you provide an historical overview, readers will expect you to connect it in some way with the current situation; therefore, show how historical perspectives have value for today.

5. If you describe your particular project, readers will expect you to generalize a bit and explain how this information matters to those in different contexts and circumstances; therefore, keep in mind that your audience is constantly wondering, "What's in here for me?"

6. If you identify a problem, readers will expect you to offer some solutions. Therefore, get into the habit of writing recommendations and discussing implications or, if the issue cannot be resolved, offer some reflections that are based on a synthesis of the research and your professional good sense.

7. If you set forth a general proposition readers will be waiting for you to provide specific instances of the concept; therefore, collect compelling examples to illustrate key points.

8. If you write a title or an abstract for an article, readers will expect that title to fulfill its promise and the abstract to succinctly summarize the content. Therefore, remember to revisit your title and abstract after the manuscript is fully developed to make certain that they match the manuscript.

If you fail to do any of these eight things, you can expect that readers will leave in disgust. Now that you have a specific audience clearly in mind you are ready to choose a basic article type and locate suitable outlets.

THREE BASIC TYPES OF ARTICLES

In general, journal publishers emphasize one or more of three types of publications. *Practical* articles deal directly with the situations facing practitioners in the field. Often, they take the "how to" approach. They keep readers abreast of new developments in the field.

One specific type of practical article, for example, is the project report. Those who are inexperienced at writing project reports frequently make the mistake of generating manuscripts that read like excerpts from a grant proposal, a local newspaper account, or advertising copy for a brochure. If it is to be an article with appeal for a wider audience, the approach should not be "Let me tell you all about my project." Rather, it should be to think in terms of the project's significance for others. Keep in mind that many of your readers might be interested in doing something similar. Be generous with suggestions that will save them time or money. Be candid about glitches and how they were addressed.

Situate your project in the larger context of similar projects by reviewing the literature and showing how yours fits in. You may find an article about the characteristics of successful intervention programs, for instance, and realize that your project incorporated all of these attributes. Unless your project was truly remarkable in some way, it might be more helpful to write a review of successful programs and use your project as just one example. You will also need to be realistic about whether your project, however much it was appreciated locally by those who participated, really merits a state, regional, national, or international audience. If you fail to consider such things, your manuscript will be of little interest to a professional journal or magazine.

One familiar "how to" structure for a project report is chronological:

- The needs assessment (Why this project at this time?)

- The planning phase (What were the goals and objectives established at the outset?)

- The implementation phase (What materials, strategies, and events occurred?)

- The evaluation phase (What was accomplished? Why was it successful? Were there any unanticipated outcomes? How might it have been improved?)

There are other types of practical nonfiction articles that might be categorized by their primary purposes, such as the persuasive article, where you are trying to convince others in the field to do things differently; or the informative article, where you are attempting to update knowledge. Whatever the particular type, practical articles are, first and foremost, intended to improve practice.

Review or theoretical articles synthesize and critically evaluate material that has already been published. They tend to be "think pieces" that urge readers to reflect on issues of some concern. Before endeavoring to publish a review of the literature, realize that a publishable review is about as different from most college assignments as a junior high school student's first research paper is from a dissertation. First of all, inexperienced reviewer/writers seldom present a mental map of the entire landscape of the field, whereas publishable reviews of the literature typically do. Secondly, college papers tend to indiscriminately include any source that happens to mention the topic; whereas, a published review of the literature tends to limit itself to authoritative sources from respected, peer-reviewed publications, to synthesize actual studies (rather than relying on opinion pieces), and to present both sides of an argument. Third, student writers of assigned papers seldom take a stand on the issue. Authors of published reviews of the literature have a unifying thesis and take a stand that is supported by the review. And finally, published reviews of the literature frequently conclude with research-based recommendations, a section that is not included in most student papers.

Research articles report the results of original research conducted by the authors. Quantitative studies are typically organized by headings such as background/problem statement, subjects, method/procedures, results, discussion, and recommendations and conclusions. When writing quantitative research articles, think about reliability and validity and keep in mind the overarching goals of empirical research: generalizability and replicability. In empirical research, authors tend to say a little about a lot of participants (e.g., a national survey). You'll need to provide at least enough detail for readers to decide if your conclusions were warranted. Qualitative research, on the other hand, more often takes the form of case studies, interviews, narrative research, and various types of ethnography. When writing qualitative research articles, think about key words and phrases from your participants that demonstrate how you arrived at patterns and themes from the mass of words you recorded. Keep in mind the goals of qualitative research: rich description of individuals or cases that have the power to illuminate larger issues. In qualitative research, you'll tend to say a lot about a few individuals or cases. You'll need to be credible—in qualitative research, this means you went deep and the sheer amount of information collected over time is compelling. Your readers need to be struck by the "slice of life" quality of your work that is captured in rich detail.

Here are a few words of caution about the research article. Actually, a very tiny percentage of what is published in the professions, at least in the social sciences, qualifies as original research. Do not try to make a review/theoretical or practical article sound like a research in title or format in the hopes of impressing someone. Going to the library does not make it a research article. If you have conducted research as part of your college studies, resist the temptation to drop your thesis in the mail like a raffle ticket and realize that a publishable article is a totally different undertaking from writing for class. At this very moment, I have three copies of a 60-page thesis sitting on my desk. It was submitted to a journal that has an absolute maximum page limit of about one-third of that. Nor will the editor take responsibility for saying what has to be cut. That is the author's job. I know that the journal will never publish 14 data tables. The author will have to be selective. Furthermore, it is rare for a one-shot study to be published in a leading journal. More often, a series of investigations has been conducted and the article reports on that line of research. Figure 5.1 summarizes the three basic types of journal articles.

Authors who are trying to decide which type of article to write would do well to consider what type of manuscript they generally prefer to read. Some authors attempt to write research articles when they are (evidently) the type of readers who skip over the technical parts in a research article. As a result, they have not internalized the style and format of the research article. It is better to write a solid practical article than to write a research article badly, have it rejected repeatedly, and have nothing at all published five years hence. Practical articles may be a place to begin, or they may be the type of article you will prefer to write throughout your career. It is better to contribute something of value,

Practical—Articles written for practitioners in the field.

Purpose: To explore the practical implications of theory and research and improve professional practice.

Structure: Often centered on questions or issues of concern to those in the field.

Research—Reports of original research that include data collected by the author(s).

Purpose: To provide sufficient information for other researchers to understand how they might replicate the study.

Structure: Typically follows a structure such as background/review of literature, research purpose/questions, subjects, methods/procedures, findings/results, recommendations/conclusions.

Review—Reviews of theory/research.

Purpose: To synthesize previously published research.

Format: Often organized around themes or trends in the research literature identified by the author.

Figure 5.1   *Three Basic Types of Journal Articles*

however small, than to perpetually daydream about publishing the definitive piece of research or the theory that will revolutionize your field (this is what editors refer to as a seminal work). Use the self-assessment in Figure 5.2 to determine which type or types of articles you might be best suited to authoring, at least at this point in your career.

"But," you may be asking, "don't all good articles include elements of one another?" Good question. A research article that has no connection with theory or practice is tragically flawed and a practical article that recommends professional actions without any basis in theory or research deteriorates into gimmicks. Nevertheless, authors need to decide what category of article, in the main, they seek to produce. Attempts to mix these article types are like home remodeling efforts that disregard the era and style of the home—they are badly muddled. Generally speaking, editors and reviewers don't know what to do with feature-length articles that are not one of the three types. Frequently, these muddled manuscripts attempt to do too much and, consequently, fail to do anything well. Thus, they are routinely rejected.

After settling on a category of article, you can begin scouring through the literature, paying particular attention to both classic and current authoritative sources. The nonfiction author's motto could be, as Higgins notes, "You cannot write well without data" or, as Epstein writes, "Facts are eloquent" (in Winokur, 1999, p. 82). Do not skimp on this process of reviewing the literature or you will make some embarrassing mistakes, such as failing to realize that someone

1. Is the primary purpose of the article to
   a. describe and inform practitioners?
   b. present findings from original research?
   c. criticize and analyze major trends in the field?

2. Does the intended audience consist *primarily* of
   a. practitioners?
   b. researchers?
   c. scholars in the field?

3. Is the writing style of the piece closest to
   a. a journalistic "newspaper" style?
   b. a research report style?
   c. a graduate-level textbook style?

4. Does the tone of your writing tend to be
   a. down-to-earth and practical?
   b. consistent with the style of qualitative or quantitative research?
   c. more scholarly and formal?

5. Do the ideas in the manuscript tend to be
   a. concrete and specific, based on direct experience?
   b. richly detailed (qualitative) or statistically precise (quantitative)?
   c. more philosophical and theoretical, stressing analysis, synthesis and evaluation?

Count your answers: _____ a _____ b _____ c

The *a* answers relate to ***practical*** articles that strive to apply theory and research to the situations confronted by practitioners in the field.

The *b* answers relate to ***research*** articles that report on original studies conducted by the author(s). These articles are often organized into sections titled introduction/problem statement, review of the literature, subjects, methods/procedures, results, discussion, implications.

The *c* answers relate to ***review/theoretical*** articles that synthesize and critically evaluate previously published material and tend to focus on trends, issues, and controversies in the field.

Figure 5.2 *Self-Assessment: What Type of Article Should You Write?*

(or, worse yet, many others) have already published what you decided to write about. If someone has written a noteworthy piece on a topic and you never heard of it, you could be certain of a reviewer comment such as, "There are several notable works on this topic of which the author seems unaware."

After you have amassed extensive, high-quality information on the topic and settled on an article type, you'll need to think about outlets. Although many inexperienced authors assume this is the final step, it actually should occur very early in the process in order to maximize chances for acceptance.

SUITABLE OUTLETS FOR MANUSCRIPTS

"We wish you success in finding a suitable outlet for your work." So reads the standard rejection letter used by many publishers. What, exactly, does this mean? In many instances, manuscripts are rejected purely because they do not suit the particular audience and style of the intended publication. Although rejection rates of 80 to 90% sound dauntingly high, the reality is that many of the manuscripts in the mail are on the way to the wrong outlet. Mainly, this occurs because authors are not thoroughly familiar with outlets.

Speaking as a journal editor, I have received manuscripts submitted in a scattershot way on numerous occasions. It is obvious the manuscript is being submitted indiscriminately. The pages are crumpled, have stray pencil marks here and there, and often there is a coffee stain or greasy thumbprint. The authors do not have even a fleeting familiarity with the mission, content, or style of the journal. Other equally ridiculous submissions are entire dissertations or theses with cover letters directing me to read 300 pages and let the author know if there is an article in there somewhere!

Successful authors have learned to be matchmakers. They put a manuscript into the hands of editors, reviewers, and publishers who will love it and want to marry it. First, they decide which of the two broad categories of professional publications they wish to pursue, journals or magazines. Professional journals are the more scholarly, black-and-white publications that generally include research while professional magazines tend to be more practitioner-oriented, widely circulated, colorful publications that typically include advertising. Published authors tend to make journals their textbooks, studying them for cues on how to write and format a manuscript that will click with the outlet.

There are many tools that can assist you in ferreting out publishing opportunities with various outlets, including:

- articles about publishing articles (e.g., Henson, 1999a; Gargiulo & Jalongo, 2001)

- guides to publishing in scholarly outlets (e.g., Day, 1996; O'Connell, 1999; Kupfersmid & Wonderly, 1996; Sternberg, 2000)

- directories of publishing opportunities (e.g., Anson & Maylath, 1992; Bagnall & York, 1999; Bowker, 1997; Cabell & English, in press; Doughty, 1994; O'Connell, 1999)

- Online sources (e.g., websites of professional organizations, directories of electronic journals like King, Kovacs & Okerson (1994) or EBSCO Industries at http://www.ebsco.com/ess/services/online.stm)

Figure 5.3 provides some strategies for studying professional journals and magazines with an eye toward locating suitable outlets for your work.

As mentioned earlier, it is *not* acceptable to submit a manuscript to more than one professional journal or magazine at a time. Why? Because it wastes the time of reviewers who donate their time to expansion of knowledge and betterment of the field.

Obtain a copy of the publication—Go to the library, the virtual library, or request a sample copy to see what the publication actually looks like. Do not make wild guesses based on journal title alone. Do not submit manuscripts to publications you have never seen. Look up the publication in a directory of publishing opportunities or on the publisher's website to discover more clues about the criteria for acceptance and the goals of the publication.

Determine what is published in the journal—Read the masthead and the publisher's mission statement. Answer basic questions first: Do they publish unsolicited manuscripts? Will they consider original, empirical research and numerous statistical tables? What about qualitative studies? Is the publication practitioner oriented? Do they accept review/theoretical articles? Are there special departments or columns? Are they written by the Department Editors? Answer questions about more subtle features next: Do you notice anecdotes or case studies in the articles? Do the authors dare to use "I" and write about personal experience? How much use is made of quotes from authorities? Are the reference lists extensive? What, if any, types of figures, illustrations, and photographs generally are included?

Psyche out the audience—Scan the letters to the editor and look at the advertising, if any. What can you infer about the characteristics of the audience? Are they scholars? Administrators? Practitioners? Conservative? Liberal?

Obtain authors' guidelines—After identifying several journals that look promising, obtain a current copy of instructions for authors. Note such things as the type of material published, page length requirements, referencing style, and so forth.

Determine what topics have been (or will be) treated—Use the back stacks or the virtual library to scan through the table of contents for several issues/years. Notice how the titles are written. Determine if your topic has been addressed recently. If available, look at an editorial calendar or a call for manuscripts. Does your article fit into any of these forthcoming issues?

Figure 5.3   *Strategy for Finding Suitable Outlets*

continued on next page

Figure 5.3   *continued*

Choose outstanding examples—The most successful articles are sometimes reprinted elsewhere—as book chapters, sold as reprints, in collections of best articles from the publication. Do some detective work
to find out which articles have been acknowledged in this way. A
good source for some of the best articles published each year is the
Dushkin/McGraw-Hill series *Annual Editions*. The table of contents for
each volume is available on their web site at *www.dushkin.com*. Identify a couple of articles that are similar to yours, not in *content* but
in *style* and *format*. Note such things as the length (a 4 page journal
article is about 16 double-spaced, 12 point print pages of typed copy),
use of headings, examples, support from the research, use of figures,
and whether an abstract is required.

One way of getting around this problem is the query letter. A query letter,
also called a letter of inquiry, is intended to identify the outlet that would be most
interested in your manuscript prior to actually submitting the manuscript for
review. It takes the form of a concise business letter and, increasingly, uses e-mail
to expedite the process. Figure 5.4 offers guidelines for composing these inquiries.
Even if you never send out the query, you may find that writing a letter about
your manuscript is a good way to start because it forces you to think about your
thesis statement and how you would "sell" someone on your idea.

One category of outlet that should not be overlooked is the electronic journal. The advantages and disadvantages of publishing electronically have been
hotly debated (see Figure 5.5), but publishing undeniably is moving into the
electronic age.

THE MANUSCRIPT DRAFT

How do authors get started writing an article? Herbert and Jill Meyer suggest:

> The absolute first thing to do when you launch a writing project is
> to resist the impulse to start writing. You need to relax, to settle down
> and, above all, YOU NEED TO THINK. Don't worry about wasting
> time; it's never a waste of time to get your thoughts in order. Who has
> asked you to write something? Who will read it? What purpose is the
> piece intended to serve? To persuade? To inform? To trigger action?
> Ask yourself all these questions . . . and when you feel you've got it
> right, then—and only then—should you move on to the first real step
> in the writing process: The correct category of writing product. (Safire
> & Safir, 1992, p. 102)

Why Inquire?

- To obtain information, in advance, that the manuscript is of interest to the publisher.

- To avoid wasting time submitting a manuscript to a journal or magazine that is unreceptive to the topic, approach, or format.

- To make contact with an editor and give yourself some encouragement to get the manuscript out the door.

- To determine if the editor has already committed to publishing manuscript(s) on your topic that has not yet appeared in print (this is particularly helpful for "hot" topics that are very much in the literature or other time-sensitive material).

When to Write a Letter of Inquiry

- After you have checked editorial policies to make certain that the editor will respond to queries.

- When you are first getting started with writing and want to make certain that your impressions of what would be acceptable for a particular outlet are accurate.

- If time is of the essence and you cannot afford to wait for your manuscript to be reviewed by several outlets, one at a time.

- If you are being invited or commissioned to write an article and want to make certain that what you have in mind would meet the publication needs of the outlet.

What Should a Query Include?

- Evidence that you are familiar with the outlet and its readership.

- A one or two sentence summary of the manuscript's purpose, content, focus, and relevance for a clearly identified audience.

- A one sentence indication of your qualifications to undertake the task.

- All the elements of a good business letter—clear, concise, to the point, making it clear what action is to be taken.

- Assurances that you understand that the manuscript would need to be reviewed and you realize that a positive response does not guarantee publication.

Some Caveats About Query Letters

- Do not write a letter unless you actually have a manuscript ready to submit.

Figure 5.4   *The Query*

continued on next page

Figure 5.4 *continued*

- Some journal editors only will respond to entire manuscripts, not to queries.
- Do not use such letters to get an "assignment" out of the editor; finding a topic is your job.
- Do not attempt to flatter the editor into considering your work (e.g., "I would be honored to be published in your prestigious journal"), use a hard sell approach (e.g., "This is the article the field has been waiting for because . . . "), or imply that you want to keep the work from being disseminated or intend your manuscript to be a sales pitch (e.g., "My innovative program, _____ © has been well-received throughout the United States.")

Sample Query Letter

Insert Date
Insert Current Editor's Name
Editor, *XYZ Journal*
Street Address
City, State, zipcode

Dear (insert editor's name):

I have written a manuscript entitled "_____" that appears to be appropriate for the audience of *XYZ Journal*. This article:

[Explain the manuscript's major thrust in a sentence. Use words like defines, summarizes, compares/contrasts, reports, analyzes, evaluates, recommends.]

Although I recognize that the manuscript must go through the peer review process, I would appreciate your initial reaction to the concept.

As a [describe your professional role briefly], I [tell why you are qualified to write about this topic, why you selected it, and/or what other related work you may have published].

Please reply to the above address, by fax (insert number) or by e-mail (insert e-mail address) at your convenience. I will look forward to your reply.

Sincerely yours,

Your Name
Your Title

For the Author

Advantages: rapid publication of work; wide dissemination of work

Disadvantages: work may not be peer reviewed or may be perceived as less of an accomplishment; work can be more easily plagiarized by others

For the Reader

Advantages: instant access to a wide array of published material; opportunities to download and pay only for what is useful and of interest

Disadvantages: difficulty of reading on screen or marking up text for later reference; most readers find it necessary to download and print out longer texts

For the Publisher

Advantages: Production tasks can be automated; advances in technology make it possible to produce an electronic journal that mimics the appearance of the paper version; expanded opportunities for international readership

Disadvantages: Intensified competition for subscribers;

Need for more sophisticated equipment and higher levels of staff training to use the technology

For the Librarian/Archivist

Advantages: less physical space for storage is necessary; search processes are facilitated

Disadvantages: inability to operate when the systems are down; potential for loss of material is great as new systems replace old

---

For a bibliography of works that treat these issues in depth, see *http://info.lib.uh.edu/sepb/bgen.htm.*

Figure 5.5   *Issues in Electronic Publishing*

In the main, the task of all nonfiction writers is to make readers comfortable with what is unfamiliar or provide them with fresh perspectives on what is widely known. Making the new familiar consists of accessing readers' prior knowledge and reassuring them that they really do know something about your topic, no matter how unique or surprising. That way, they don't begin reading about an innovation and think to themselves, "Ooooh, that's really different. I'm not so sure I want to go in there—I could be way out of my depth." Making the familiar seem new is just the opposite stance; the writer's task consists of taking a timeless message and freshening it up so that readers don't say to themselves, "There's nothing new here, I've read all of this elsewhere before."

What about the role of ideas? Many new authors are convinced that ideas are everything. What they fail to realize is that, at least when writing nonfiction, interesting ideas emanate from this process of bringing information, audience, and purpose together rather than dropping down from the sky as pure inspiration. Although the ability to generate ideas is undeniably important in writing, keep in mind the psychologist's definition of creativity: the ability to recombine and juxtapose existing materials and ideas in to new, interesting forms. In other words, as my Italian grandmother used to say, "There is nothing entirely new under the sun." So, most of the time you will be in the position of making something new from the old and familiar—the very essence of creativity.

Do not allow yourself to be stymied by waiting around for an idea nor to pursue an idea merely because it sounded good at the time. In an interview with the best selling author of the Harry Potter children's books, J. K. Rowling, she had this to say about ideas: "I have a few ideas sitting in my filing cabinet at home. Maybe I'll go back and do something with them, but maybe when I go back to them, I'll find out they're complete rubbish. . . . The things I'm best at writing I absolutely adore. . . . The idea has to grip me from the start" (quoted in O'Malley, 1999, p. 36).

Some authors have the problem of being so wedded to arriving at a perfect plan that they cannot seem to write anything, while others have the problem of writing on and on without any idea about where they are headed. You may find that reflecting on some key aspects of the writing task will help you to get your bearings. Try the set of questions in Figure 5.6 as a mechanism for aiming your writing in a productive direction before you begin to write.

Now that you have the *what* (a topic and perspective on it), the *who* (a particular audience), and the *why* (purpose for writing) figured out, the next step is *how*. In other words, you will need to settle on the structure, approach, and format that do the best job of bringing your material and audience together.

THE PUBLISHABLE MANUSCRIPT

Now that you know your audience, topic, and focus, you can concentrate on completing the manuscript. As you do your homework studying the journals, select a few that appear to be most promising and examine the structure of the articles that are published there. The full-length or feature article typically follows the pattern outlined in Figure 5.7.

It sometimes happens that, while searching through the journals, you discover that someone already wrote and published the article you have in mind. What could you do to salvage the effort expended thus far?

- *Change the outlet*—Send it to a different publication that has not treated the topic recently.

- *Change the audience*—Write it for a general audience instead of fellow professionals; write it for professionals in another field who may be less familiar with the topic.

- *Switch the article type*—If you were writing a review of the research literature, write an article that offers research-based recommendations to practitioners instead.

Working Title _____

Article Type (check one)

____ Theoretical

____ Review of Research

____ Practical

____ Original Research

Content/Approach—What aspect of this topic can you address adequately in no more than about 18 double-spaced pages?

Thesis—What is your perspective on the topic, issue, controversy, etc.?

Main Points to Be Addressed— (provide a bulleted list)

Specific Audience—Why bring this topic and audience together?

Concrete Examples—What specific examples do you intend to use (e.g., quotations from people who participated in the project, excerpts from journals, samples of student work, anecdotes, drawings/ photographs/other types of illustrative material)?

Major Sections—Make a one-page outline, web/map, or overview.

Possible Outlets—Obtain author guidelines from the journal or off the Web, an example of a table of contents from the journal, and one exemplary article).

References—Produce an annotated bibliography that is specifically linked to your topic. Annotations should be one or two sentences about the content of the article. Be certain to refer to the correct style manual, such as American Psychological Association style, as you prepare your final reference list. When writing for publication, include only those items that were directly cited in the work, not everything that was read in preparing the manuscript.

Figure 5.6   *Preplanning Worksheet: Professional Journal Articles*

- *Take the opposite stance*—If you were writing about the positive effects of mentoring, for instance, consider writing about what goes wrong with mentor/protégé relationships.

You may want to follow a procedure similar to that in Figure 5.8 for generating articles. As you discover more about your personal work habits and writing style, amend that process to maximize your productivity.

When writing nonfiction articles, remember that you don't have much space and you have even less time to get your reader interested—just a few seconds, at most. As Donald Murray (in Winokur, 1999, p. 68) advises,

> Don't begin with the background of your subject, how you happened to get interested in it, why the reader should read it, or how you obtained information for it. Begin your article with conflict that produces tension, often revealed by including a brief example or anecdote and problem that will be resolved at the end. It's a good rule to start as near the end as possible and then plunge your reader into the central tension. When you've involved your reader in this way, weave in background facts or information as you think your reader needs it to understand the purpose and point of your piece (in Winokur, 1999, p. 68).

The Train	The Exclamations
	!
Cowcatcher—clears the track with a strong lead that grabs attention	**Hey!**—Is the "hook" that draws the readers' attention in 5 seconds and compels them to read on
Locomotive—gives the power thrust that contains the focus statement	**You!**—Gives the "what's-in-it-for-me-the-reader?" statement
The cars—provide the key main points in your argument and authoritative support	**See!**—Is the body of the article that highlight key points and supports them with evidence
The caboose—brings the train to an anticipated and satisfying end	**So!?**—Is your conclusion and a thought to take away

Adapted from: Henry, O. (1967) *Writing and selling magazine articles*. Boston: The Writer. Campbell, W. (1949). *Writing nonfiction* (rev. ed.). Boston: The Writer.

Figure 5.7   *Two Metaphors for the Structure of the Journal Article*

1. Before you begin to write, complete the following sentence: "I contend that . . ."

2. Next, ask yourself
   - If somebody else's essay were arguing the same thesis, would *you* be intrigued by it?
   - Is it new? True? Important?
   - Have you really taken a stand or are you waffling?
   - What authoritative evidence have you collected (concrete details and apt quotations) that would convince your readers that you have done your homework?
   - What are you *really* trying to say?

3. Now, stride confidently into your topic and get directly to the point. Avoid long warm-ups and do not waste words.

4. Look through all of the materials that you have collected and sort them into meaningful categories. Arrange them on a computer file by category.

5. Sketch out a plan for the body of the piece. You may find it helpful, at least at first, to write in a question-and-answer format, allowing the questions to serve as section headings. Generate one concrete example (e.g., anecdote, direct quotation, analogy) for each main section heading.

6. Develop a vigorous lead. Consider beginning your manuscript with a brief anecdote that illustrates the main point, a startling, current, and relevant statistic; an interesting paradox; a persistent debate in a nutshell; and so forth. Consider saving the strongest statement of your thesis for the last sentence of the first paragraph.

7. Within the first page or two, clearly state the purpose and focus of the manuscript. Identify your theme and stick to it throughout the work.

8. Write in simple prose. Strive to make your ideas impressive rather than overloading the piece with verbiage. Remember that you can always go back later and dress things up as necessary.

9. As you draft the body of your paper, strive for balance. One section should not be three pages long and the next, just two paragraphs, for instance.

10. Provide evidence of a recent and balanced review of the literature. Rely on original sources rather than secondary sources (e.g., textbooks).

Figure 5.8 *How to Write a Nonfiction Article*

continued on next page

Figure 5.8   *continued*

11. Remember that, in the words of editor Jack Frymeir, "all good writing moves back and forth between the general and the specific." For most nonfiction pieces it is preferable to weave together theory, research, and practical ideas rather than arrange this material in the most pedestrian fashion with all of the theory in one spot, all of the research in another, and all of the practical ideas in a separate section. Organize your material around key concepts and main points.

12. If you reach a point where you are describing something and it is getting bogged down in words, see if an illustration, diagram, figure, or table would help. Look through several examples of outstanding articles published in the outlet(s) you have in mind. Note how they use illustrative material effectively.

13. Show evidence of commitment to the writer's craft. Study exemplary journalism as represented in *Harper's*, *The Writer*, or *The Atlantic Monthly*. Avoid sexist language (Schwartz, 1995), clichés, excessive jargon. Consult the appropriate style guide/publication manual—American Psychological Association (APA, 2001); University of Chicago Style; Turabian, (1996), or Modern Language Association (MLA, 1998). For more on style, see Hacker, 2000.

14. Remember that every successful essay has: "1) a well-defined thesis, 2) a clear strategy, 3) strong evidence, 4) a clean narrative line, and 5) a persuasive closing" (Trimble, 2000, p. 35).

15. Recognize that even quality manuscripts are sometimes rejected due to limitations in space, etc. Consider giving your manuscript a different focus and resubmitting it.

Read the following paragraph from "On the Rez," Ian Frazier's (1999) article about Indian reservations in *The Atlantic Monthly*. Notice how he gets straight to the central tension, weaves in details, and addresses many of the questions that are apt to be lingering in readers' minds (e.g., What is life like on a reservation? Which tribe will be discussed and where do they live? How do the Native Americans view life on the reservation? Is the author a Native American and, if not, what qualifies him to be spokesperson?).

> This article is about the Oglala Sioux Indians who live on the Pine Ridge Reservation, in southwestern South Dakota, in the plains and badlands in the middle of the United States. When I describe this subject to non-Indians, they often reply that it sounds bleak. "Bleak" is a word I have never heard used by Indians themselves. Many thousands

of people—not just Americans but German and French and English people, and more—visit the reservations every year, and the prevailing opinion among the Indians is not that they come for the bleakness. The Indians understand that the visitors are there out of a sense of curiosity and out of an admiration which sometimes reaches such a point that the visitors even wish they could be Indians too. I am a middle-aged non-Indian who wears his hair in a thinning ponytail copied originally from the traditional-style long hair of the leaders of the American Indian Movement of the 1970s, because I thought it looked cool. When I'm driving across a field near the town of Oglala, on the Pine Ridge Reservation, and I see my friend Floyd John walking across the other way, I stop, and he comes over to the car and leans in the window and smiles a big-tooth grin and says, "How ya' doin', wannabe?" (Frazier, 1999, p. 53)

This article was a great read, a piece that grabbed me on page one and never let go. I didn't want to put it down; as Stein (2000) puts it, it defied interruption. Another part of making a manuscript publishable in your field is writing in a professional style and voice. Take a look at this sentence from a student paper: "There is no evidence that today's parents care any more or less about their children than in previous generations; however, what has changed is the loss of community, an increase in splintered families, as well as keeping in touch with one another while being on the go." If you are thinking like an editor, you are put off by that last part—"splintered" families sounds a bit melodramatic and judgmental while "keeping in touch" and "being on the go" are clichés that have very little to do with the professional journal article. Here is a rewrite: "There is no evidence that today's parents care any more or less about their children than in previous generations; however, significant changes in families undeniably have occurred. Included among these changes are a decline in the sense of community, an increase in nontraditional family structures, and a decrease in opportunities for family members to spend time together." Note how the revision makes the writer's meaning clearer and is easier to follow because the list is in a consistent format (a decline . . ., an increase . . ., a decrease . . .). The writer would also be expected to provide a citation of support for such claims—yet another distinction of writing for fellow professionals. Remember to make your lists consistent and to support what you say. When an editor has to choose among many high quality manuscripts, several awkward sentences can be the basis for rejection. Strive to make every sentence the best that you can write before you subject your manuscript to review.

MANUSCRIPT MARKETING STRATEGY

Even if you have never published a journal article in your field, you have internalized what makes articles successful by being an intelligent consumer of articles. If you are like most readers, you scan for information that is of interest at the time and disregard much of the rest, so matching topics to your audience is important. If an article is well written, informative, and helpful, you will take the time to read it and go to the trouble of copying it or at least recommending it to others, so it is important that an article be helpful and insightful. If an article is garbled, incorrect, or has little to offer, you will pass it over or criticize it in private or perhaps even in public in the form of a letter to the editor.

Journal article authors may donate their work to the betterment of their fields, but the work still has to be marketable, at least in the figurative sense. This means that editors and reviewers will want to publish it and the intended audience will want to read it. The good news is that you already know something about how to sell yourself. You have been exposed to thousands of advertising messages and you probably have been interviewed or perhaps have interviewed others for jobs. If you soften those approaches a bit, many of those basic principles apply to marketing your writing as well. The talent in marketing a manuscript is a curious balance of giving readers timely content (something that is fascinating to the audience), in the ways they expect it (an appropriate format and style, all the while pleasantly surprising them (with original ideas and interesting uses of language). If you can achieve this and you are persistent, your manuscripts will be warmly accepted.

What will "sell" the editor on your work? I suggest this list:

- Appropriate for the audience

- Admirable writing style

- Significant and authoritative content

- Concise and clearly focused

- Clear organization

- Freshness and originality

- Correct format

- Error-free copy

Unless you are an accomplished author you will be in the position of asking others to publish your work rather than being invited to write for a particular outlet. Manuscripts that are proffered to the publisher by the author are referred to as unsolicited; manuscripts that are sought by publishers from authors (usually the established, well known authors) are solicited or invited. That puts aspiring or less accomplished authors in the position of having to market their own work. This is a critical step that novices tend to skip over, much to the detriment of their self-confidence and their publication track records.

Approach the task of submitting your manuscript much as you would an important interview or audition. Strive to create a favorable impression. Be courteous, professional, business-like, and conform to the policies and procedures of the outlet.

- *Correspond with the editor in a professional manner*—Make sure you know the current editor's name; some journals change editors annually. Do not try to flatter the editor. Evidence of familiarity with the publication and its readership is sufficient.

- *Include a brief cover letter with all manuscripts*—It is amazing that the same person who wouldn't dream of putting an item in a colleague's mailbox without a note of explanation would submit a manuscript to a publisher without a cover letter. Strictly speaking, the editor is under no obligation to send it out for review because you have not directed her or him to do so. A cover letter for a first submission should warrant that the work is original and not under consideration by another publisher; a cover letter for a resubmission should explain how the reviewer's suggestions were addressed. When you refer to your work, call it a manuscript (which editors abbreviate as ms. or, for more than one, mss.) It is neither a paper (this sounds sophomoric), nor is it an article (not until *after* it is published). See Figure 5.9 for a sample cover letter.

- *Follow the specific submission policies of the journal*—If a copyright release is required, provide it. If a brief blurb about the author is required, look at past issues of the journal and infer how it is done rather than bothering the editor about how to write it. If the journal requires a particular style sheet and your manuscript was prepared in another bibliographic style, don't be lazy. Convert it. All of these specific requirements usually are on a website, printed in the journal, or can be requested by sending a self-addressed, stamped envelope.

When you produce a manuscript, don't forget to invest a reasonable amount of care in the physical preparation of the manuscript. Most peer-reviewed journals require

- A cover sheet with the author's (s') contact information

- Multiple copies (make sure each copy is complete and in the correct order)

- Print on one side of the paper only

- Numbered pages

- No identifying information about authors on the pages of the article (since it is being reviewed anonymously)

- 12-point print in a conservative typeface (e.g., Courier or CG Times)

- At least 1-inch margins all around

- A large envelope with sufficient postage to get everything returned to you

---

About the Content

- Briefly describe the manuscript you are sending. Give your manuscript a descriptive title and list the major points in a sentence or two (e.g., "Enclosed is a manuscript entitled "____" that a) defines ____, b) identifies ____, and c) makes recommendations ____.")

- Briefly explain who you are and how you are qualified to write on the topic (e.g., "I have been a practicing clinical psychologist who works with young children and their families for seven years.")

- State why you have selected this particular outlet (without resorting to a "hard sell" approach). Demonstrate familiarity with the outlet and stress how your manuscript would be of value for the particular audience.

- Warrant that the work is original and not in review with another publisher (e.g., "I warrant that this manuscript is my original work and is not under consideration by any other publisher."

About the Format

- Follow all of the procedures for a business letter. Your letter should not exceed one page of 12-point print.

- Address the correspondence to the editor by name.

- Enclose a large, self-addressed envelope with sufficient postage (e.g., Priority Mail) to return the manuscript to you in the event it is not accepted.

- Be certain that everything in the submission package conforms to the specific outlet's requirements for preparation of a manuscript.

Figure 5.9   *The Cover Letter*

Speaking now as a reviewer and editor, time after time, the authors who do everything right procedurally are also the ones who submit better quality manuscripts to begin with. More often than not, the authors who fail to comply with these simple submission guidelines also submit a manuscript that includes errors in fact, spelling, grammar, or referencing style. They also neglect to produce something in the proper format. Because the editors of peer-reviewed journals send manuscripts out for anonymous review, it is particularly annoying when an author puts his or her name on every page because it will have to be removed prior to review. Some authors neglect to number the pages, fail to arrange all pages of the copies in the correct order, or have missing (or repeated) pages in the copies they've assembled. All of these mistakes mount up until the manuscript is tarnished in reputation and the editor's and reviewers' patience has been sorely tested.

As a journal editor, I take no pleasure in rejecting people's work but I also have better things to do than clean up after inconsiderate people I don't even know. Most editors try to be understanding about beginner's mistakes and try to give the authors the benefit of the doubt, but their tolerance for shoddy work is understandably low. Your work is called a submission with good reason: you are saying, in effect, "Here is the best I can do. I submit my work to peer review and will consider any reasonable recommendations for improvement."

MULTIPLE PUBLICATIONS FROM ONE BODY OF WORK

Most professionals can think of prolific authors in their fields who have published several articles in different outlets on similar topics. Evidently, getting more than one article out of a body of work is as appealing as a getting two items for the price of one at the grocery store. How much of this overlap is permissible from one work to the next and when does it deteriorate into blatant duplication? The answer lies in the manuscripts themselves. You don't want to "imitate your first successes, straining hot water through the same old tea bag" (Erica Jong quoted in Winokur 1999, p. 178).

Before you become enamored of writing yet another article on the same topic, realize that it isn't always a tremendous timesaver. Occasionally, I delude myself into thinking that if I have already written on a topic, it will be comparatively easy to write about it again. It isn't. More often than not, returning to a topic written about previously is comparable to cleaning a spot on a dirty wall. The moment you change the appearance of that little section, everything around it looks shabby and needs to be modified too. The well organized manuscript has an infrastructure that is difficult to tinker with. Besides, if you have already written about a topic recently you may not have much that is new to say, and if you don't have anything further to say, there isn't a very compelling reason to write. Before it is all over, that "spot job" that you hoped for will become a exhausting, floor-to-ceiling, scrub brush and bucket of soapy water activity. Writing revisited seldom offers tremendous advantages over writing afresh.

Getting two or more manuscripts from one basic body of work can be achieved, however, by using one of the following mechanisms.

1. *Writing two articles at the same time*—After conducting a review of the literature, I wrote two manuscripts on the same topic for two different audiences or with two different slants (e.g., one article on the importance of listening skills for preschool/primary, another for intermediate through high school).

2. *Writing very different types of manuscripts*—I once conducted a review of the literature on the publishing productivity of higher education faculty. From that work, I generated a faculty professional development grant funded by the Provost, a national conference presentation, a newsletter article, and a peer-reviewed journal article for *Educational Forum*. That article subsequently earned

the Association for Higher Education's "Best Essay" Award—a satisfying "four for one" from (pretty much) the same basic review of the literature.

3. *Revisiting a topic after gathering a substantial file of new material*—In a field that is constantly developing, you may find that topics are ready for an update after a few years. I wrote about what makes an article publishable for an editorial and expanded those ideas for this chapter after conducting numerous conference sessions, reading scads of manuscripts, and reading the latest information on the topic.

Remember that there is a useful distinction between variations on a theme and obvious double dipping; strive for the former rather than the latter.

CONFERENCE PRESENTATIONS TRANSFORMED INTO ARTICLES

A distinguished professor and leading author was chatting with an assistant professor and inquired about her professional activities. She related, with some pride, that she would be making three national conference presentations. The senior faculty member said, in a kindly way, "It sounds as though you already know how to write proposals that get you on the national conference program. Now, what do you plan to do for the *next* 25 years of your career?"

The experiences of my recently graduated doctoral students further underscore the professor's point. Often they will submit four or five conference proposals, thinking that, if good fortune smiles upon them, maybe one or two will earn a place on the program. But because they have mastered the form, what tends to happen is that all of the proposals are accepted; and they are racing around the country at a time when few of them have travel money. For them, and perhaps for you, it might be time to develop a successful conference presentation into a publishable article.

Professional presentations are a good starting point for writing for publication for at least five reasons. First, *most professionals make oral presentations regularly*. They teach, consult, and present—all activities that require extensive preparation/ planning, skillful organization, and thoughtful self-evaluation. Using a presentation as the basis for writing an article can jumpstart the writing process, because the material is already assembled and structured in a logical way.

A second reason to draw upon oral presentations is *that at least some writing has already been accomplished*. When you prepare an all-day training session, you probably have PowerPoint© transparencies and handouts for the audience; when you apply to make a presentation at a competitive professional conference, you have the proposal written; and when you present the highlights of a completed research project, you probably have written an executive summary and have data tables prepared. The publication becomes an extension of previously completed work and writing.

Take, for example, the task of writing a brief session description that will be published in the conference program. Chances are it takes the form of a) a descriptive title, b) a first sentence that provides a general context and targets the audience, c) a list of the main points/activities in the session, and d) a wrap-up that stresses benefits/outcomes for participants. In many ways, it is quite similar to the abstract that authors are asked to write for a journal article. So, if you presented on your topic first, you may have the basis for an abstract in hand. Figure 5.10 is an overview of the types of presentations and their corresponding journal article possibilities.

A third advantage of beginning with a presentation is that *the content is already audience-centered* and tends to be concise and practical. The material is peppered with examples, cases, and stories that could be abbreviated and incorporated into a publication. Your audience, no doubt, has added to this reservoir of practical ideas and illustrative material. Moreover, one common problem of writers—that of producing much more material than they can actually use—may have been addressed already by the time limitations imposed on a presentation.

A fourth advantage of using an oral presentation is that *peers have already reviewed and responded to the work.* A presenter can go back and analyze the written feedback that audience members have provided to get a clearer sense of which points were well received and which were less so. Written feedback often identifies persistent issues that require additional reflection and evidence as well. Your ideas have been enriched and expanded by the questions and comments of a real, live audience.

A fifth advantage of using a presentation as the basis for a publication is that, if the session was well received, you may have *greater motivation to pursue the topic further.* You may be thinking already about another presentation on the same topic. Perhaps members of the audience stayed afterwards to talk, or later contacted you by e-mail. You might even have the good fortune to have a journal editor in your audience who shared a business card and urged you to write something.

Before you begin, make these adjustments in moving from talk to print:

- When speaking face-to-face, it is easier to convey your commitment and enthusiasm; you'll need to figure out how to communicate the emotional impact of your message.

- Presentations are sometimes on popular topics that are already well represented in professional publications; you may need a unique "slant" and original thesis for an article.

- Presentations are sometimes fairly generic and cover quite a bit of territory; you'll need a sharper focus for a manuscript.

- The audience for a conference presentation may be more alike in that, presumably, they all have a special interest in the topic; when writing, your audience will tend to be more diverse and some of your readers (e.g., reviewers, editors) may not share your enthusiasm for the topic.

- Presentations can sometimes be fairly freewheeling and informal; if so, you will need a much tighter organizational pattern and perhaps a more formal tone for your written work.

- Some forms of representation used during a presentation may be highly visual (e.g., a video); you will need to figure out how to convey that information meaningfully in print.

Some tips for converting a presentation into a publishable piece are summarized in Figure 5.11.

Presentation Task	Initial Writing Investment	Potential for Publication
Workshop/ Training	Objectives, activities, key points, packet for participants, reference list	Lends itself to a "how to" practical piece designed to extend or update the knowledge of professionals—Could be disseminated initially on Internet or through a clearinghouse (e.g., ERIC) then written as an article and submitted to a professional newsletter or journal
Speech	Overview of entire speech that conforms to time restrictions, identification of a thesis and key points, specific examples/anecdotes	Lends itself to a theoretical "think piece," position paper, or editorial that takes a stand on an issue and sets forth a logical argument for that point of view
Research Paper	Overall research plan, collection and analysis of data, conference proposal, entire paper or abbreviated version as required by conference to distribute to participants	Lends itself to a quantitative or qualitative research article that reports on an original study—Could be published as conference proceedings or as an article submitted to a research journal

Figure 5.10   *Types of Presentations and Publications*

Reflect—What parts of your presentation evoked the greatest response from the audience? When were they . . . nodding in agreement? Sharing experiences? Discussing and disagreeing? Smiling and laughing? Use this analysis to find the focus for your written manuscript.

Sift and Synthesize—Go through all of the materials that you prepared for the presentation. What parts might be omitted next time around? Might there be a more effective way to present some of the material (e.g., as a checklist, a self-quiz, a diagram, a table)? How could you go about taking several of the sources you collected and synthesize them into one particularly helpful item (still giving all of the original authors credit, of course)?

Correct—Presentations are notorious for incomplete or incorrect citations—material derived from secondary sources, misspelled authors' names, quotations that are not correctly attributed, and so forth. How will you make certain that all of your documentation is precise and that the material is error free?

Examples/Anecdotes—What were the most memorable experiences that were shared? How might you use these "voices from the field" to begin the article, make a point, or bring an article to a satisfying conclusion?

Style—How will you capture the passion that you have for your topic in the new medium of the written word without coming across as grinding an axe or being biased?

Questions—What burning questions did the audience have? Were there any questions that surprised you? Read through the evaluations. What questions remained? How might you organize your written manuscript around those pressing issues/questions?

Investigate—For what contingent of the audience was your presentation most interesting? Which outlets match this audience? Which outlets might be most receptive to the subject matter and approach that you have in mind?

Figure 5.11 *From Conference Presentation to Publication: The Process*

ARTICLES WITH A TIMELESS QUALITY

One editorial task that I have performed is reviewing the position papers of a professional organization. These articles were intended to provide helpful, authoritative guidance to teachers and several were previously published; some were nearly 10 years old. The surprising thing about reviewing these position statements was that much of the content was just as relevant today as it had been years before and, aside from some changes in the politically correct terminology or the formality of the writing style, most position papers were worthy of being updated, rather than scrapped. Apparently, these authors were capable of producing articles with a timeless quality. They were classics. Striving for timelessness also addresses a question that is raised frequently by authors about whether it is best to be trendy. They make an effort to be forward thinking and timely, yes, but they do not simply follow along with whatever "hot" topic is everywhere in the literature at the moment. Writing articles that will endure requires a certain amount of resistance to prevailing trends; it requires groundbreakers rather than bandwagon jumpers. A person who adopted the majority's attitudes toward African Americans in Alabama in the 1950s could not have written something of value about race relations in the United States for today. The most admirable authors tend to resist facile viewpoints adopted from the crowd and to be ahead of their time rather than an obvious product of it.

Good thinkers also find that, over the course of their lives as writers, their thinking develops further and they may no longer entirely agree with themselves. Personally, I am always impressed by authors who don't take themselves too seriously and are willing to revise their points of view, such as Harvard researcher Howard Gardner who proposed seven distinctive forms of human intelligence with the caution that he could be wrong, that there could be more (and there were).

If the articles of authors intent upon latching onto a trend and prone to sloganeering usually do not wear well, perhaps it was because their motives were impure. They sought to make a name for themselves quickly rather than to make an enduring contribution.

CONCLUSION

In some ways, producing a successful article is comparable to recording a hit song in music, because

- *Getting someone to hear you out is important*—The opening number and the big finish frequently are expected. If you begin weakly, some members of your audience may give up on you rather than listening; if you conclude poorly, you will leave readers feeling dissatisfied.

- *Being alert to opportunities is important*—Just as musicians seek out chances to perform, journal article writers are alert to publishing opportunities and seek more challenging outlets over time. They watch for calls for papers, read editorial calendars published in the journals, scan professional newsletters, attend publications committee meetings at conferences, search online for calls for electronic journal articles, and pursue collaboration with established authors.

- *Mistakes can be costly*—Every error undermines confidence in your ability to perform. Just as the vocalist practices until he or she can sing confidently without faltering, the journal article author polishes the manuscript until it flows and is relatively error-free.

- *Satisfying your audience is essential*—A musician needs fans and a writer needs readers. If an article is requested often (e.g., to copy, to warrant being published as a reprint or brochure, to be included in edited collections) your reputation as a writer is enhanced because your audience found it worthwhile.

- *Style is what differentiates you from the crowd*—Think of your favorite artist in music. You could listen to hundreds of songs played on the radio and reliably identify the artist, based on a distinctive voice and style. The same holds true for journal authors. Those whose articles are eagerly anticipated have acquired a one-of-a-kind style and voice.

- *Selecting the right material to showcase your talents matters*—Successful musicians choose material that they can perform exceptionally well. Likewise, successful article writers learn to select the article types and topics best suited to their talents and interests.

- *Good business strategy is essential*—Just as musicians need to find a recording company, writers need to find a publisher. Keep track of your manuscripts' progress. Unless you are prolific, something fairly simple should suffice, such as maintaining a separate file for each submission, making a grid or marking your calendar with the dates when each was submitted and the disposition of each work.

As we have seen, the attraction of writing the professional journal article has less to do with fame and fortune and more to do with participating actively in the professional dialogue and becoming an authoritative spokesperson in your field. Authors of professional journal articles have a measure of freedom to follow their interests greater than that of the freelancer—the author by trade, who goes on assignment and writes to editorial specifications in order to pay the bills. We get to write whatever we wish, whenever we want, and submit wherever we please. We get to write about what intrigues, troubles, perplexes, challenges, touches, and fascinates us. Surely, this freedom is one of the great attractions of writing the professional journal article.

REFERENCES

American Psychological Association (APA). (2001). *Publication manual of the American Psychological Association* (5th ed.). Washington, DC: Author.

Anson, D. M., & Maylath, B. (1992). Searching for journals: A brief guide and 100 samples. In K. Dahl (Ed.), *Teacher as writer: Entering the professional conversation* (pp. 150-187). Urbana, IL: National Council of Teachers of English.

Bagnall, D., & York, M. A. (Ed.) (1999). *MLA directory of periodicals: A guide to journals and series in languages and literature.* New York: Modern Language Association of America.

Bowker, R. R. (1997). *Ulrich's international periodicals directory.* (36th ed.). New York: R. R. Bowker.

Cabell, D. W., & English, D. L. (in press). *Cabell's directory of publishing opportunities in education.* (6th ed.) Cobell, TX: Cabell Publishing Company.

Day, A. (1996). *How to get research published in journals.* Burlington, VT: Ashgate.

Doughty, B. (Ed.) (1994). *Contributor's guide to periodicals in reading.* Newark, DE: International Reading Association.

Frazier, I. (1999). On the rez. *The Atlantic Monthly,* 284(6), 53-84.

Gargiulo, R., Jalongo, M. R., & Motari, J. (2001). Writing for publication in early childhood education: Survey data from editors and advice to authors. *Early Childhood Education Journal, 29* (1), 17-24.

Hacker, D. (2000). *A pocket style manual* (3rd ed.). Boston: Bedford/St. Martin's.

Henson, K. (1999a). Writing for professional journals. *Phi Delta Kappa, 80*(10), 780-783.

Henson, K. T. (1999b). *Writing for publication: Keys to academic and business success.* Boston: Allyn & Bacon.

King, L. A., Kovacs, D., & Okerson, A. (1994). *Directory of electronic journals, newsletters, and academic discussion lists* (4th ed.). Washington, DC: Office of Scientific and Academic Publishing.

Kupfersmid, J., & Wonderly, D. M. (1996). *An author's guide to publishing better articles in better journals in the behavioral sciences.* New York: John Wiley & Sons.

Modern Language Association (1998). *MLA style manual and guide to scholarly publishing* (2d ed.). New York: Author.

O'Connell, J. (Ed.) (1999). *Serials directory: An international reference book.* (13th ed.). Ipswich, MA: EBSCO Industries.

O'Malley, J. (1999). Talking with . . . J. K. Rowling. *Book Links, 8,6,* 32-35.

Safire, W., & Safir, L. (1992). *Good advice on writing.* New York: Fireside/Simon & Schuster.

Schwartz, M. (1995). Guidelines for bias-free writing. Bloomington: Indiana University Press.

Selye, H. (1984). *The stress of life* (revised ed.). New York: McGraw-Hill.

Stein, S. W. (2000). *Stein on writing.* Griffin Trade Paperback.

Sternberg, R. J. (Ed.) (2000). *Guide to publishing in psychology journals.* New York: Cambridge University Press.

Thyer, B. A (1994), *Successful publishing in scholarly journals*. Thousand Oaks, CA: Sage.

Trimble, J. R. (2000). *Writing with style*. Upper Saddle River, NJ: Prentice Hall.

Turabian, K. L. (1996). *A manual for writers of term papers, theses, and dissertations*. Chicago: University of Chicago Press.

Winokur, J. (Ed.). (1999). *Advice to writers*. New York: Vintage/Random House.

CHAPTER 6

❦

Writing Books for Fellow Professionals

❦

M y first invitation to author a book came at a time when I was poorly prepared to accept it. At the time, I had published only two articles in major journals but some kindly reviewers mentioned to one of the editors that I might make a good author for an association-sponsored publication. I was surprised and flattered by the offer, but plagued by anxiety. After several false starts and extensive editorial support, I managed to produce the book. So much had been learned along the way that I couldn't bear to think of not using that learning again to write another book. The second book was a textbook—much longer and more involved than the first. When it was finished, again I had learned so much and hated to squander that growth. Like being a toddler who is driven to practice whatever motor skills she or he has at the time, such as walking while holding onto furniture, filling and emptying containers, or operating a pull toy, I had mastered one task and felt impelled to accept another challenge.

Too many authors view writing a book as an outlandish proposal. They doubt that they could have that much to say. Don't dismiss the possibility of writing a book, prematurely, however. Although a book may seem outside the realm of possibility at the moment, you can surprise yourself. Books often have rather humble beginnings. Before they were books, books often look like piles of junk stored in cardboard boxes. In my office, there is an inverse relationship between the amount of floor space in my office and the number of books I have underway. Many of the textbooks on your shelves began as class notes for a course that was well taught. Many books for practitioners that you refer to frequently started out as a file of ideas and copies of workshop or training handouts. And the scholarly books in your professional library probably began as lively discussions with colleagues, a series of research investigations, and presentations at conferences.

SUITABILITY FOR BOOK AUTHORSHIP

Your suitability for writing a book (rather than sticking with articles or other, shorter writing projects) has as much to do with your ability to postpone gratification as it does with your mastery of the content. The following questions may help you decide if writing a book is right for you.

Can you handle a large, unwieldy project?

As E. L. Doctorow has observed, "Writing a book is like driving a car at night. You only see as far as your headlights go, but you can make the whole trip that way" (in Winokur, 1999, p. 46). Chapters of a book are more than separate articles bound together. Therefore, an important and damnably difficult part of producing a book is planning it in a way that will hang together conceptually. Even edited books, where each chapter has been written by a different author or authors, have some features that unify these disparate elements into a cohesive volume. Frequently, an editor is responsible for writing an introduction to the book and the sections of it that make these connections more explicit. The way to achieve this unity, of course, is not always abundantly clear. You need to have a healthy tolerance for ambiguity and be capable of high-level conceptualization in order to write or edit a book that flows from one chapter to the next. Console yourself with the fact that, if you average just one publishable page per day, in a year you'll have an average size book.

Will you care enough to stick with it?

Another consideration in book authorship is persistence, for books are quite demanding in this respect. Much of your dedication to the task emanates from your passionate curiosity about the topic. As Stephen King (2000) advises

> You can approach the act of writing with nervousness, excitement, hope-
> fulness, or even despair—the sense that you can never completely put on
> the page what's in your mind and heart. You can come to the act with
> your fists clenched and your eyes narrowed, ready to kick ass and take
> down names. You can come to it because you want a girl to marry you

or because you want to change the world. Come to it any way but lightly.
Let me say it again: *you must not come lightly to the blank page.* (p, 106)

Where the long-term commitment to a book is concerned, such determination is doubly important. Woody Allen once quipped that "half of life is getting it done and turning it in on time" and, surely, that is at least half of book publishing as well. Writing a book requires patience as well as persistence because, as Smith (1997) reports, the average amount of time from first idea to printed book is approximately four years.

The easiest and best way to predict who will write a book is to find someone who has already written one. Book authors need to begin somewhere, though, and this (usually) means that you have written and published a few articles before proposing a book. The articles serve as indicators that you know how to write well enough to be published and that you can finish what you start. To illustrate, within a few years after I selected several new editorial board members for the journal virtually every one of them had a new book in a publisher's catalog. Clearly, a selective bias was in operation. They had been chosen because they were experienced as journal article authors and they all were sufficiently interested in publishing to serve on the board when a free subscription was their only compensation. They had remained on the board because they provided prompt and thorough reviews of others' work. These same work habits enabled them to get their books done and turn them in on time.

Can you directly connect your book with your work life?

Most prolific nonfiction authors who write for fellow professionals link their books to their work. They tend to use their daily experience to discover projects with relevance for professional audiences and build a book around it. Everyone remarks on how "disciplined" I must be in order to write so many books but if I had that much self-control, I would be a size 10. The secret to my writing is that it is always connected to what I am obligated to do as part of my job and I see it as saving me time later on. I might be preparing to teach a class but the book is being written simultaneously. I might be writing an article but pieces of it will be useful later on in a book, and so forth. Few of us have the time or energy to write a book that is totally divorced from other aspects of our lives. Are you good at multitasking and capitalizing on work you have completed previously? Chances are you will need to be in order to succeed at book authorship.

Will your institution reward or recognize your efforts?

It is up to you to decide how (or whether) various perquisites will influence your decision to pursue publication of a book. If you are a faculty member at a research institution, there may not be much recognition for writing a textbook. Textbooks are viewed as mere transmission of existing knowledge rather than the creation of knowledge, a goal that is made possible only through original research. Timing is another issue. You may be at a career stage where it is important to produce something rather quickly, rather than wait until a book can be accomplished. If, as one professor described it, "You need *at least* a book to be awarded tenure at my university," then your only choice is between writing one and staying or failing to write one and going elsewhere.

Even if publishing a book never becomes a job expectation or is compensated with tenure, promotion, release time, or other incentives, it may be worth it to you in terms of self-esteem. According to Abraham Maslow's (1998) "Hierarchy of Needs," after basic needs are met, human beings naturally strive for belongingness and the esteem of others they admire. Several of my elementary school teacher, counselor, and librarian co-authors have had their contributions to books recognized by their employers—a copy posted on a bulletin board, a surprise wine and cheese reception, or a positive note in the personnel file. All of them considered this recognition to be a career highlight and, surely, that is worth something.

Will you make the time?

Unlike the best-selling authors who devote their lives to writing, professionals who write for other professionals seldom have the luxury of quitting their day jobs. For most of us, anyway, agreeing to a book means agreeing to another job, one that will claim wee hours, weekends, and holidays over a long span of time (at the very moment I first typed this, it was 5 a.m. on Thanksgiving Day). So, if you are the type of person who wouldn't think of going into the office on Saturday or working during your vacation, perhaps authoring a book is not for you. There will be deadlines that come due when you have a house full of company or are in the midst of a big project at work that has left you exhausted.

Invariably the stars and planets align themselves in such a way that makes all of the most time-consuming tasks at work and at the publishing house due on the same day. While writing this book, for instance, my house caught fire and nearly burned down when some plumbers were soldering pipes for a new washing machine hook up. After the blaze was brought under control, the Fire Chief allowed us to go back in and told us to take just a minute and retrieve just a few easily transportable items that were very important to us. My husband emerged with a metal file of important papers such as our marriage license and life insurance policies. The firefighters found it odd, I'm sure, when I emerged with computer diskettes! But those floppy disks were the books I was writing at the time, including this one, and losing that irreplaceable work would have made the tragedy unbearable.

Can you be realistic?

I realized early on that writing the enduring classic or Great American Novel was way beyond my capabilities. Later on, while wading through the literature in education, I fantasized about writing a textbook more engaging than the ones I couldn't wait to sell back to the bookstore, even at a tenth of the purchase price. Later still, I dreamed of producing a scholarly book better than those that could not be read in one sitting without benefit of caffeine. Believing you can do at least as well, or perhaps even better, is the first step on your journey to becoming a book author.

Don't expect to go on a national book tour and make a small fortune when freelancers—those who attempt to make a living by writing alone—report an average annual income of around $4,000 (Winokur, 1999). The experiences of best-selling novelists are nothing like the book experiences of most professionals in specialized fields. Fantasies aside, what is it really like to write and publish a nonfiction book for a small audience?

Think of book publishing as having four phases. First, there is the fun part: talking about your idea, getting a proposal put together, signing the contract and going out to celebrate with your editor. Next, there is the drudgery part: getting up (or staying up) in the middle of the night, responding to all of the criticisms of reviewers, and struggling to write in addition to everything else you have to do or want to do. After that comes the torture part: proofreading for errors; responding to a copy editor's questions about clarity, spelling, consistency, and missing references; helping with the advertising and promotion. Finally, comes the waiting part: watching for the publisher's catalog, ripping open the carton to see the finished product (which always looks so pitifully small in comparison to the time expended); hoping for a respectable showing on the royalty statement, and wondering why on earth you made such sacrifices for such a paltry pay off. Given this sobering view, why would anyone agree to write a book?

SEVEN REASONS TO WRITE A BOOK

There are at least seven good reasons to write a nonfiction book for fellow professionals.

1. *Authors learn from writing books*—The scene was Dar es Salaam, Tanzania. I had been asked to deliver one of the four keynote addresses at the first East African Early Childhood Conference. On the last morning of the conference, a breakfast was planned for all of the presenters. Because I am a better writer than I a speaker, I approached this freewheeling panel discussion with some trepidation, particularly since the spring rains had ruptured the main water supply lines to the city and everyone was looking wilted and worried about body odor. To my complete surprise, the administrator who introduced the panel decided to play Devil's Advocate. He questioned the value of early childhood education, arguing, in effect, that children were better off at home in the company of their mothers. When he finished, I said, "Of course, I disagree," but I did not stop there. I had just finished writing a textbook on early literacy and a book about the teacher's role. As a result, I was a veritable reservoir of ideas, facts, and figures. I was able to support

my assertions with research and cite authors' names and dates, even though it was a totally impromptu situation. If I had not been so clear headed about my ideas from wrangling them into logical arguments and readable prose, I suspect that the outcome would have been much different. It is no mistake that, when we want to identify someone as a real authority, we use the expression that he or she "wrote the book on it." Writing a quality book is, without question, a self-directed education for the author.

2. *Book authors can make a contribution to their fields*—Sometimes, people read my nametag at conferences or find my e-mail address and say that they have read my book or that they like my writing. If it is a textbook, they might say that they've adopted the book for a class and that it helps them to teach more effectively. Some of my textbook publishers send me a list of all the colleges and universities where the book is in use, so I have some idea of how the book is being received by peers. Students also let me know if they found the book to be informative and readable. After two colleagues adopted my book for use in class, several students stopped by to introduce them-selves and tell me that they were learning from it and enjoyed the numer-ous examples used to illustrate key points. Making a contribution to your field, however small, can be gratifying.

3. *Book authors are invited (and often paid) to speak at conferences*—Over the past 10 years or so, I have had all-expense paid trips to such interesting locales as Belgium, Switzerland, Canada, France, Russia, Germany, and many others. In virtually every case, that invitation was predicated on the strength of what I have published. I tell my husband, "This is the professor's version of winning the lottery," because, even though I work very hard at these conferences, I feel that I am well compensated by the travel support alone. Often, I can combine business with pleasure and do some sight seeing along the way.

    Another type of indirect support for book writing may come from employers. If you are a faculty member with a book contract, you may be eligible to apply for a sabbatical. As a college professor, I have earned three one-semester sabbaticals at full salary to support my writing. Thus, writing books can have delightful secondary effects.

4. *Book authors get to know other book authors*—Taken as a group, those who write and publish nonfiction books are hard working, intelligent, thoughtful, inter-esting, and outspoken. Their company can be particularly pleasurable. When book authors get together, we talk about the frustrations as well as the sat-isfactions of writing. We talk about other projects we have in the works, possibilities for collaboration, and things we might want to write in the future. These conversations are among the ones I treasure most as a profes-sional, for there is much laughter and no small talk. As a book author, you become part of a network of writers; and, surely, this is one of book writ-ing's great rewards.

SINGLE-AUTHORSHIP AND CO-AUTHORSHIP OPTIONS

As an initial step in book writing, consider what role you will play as an author. Are you going to write the entire book? Will you collaborate with one or more authors? Will you contribute no more than a chapter or two and serve as editor for chapters written by other authors? Will you edit a book of previously published material? Each of these approaches to producing a book has advantages and disadvantages. If you are a single author, you will have more work to do but you can do it at a pace that suits you and you will receive full credit. This may be important to you if you are a faculty member and your tenure/promotion committee gives you more points for a single-authored work. If you are collaborating with one or more authors, you will have a bit less work to do, assuming that all goes well; but you will have to invest considerable energy in orchestrating the effort and share the credit. Many tenure and promotions committees at universities will require you to document exactly what your contributions to the project have been and to report a percentage of the work for which you were responsible. Although it is tempting to think, in divide-and-conquer fashion, "There will be ten chapters and each one of us will write five," the cohesiveness and consistency of the work will suffer if you or your co-author(s) do not read and edit one another's work. What will you do if your co-author fails to deliver quality work when you are counting on this book to further your career? Be practical about these issues and discuss them openly before problems arise, realizing that co-authorships can sour and and jeopardize the work. Nevertheless, due to the sheer magnitude of the project, a book proposal often involves more than one author. Figure 6.1 provides some guidelines for identifying co-authors and collaborating more successfully with them on book projects.

If you have an idea for a much-needed book and good contacts in the field, an edited book may give you some of the advantages of book authorship without the staggering responsibility of writing it entirely yourself. Some pointers on writing edited books from Christopher-Gordon Publishers are included in Figure 6.2.

TYPES OF BOOK PUBLISHING OPPORTUNITIES

Before I pick up my new glasses at the optometrist's, I always ask, "Is Barb there today?" because she usually can adjust them right the first time. It seems that others follow some sort of routine, but I always catch Barb really studying my face. Perhaps this is important because faces aren't truly symmetrical—I once saw a series of photographs of famous people in which one side of their faces was made the mirror image of the other, and all of them looked very strange! Add ears into the mix, and it is gets even more complicated. Personal preferences no doubt enter into the adjustments as well. I happen to like my glasses practically riveted to my nose, yet I know others who have made pushing glasses up their noses into a life-long habit. And so it is with book publishing. There are just a few editors who

Fair, Reliable, and Trustworthy

- What evidence do I have that this person will complete the book?

- Has this individual established a reputation for honorable, principled, ethical behavior?

- Can we achieve consensus regarding each collaborator's contributions and the allocation of credit prior to beginning the book?

Mutual Admiration and Respect

- Do I hold this person in high professional esteem?

- Does he or she have similar confidence in my capabilities?

- In the event that our book authorship roles change in unanticipated ways, could we renegotiate our writing arrangement?

Complementary Strengths

- Will the tasks and chapters that each of us agrees to undertake match our competence?

- What expertise, perspectives, or work style do I bring to this book that my partner(s) cannot?

- What will we accomplish as co-authors that would be exceedingly difficult to achieve independently?

Shared Commitment

- How important is this book to my career and to me?

- Does my collaborator have similar priorities?

- What will we do in the event that our book-length manuscript is rejected?

Figure 6.1   *Selecting a Co-Author*

We believe that edited volumes have several advantages:

- An edited volume can be written and produced in a very short time, meaning it can be in the marketplace quickly to meet developing needs.

- The format of an edited volume is more flexible; it encourages individual expression.

Figure 6.2   *The Edited Book: Christopher-Gordon Publishers*

Figure 6.2 *continued*

- No one person is responsible for a large amount of text.
- A chorus of opinions may offer a wider perspective on new information.
- Active contributors in a particular field are not limited to a single project. They are able to present their views in a number of forums.
- Edited volumes can be valuable signposts in the evolution of a line of research and practice.

The Editor's Role

- Editor works with publisher to define the target audience, select topics for inclusion in the book, and develops a list of potential contributors.
- Editor works with publisher to decide whether the editor, publisher, or both make the initial contact with contributors.
- Editor reads chapters as submitted and makes recommendations as follows: a) returns manuscripts to contributors for revision with deadline for resubmission; b) submits manuscripts to publisher for outside review; c) after review, advises contributor of changes needed and deadline for resubmission.
- Editor advises publisher in the event that a piece needs to be cut.
- Editor will keep publisher apprised of progress on project and may ask publisher to remind contributors of deadlines.
- Editor submits own material (one or two pieces) to publisher for review and revision suggestions.

The Publisher's Role

- Publisher invites contributors to participate if editor so wishes.
- Publisher sends confirmation of financial arrangements and schedule, along with guidelines explaining the overall project and the desired structure for the chapter.
- Publisher, upon advice of the editor, will guide and direct contributors in such matters as time lines, permissions, necessity and degree of revisions, manuscript preparations, or any matter pertaining to suitability of material or performance of contributor, including termination of chapter.

Source: *The Author's Guide*, Christopher-Gordon Publishers.

are a perfect fit for your book. They are the ones who are willing to study your proposal and be receptive, within reason, to your ideas and preferences.

After you have determined who is doing the writing and what your role in the project will be, the next step is deciding on the type of book project. Figure 6.3 highlights the main categories of nonfiction books professionals who would be likely to write for those in their fields.

If the book you imagine writing is an outgrowth of your work in professional training or teaching, you may have considered writing a textbook. If so, use the material in Figure 6.4 as a way to decide if this type of manuscript is suited to your strengths. The real challenge in textbook writing is to make your

---

- **University presses**—Outlets for book-length manuscripts, monographs, and journals. Nonprofit. Most underwritten to some extent by the institutions, private foundations, or government agencies. Some have endowments for books in certain fields. There are about 141 university presses in the United States (Lamb, 1997).

  Examples: Harvard University Press, State University of New York Press, Cambridge University Press, University of Kansas Press; for a complete list, *see The Association of American University Presses Directory, 2000-2001* (AAUP, 2000).

  Purpose: to disseminate knowledge, to make research accessible to a wider audience.

  Marketing: Usually through direct mail flyers and brochures. Larger publishers do exhibits at professional conferences.

  Review Process: Often has a faculty committee of reviewers.

  Misconceptions: University presses are concerned with salability even though they are nonprofit. They do not exist to publish the work of their own faculty. Many pay small royalties. They usually provide extensive review systems and editorial support.

  Products: Although these books may be adopted as college-level texts, that is not their primary purpose. In the main, university presses exist to publish research; and, because they are sponsored, they can afford to publish at least some works that may not have a large audience.

  ───────── ✿ ─────────

- **Commercial Scholarly Publishers** are profit-making scholarly publishers.

  Examples: Jossey-Bass, Greenwood, Springer-Verlag, Elsevier.

Figure 6.3 *Categories of Book Publishers*

Figure 6.3 *continued*

Review Process: Usually a small, in-house staff and reviewers from other parts of the country or world.

Marketing: Tend to have well-developed mailing lists, exhibits at professional conferences, and some advertising in journals.

Products: Scholarly works that are well documented and produced by leading authorities in a particular, sometimes highly specialized, field. May produce books in a series that are edited by prominent authors, such as yearbooks on particular topics.

———————————— ✿ ————————————

- **Tradebook Publishers** are usually publishing giants that produce books for general audiences. Often, after an author of scholarly works establishes a national reputation, she or he will produce a tradebook that makes the work understandable to general audiences.

Examples: HarperCollins, Basic Books, Simon & Schuster.

Purpose: To produce accessible works by great thinkers in the hopes of making *The New York Times* best-seller list.

Review Process: Tradebook publishers typically invite highly visible and acclaimed authors to write for general audiences.

———————————— ✿ ————————————

- **University Centers or Institutes**—Research and development centers where a variety of materials related to very specialized topics are produced. Such centers often begin as grants and frequently depend on various funding streams to continue.

Examples: University of Michigan Faculty Development Center, ERIC Clearinghouse.

Purpose: The main purpose of these publications is to disseminate specialized, current information to other academics who have an interest in a particular area of a field. Informational brochures, conference papers, and monographs on specialized topics are produced at a low cost, or mailed for the price of the postage as a service.

Products: Often these publications are not typeset but produced instead from camera-ready copy. Most of the publications from these centers and institutes are of the desktop publishing variety. They may not be casebound, but stapled or spiral bound. Increasingly, they are disseminated through electronic means.

continued on next page

Figure 6.3 *continued*

Review: Often accomplished by an in-house board.

Marketing: Usually done through internet, direct mail, and through center-sponsored conferences for clearly defined groups of scholars or general audiences.

- **Learned Societies/Association Publications**—Publishes for a specific organization and clearly specified professional audience.

Examples: National Council of Teachers of English, American Association of University Women, Phi Delta Kappa Fastback Series.

Purpose: To provide timely and authoritative information at a reasonable price for members and other audiences that would have an interest in the field.

Review process: Usually uses association members as reviewers.

- **Commercial Textbook Publishers**—Produce instructional materials for teachers and schools from basic education through postgraduate study.

Examples: Prentice Hall, Allyn & Bacon.

Purpose: To provide instructional materials for preservice and inservice professionals enrolled in college/university courses or in professional development workshops, institutes, etc.

Review Process: Uses outside experts who represent different regions of the country and different types of institutions to try and get the broadest acceptance possible.

Marketing: Usually has a sales force that calls on faculty to secure book orders.

Products: Books typically contain a wide variety of instructional materials (e.g., photographs, drawings, exercises, case material) and ancillaries (e.g., instructor's manual in hard copy and CD, Web-based study guides, audio or video tapes, and transparencies).

---

book enough like its peers and siblings in the book industry that it will be embraced by the audience, yet sufficiently distinctive that it will prompt a college instructor to abandon a satisfactory book in favor of your new (and presumably better) one. Above all, the successful textbook convinces instructors that it can help them to become more effective teachers.

THE BOOK PROPOSAL

One of my editors reported that it costs her company about $20,000 to produce a "plain vanilla" textbook (e.g., black and white inside, few photos and drawings, ordinary cover, about 300 pages). With that investment in mind, it is easy to see

---

1. *The leading edge*—You are a voracious reader who not only remains current in the field but also has a sense of where it might be headed next. After you review all the books that would compete with the one you are considering, you have a clear picture of an innovative approach that would represent a stride forward.

2. *The track record*—You have written several articles and/or book chapters and would like to take on a new challenge and pursue a topic in greater depth. You have a reputation for meeting deadlines, task persistence, and high standards, and quality work.

3. *The field-testing*—You have extensive notes and successful activities that have been used several times as the basis for teaching a particular course. You are a collector of all types of material related to the course, such as exemplary responses to various assignments produced by students.

4. *The beginner's mind*—You are skilled at explaining difficult or unfamiliar concepts in ways that even novices can understand. When students evaluate your teaching they comment on your repertoire of teaching techniques, ability to provide interesting examples, and commitment to fostering their progress as learners.

5. *The market analysis*—You have discussed textbook choices with long-distance colleagues at other institutions who teach a course similar to the one that you teach. They concur that it is difficult to find an acceptable text and most are using a text that is not particularly satisfactory, portions of multiple texts, or collections of readings.

6. *The specific approach*—You have spoken with sales representatives about books and approaches that other professionals in the field are seeking and prefer. You have analyzed other authors' approaches to your topic.

Figure 6.4 *Should You Write a Textbook?*

continued on next page

Figure 6.4 *continued*

7. *The thick skin*—You respond well to criticism and regard it as an opportunity to improve rather than an ego threat. You are accustomed to dealing with multiple perspectives on your work and possess sufficient confidence to rebound from less-than-glowing responses to your writing rather than abandoning the project.

8. *The work habits*—You are commonly perceived as a person who is well organized, knows how to prioritize, attends to the details, and is a bit of a perfectionist. Still, you manage to be very productive and do not allow yourself to get derailed when problems surface.

9. *The creative fluency*—You have good ideas, and lots of them. When you teach classes, even classes on the same basic topic, each one is distinctively different. You are the type of instructor who revises the syllabus every semester because you are constantly striving to improve the course and tend to generate new ideas time after time. When new courses are developed or existing courses undergo major revisions, you are often the person involved.

10. *The practical perspective*—You are not so immersed in theory and research that you fail to pursue the practical implications of scholarship. For you, the theory/research/practice connections are clear and important. You regard yourself, first and foremost, as a teacher and as an advocate for students.

11. *The right motivation*—You are entering into this endeavor with a desire to contribute to the field by helping others to teach a class more effectively. You are patient, or at least have learned to be, when it comes to attaining major professional development goals. You do not expect fame, fortune, and early retirement opportunities to emanate from this project.

12. *The interpersonal skills*—You know when to lead and when to follow. You have good sense about when to ask for assistance and who is most able to provide it.

13. *The persuasiveness*—If an opportunity to discuss your book project with an editor would arise, you could be clear about what your project is and why it is worthy of financial support. You would not lapse into lecture or bore the editor with a long-winded explanation of the intricacies of your field. Rather, you would approach the editor in a business-like way and succinctly sell your idea.

why the acquisitions editors, (those who find and sign authors, including the first timers), would be cautious about entering into such agreements. It would be entirely accurate to say that the acquisition editor's job depends upon making wise decisions about which projects to support. Some criteria for rendering such decisions include the following:

- Is the idea/project worth doing?

- Is it right for our publishing house's market niche?

- Is the book likely to be profitable?

- Can I convince my editorial colleagues to support the project, using material from the book proposal written by the author as support?

- Does the author or team seem to be equal to the challenge?

- Is the publisher willing to invest three to four years of work in this author and project?

Realize too that "Serious publishers undertake to publish an author, not only a book. We're looking for writers who will go on writing, and, ideally, grow and develop, not just for a person who is momentarily with book" (Vaughan, 1985, p. 48).

Before you begin writing, analyze the marketability of your idea. Some questions to ask before you begin include:

- *The Larger Context*—Am I aware of some national trends that might affect the content or type of book that would meet the needs of readers?

- *Competition*—Have I really studied what is out there, made a grid of features, and analyzed how my book might represent a stride forward while building on the strengths of previously published works?

- *Market*—If it is a textbook, how many postsecondary institutions offer a course for which my book is suitable as a primary text? If it is a scholarly book, how many people would be willing to spend their money on my book?

- *Reputation*—How well known are my work and my name? Is it realistic to think that faculty would choose my text over those already in existence? If a scholarly book, are libraries likely to include it in their standing orders?

Try using the questions in Figure 6.5 as a way to begin planning your nonfiction book.

Publishers of nonfiction for professional audiences generally do not require you to write the entire book before rendering a decision. In fact, they generally prefer to work with you as the book is being developed and obtain reviews along the way so that the project has a better chance of being well received by professionals in the field after it is published. It is customary to use a book proposal, brief plan for the book, and a couple of sample chapters as the basis for rendering this decision. This book proposal, often referred to as a book prospectus, has some key ingredients. Figure 6.6 is an overview of the components typically required in a book prospectus. Publishers have a set of more detailed and specific guidelines that generally can be requested in person at a conference booth, via mail or e-mail, or printed out from a website. Be certain to study the requirements prior to beginning your book prospectus and follow them carefully.

Do not allow yourself to be daunted by the prospectus. Focus on how your book represents an improvement over what is out there—a fresh perspective, an emerging need, a significant trend. Although many authors assume that it must be far more difficult to get a book contract than it is to publish in a professional journal, it is sometimes *easier* to get a book contract than it is to have an article accepted for the top journals in your field. Think about it logically. There are many professionals who will commit to producing an article-length manuscript and competition is keen for the few slots in any given year in the leading journal in your field. Your odds of getting a contract are about 1 in 45 (Smith, 1997);

---

1. The subject matter of my book is:

2. The focus, thesis, or approach of my book is:

3. The specific audience for my book would be:

4. This topic and focus are suited for this audience because:

5. This book is timely and would sell because:

6. Three publishers who produce this type of book are:

7. Other books written on this topic for my audience include:

8. Specific features of these competing books are:

9. The book I am proposing is different from or better than these books because:

10. The resources that I will need to produce the book include:

11. The book would probably be about ____ pages with ____ chapters.

12. Distinguishing features that make my book unique are:

13. My qualifications to write this book include:

Figure 6.5   *Planning a Nonfiction Book*

not that bad when your odds of winning the state lottery are about the same as being struck by lightning.

Post-contract casualties in book publishing, however, are high. Of the thousands of books awarded contracts, only about half will survive the rigors of authoring, critical review, and production processes (Smith, 1997). And, finally, even after books are published, only about 5-10% of those produced go into subsequent editions and become profitable for the authors (Smith, 1997). This puts acquisitions editors in the position of constantly trolling the professional waters for new projects. They dream of signing authors capable of dethroning the textbook dynasties already in place or authors capable of writing scholarly books that send readers running for their credit cards and checkbooks. And, unless these

---

Cover Letter

- (one page describing major thrust of the book)

Curriculum Vitae

Overview of the Book

- its uniqueness
- how it fulfills a particular need
- the specific audience and persuasive evidence that it is salable

Market Analysis of Competing Works

Annotated Table of Contents

Two Sample Chapters

Suggested Book Format (its physical appearance)

- approximate page length
- estimate of illustrations required
- special features (index, glossary, appendix, etc.)
- anything special that costs money (e.g., spiral binding, accompanying CD, etc.)

Timeline for Completion

- Be realistic about this—most books take at least two or three years from prospectus to print.

Previous Work Done on This Project

- Have materials been field-tested?
- Is some of the material already completed?

Figure 6.6 *Components of a Book Prospectus*

acquisitions editors net a few good ones, the many books for which they are responsible (their "list") will make an embarrassingly poor showing.

NEGOTIATING THE CONTRACT

For those who are seeking to publish a book for the first time, it is common to feel honored by any publisher's offer of a book contract. But if you make all of the sacrifices to write a book, you certainly will be disappointed if hardly anyone reads it because you signed with an obscure publisher who fails to promote it. And, if one publisher is sufficiently interested to offer a contract, chances are that some other publisher would be too. Author Tina Rosenberg explained how she made her choice between two publishers who were interested in her book on violence in Latin America:

> One publisher sat down with me and said, "We're going to make you a star." And the other publisher, [William] Morrow, sat down with me and said, "We're going to help you write the best book that you can write." I chose them. (cited in Lamb 1997, p. 300)

Approach your connection with a publisher with all of the caution you would exercise when purchasing an expensive piece of jewelry—choose someone reputable who has merchandise within your range. Find out something about the publisher before you sign. In the book industry, there are huge publishing houses with instant name recognition and massive advertising budgets as well as small presses that can barely afford to have a website. Both may be equally reputable, but one may be a much better match for your particular book project at this stage in your career. When researching a publisher, try the strategy outlined in Figure 6.6.

Some authors may feel that it is crass to discuss financial issues with a publisher or that arguing for better terms might cause the publisher to back out of the deal. Other authors are excessively suspicious, have an inordinate fear of someone pirating their ideas, and are convinced that they need at least one literary lawyer and one agent to protect them from the evil publishing industry. Somewhere between these two extremes is about right. Most publishers have a standard contract, not unlike the typical renter's agreement. Usually, it is written to the publisher's advantage without crossing the line into unethical or unscrupulous practices. Because the profit margins on books for fellow professionals are so small, the services of an agent or lawyer are seldom necessary. It will probably be sufficient to be well informed about publishing terminology (see Figure 6.8), to avoid being overly eager to sign, to discuss the contract with a successful and savvy author, and to negotiate a contract that is at least a bit better than the preprinted one. Make certain that the contract applies to the first edition only so that you can renegotiate if your book becomes successful. Contract terms should become more favorable to the

Look on the bookshelf—Scan the books on your shelf, at the bookstore, or at the library while paying attention to the publishers. Does the publisher you are considering have name recognition in your field? Does it produce books that are highly respected in the field?

Scan through the publisher's catalog—Is there a gap in their existing list that your book might fill? Or, are there several other titles with topics similar to your own and does it look like this publisher wants to corner the market on the topic you have in mind?

Visit the conference booth—Does the publisher have effective promotional materials and competent sales personnel? Does there appear to be interest on the part of the conference participants in the publications of this company?

Talk to your colleagues—Does the publisher have a good reputation for service, quality, and creativity? Are there several books that have made it past the first or second edition?

Chat with authors—Does the publisher get good reports from authors who have worked with them? Do they have editors with reputations for being ethical, supportive, innovative, and knowledgeable?

Check the Internet—Visit the publisher's web site. Is it of high quality? Look into the publisher's profitability by reviewing the company's stock history. Does the company appear to be solvent? Any talk of mergers or institutional reorganizations?

Consult reference tools—Refer to directories that provide information about various publishers (Bowker, 1999; Bowker, 2000, see www.bowker.com for the latest book directories) or general resources on the world of academic book publishing (Epstein, 2000; Germano, 2001). What is within the publisher's range of interest? What niches have they established or do they hope to establish? What other books have been published on the topic? Check www.booksinprint.com.

Figure 6.7 *How to Check Up on a Potential Publisher*

author as your publisher's risk is lowered. Figure 6.9 offers suggestions on contracts and copyright issues.

DEVELOPING THE BOOK

Now that you have secured a contract, there is more work to be done than you can begin to imagine. At times, you will feel like the young girl in the fairy tale

Financial Terminology

The **gross** is the total amount that the book earns. The **net** is the money that is left after all of the expenses are paid, such as paper, printing, advertising, paying the sales and editorial staff, and so forth. The net is usually about 30-40% of the gross. Suppose that a publisher charges $40.00 for a book. Of that amount, about $9 goes to reviewing, design, paper, printing, production and editing; $7 goes to pay sales reps, produce advertising, marketing, mailing, and free desk copies; $4.00 goes to bookseller's profit. This means that if the advertised price of the book is $40.00, the net is approximately $12.00.

Royalties refer to the profit share given to the author. Using the net example above, if you get a fairly typical royalty rate of 10% and have one co-author, you and your co-author earn $1.20 per book and your share is 60 cents per book. Read the contract carefully—rates are often lower on international sales or direct sales, you get no royalties on used books, and many professional associations do not pay authors royalties. Be cautious, also about signing away electronic rights or translations. If the book is a huge success, you may want greater flexibility in negotiating those royalty rates. Make sure that your contract would allow you to renegotiate in the event that the book goes into a subsequent edition.

A **grant-in-aid** is money that the publisher pays to support the work (e.g., money toward a computer) or as an incentive to sign (e.g., money to attract an author with another offer). Grants-in-aid are sometimes used to compensate the author for ancillary projects (e.g., producing a computer disk to accompany a book). Grants-in-aid are not deducted from royalties later on, they are an outright payment. However, if you fail to produce the book, you may be obligated to pay them back.

An **advance against royalties** is simply a mechanism for getting some money to you without waiting until 6 months to a year after the book is published. It is a deduction from future book earnings.

Deductions against royalties are sometimes an unpleasant surprise for authors. Who will be responsible for contacting other authors and securing their permission to use their work? Who will pay for it? Who will render the line drawings? Who will supply the photographs, if any, and at what cost? Who will index the book and how much will it cost? Who will produce ancillaries, if any, such as a companion website, instructor's guide, accompanying computer disk, etc.? Publishers often deduct all of these expenses from the royalties and they can become quite expensive—a book indexing costs about $800.

Figure 6.8 *Contract Terminology*

1. Remember that this is a business, no matter what publisher you are dealing with or how delighted you are to be awarded a contract. Think about which publisher is well positioned in the market to promote your particular work and sell it successfully. Do not allow yourself to be flattered by any offer and sign with any company who offers to publish.

2. Treat every contract as a rough draft or work in progress. Just because it is printed does not mean it cannot be changed. If you sign a "boilerplate" contract, you probably are not getting the best offer for your work. If there is a clause in the contract you cannot abide by, cross it out and initial it. Some publishers have a "noncompeting work" clause that prohibits you from writing another book on the same topic for a specified number of years. You may not want to agree to that condition.

3. Realize that those who write contracts give themselves the advantage without doing anything unethical or illegal. Just as a salesperson at a car dealership will cheerfully allow you to pay full sticker price for a new car, publishers will allow you to write a book with the bare minimum of support.

4. Speak up for your own good and that of the project. Think about what you will reasonably need in order for the book to be successful and argue for that. Will the book need line art rendered by an artist? Photographs? Supplemental materials? Do you need technology support to produce a website?

5. Learn publisher's terminology. An advance is money paid to the author before the book is written, but there is an important distinction between an advance against royalties (this means it comes out of your royalties later on, after all other expenses are paid) and a grant-in-aid (that is a sum of money paid to support you that is not deducted from future earnings). If, for some reason, you don't produce the book, you may be obligated to pay back an advance. Royalties are a small percentage of the net, not the gross, earned from the book. But there are different types of royalties. For instance, you may want an escalation clause in case the book is wildly successful. It would allow you to earn royalties at a higher rate after a specified number of copies has been sold. The royalty schedule may be different for books sold in different ways (e.g., direct sales at a conference) or in different formats (e.g., electronic) or translated into different languages (e.g., Chinese). In today's publishing environment, think carefully about signing away electronic rights.

Figure 6.9 *Suggestions on Contracts and Copyright Law*
continued on next page

Figure 6.9   *continued*

6. Think about your rights as an author. If your book goes out of print, who owns it? Some publishers retain the rights but you may want them to revert to you as soon as the book goes out of print. Contracts sometimes include what publishers call a "kill fee." This means that, if the book you produce is "unacceptable" to the publisher, they may pay you a specified amount or allow you to keep the advance but never publish the book.

7. Consider the liabilities you may encounter. Most book contracts make you responsible for things that are "scandalous, libelous, or unlawful" so be particularly careful about getting everyone's permission to use any of their words or work, even if it is very complimentary, in your view and even if the person is a friend or family member. An excellent resource on permission is Allyn & Bacon's Author Center at (www.ablongman.com/author/1,2185,,00.html). It contains sample permission letters, a model release form, and other useful information. Many book authors begin by imagining all of the material they will collect from others' work and include, but the permissions fees could leave you penniless. You will want to follow the "fair use" copyright guidelines (www.loc.gov/copyright and http://www.benedict.com/).

As a rough estimate, you can use about 50 words from an article and about 500-1,000 from a book, depending on the overall length and providing that you give credit. (For more on libel and copyright issues, see Jassin & Schechter, 1998; and Copyown: A resource on Copyright Ownership for the Higher Education Community at (http://www.inform.umd.edu/CompRes/NEThics/copyown/). And the position statement of the National Humanities Alliance, Committee on Libraries and Intellectual Property at (http://www.nhalliance.org/ip/ip_principles.html).

"Rumplestiltskin" who is locked in a room full of straw and directed to spin it into gold. Surrounded by piles of books, papers, and notes, you are expected to weave them together with your experience and generate a book. There will be times when you despair of this ever happening. There will be times when your editor calls to inquire about the status of the manuscript and you feel compelled to produce a litany of excuses or perhaps even lie in hopes that it will force you to get back to work. Annie Dillard (1999) captures the relationship between author and book when she writes.

> I do not so much write a book as sit up with it, as a dying friend. During visiting hours, I enter its room with dread and sympathy for its many disorders. I hold its hand and hope it will get better.
>
> This tender relationship can change in a twinkling. If you skip a visit or two, a work in progress will turn on you.
>
> A work in progress quickly becomes feral. It reverts to a wild state overnight. . . . It is a lion you cage in your study. As the work grows, it gets harder to control; it is a lion growing in strength. You must visit it every day and reassert your mastery over it. If you skip a day, you are, quite rightly, afraid to open the door to its room. You enter its room with bravura, holding a chair at the thing and shouting, "Simba!" (p. 52)

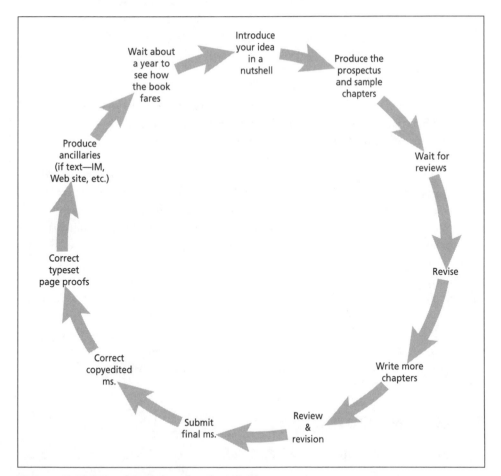

Figure 6.10 *The Book Production Cycle*

More often than not, you will fall behind schedule, particularly if it is your first book. Even though your contract says that the publisher can withdraw the offer if you fail to meet the deadlines, most editors expect delays and will forgive you, unless you are on their editorial calendar to go to press. "Why isn't the manuscript ready? Because every book is more work than anyone intended" (Vaughan, 1985, p. 43). Expect that you will tell yourself (and maybe even assure your editor) that chapter 4 is ready to submit and then be ready to scrap it after reading it on a dreary afternoon. You will beg others to read it for you and then be irritated when they fail to get your meaning or suggest a rewrite.

Book production is a roller coaster ride of hurrying up alternated with unbearable waiting—hurry to create the prospectus, then wait for the contract; hurry to complete the manuscript, then wait for the reviews; hurry to make final corrections, then wait for the book to be published. As Vaughan (1985) notes:

> Among the most formidable problems an author faces are the silences: first, your own in the long process of writing the book; second, the silence that follows the first submission of the manuscript; then that between the occasional communiqués from the editor. Why is your editor so silent and so bafflingly slow? (p. 44)

In the interest of survival, your editor is going to move quickly on sure things (well established authors going to subsequent editions) and bright hopes (new projects with rave reviews). If your book is neither, it is a long shot and will get a modicum of polite ministrations from the editorial staff. One publisher I know has a rating system for books that ranges from *AAAA* grade down to a *C-,* based on market size and advertising budget. Most editors have a group of authors for whom they are responsible that would rival a big city social worker's caseload. Under these conditions, editors will understandably lavish more attention on the *AAAA* book. Not one of my books has hit those top categories, but it doesn't really matter. Fortunately, book royalties are not my sole source of income.

Many authors bail out of book projects after the first round of reviews. Still flushed with pride over being awarded a contract, they expect unconditional acceptance and accolades from reviewers. Instead, the response is critical and challenges them to rethink portions of the work. What standards do reviewers use to render these decisions? Figure 6.11 is an example of specific criteria for evaluating book proposals made to Christopher-Gordon, the publisher of this book.

EVALUATING OUTCOMES

A prolific textbook author remarked, "I don't write textbooks with the expectation of making big money. If I clear enough in royalties to take the kids down in Disney World in Florida for a week, I'm satisfied." Authors who are considering writing a book while visions of six-figure royalty checks dance in their heads may be shocked by this blasé attitude toward profit. The reality is that just about any book you might write for fellow professionals is a small market and, even if you could capture a major share of the market, there is about a 90% chance that it won't make big money. In a recent review of the business of scholarly communication, the researchers concluded that "any excess of revenues over expenses is typically dependent upon the profits earned on the last 10-15% of copies sold beyond a specific break-even point. Many serious books and journals reach such a break-even point only after a number of years—and a disconcertingly large percentage never meet it at all" (Abel, 1999, p. 4).

---

1. What is your overall opinion of the material? Does it appear to meet a specific need?

2. Who is the primary audience for this type of material? Will the intended audience find the book useful? How do you see the book being used?

3. How does the philosophy behind the book fit into current thinking about teaching and learning? Is the book's structure helpful? Do you think there is much redundancy across chapters?

4. Are there any topics that have been omitted? To your way of thinking, are these omissions critical; that is, will their absence adversely affect the sale of the book, or do they outweigh the positive features of the material?

5. What is your opinion of the writing? Is the author writing for the intended audience?

6. What, in your opinion, are the material's greatest strengths? Please be specific. What are the greatest weaknesses, and what would you do to strengthen those areas?

7. Do you think you would use the finished book based on the material you have seen? How? Would you recommend the book to your colleagues? Why or why not? Are there any organizational devices that would make the book more useful?

8. Which books, if any, do you see as this book's primary competitors? Does this project compare favorably? Unfavorably? How?

9. Are there any particular chapters that are exceptionally good, or on the other hand any that you find lacking in comparison to the others? What ones, and why do they stand out to you?

10. Is the title appropriate? Does it accurately describe the book's content?

Figure 6.11   *Reviewer Questions—Christopher-Gordon Publishers*

Books involve so much time and effort that authors' feelings about books that fail are particularly intense. Most book authors have a few war stories to share about bad editing, paltry royalties, and insufficient promotion of a book, questionable policies, or inappropriate cover designs. Some of the more common complaints about publishers are reflected in the following comments I have heard from book authors:

- "My book came out at the wrong time. I made my deadlines, but the publisher didn't make theirs and now I've missed the fall book orders."

- "The publisher did not advertise it enough. One time in a direct-mail catalog is not sufficient."

- "There were hidden costs—indexing, photographs, artwork. In my first royalty statement, *I* owed *them* money."

- "After I put the manuscript in the mail and I thought it was finished, there were constant demands on my time."

- "I didn't realize that it was such a small market. I had visions of selling about 20,000 copies of my textbook. Instead I sold only about 5,000 in four years—and this, I later learned, is considered a respectable showing for my highly specialized field."

What follows are the most common sources of conflict between editors and book authors, identified by Luey (1995), which I elaborate on here:

Fundamental differences in perspective—Academics are sometimes put off by nonacademics who are making decisions about their works. When I observe professors at conferences standing at the publisher's display booth and bending an editor's ear about their ideas for books, I have to laugh. The academics seem to think that they are at the doctoral exams and are dropping names of theorists and researchers right and left. Meanwhile, the editor is a tough-minded business person who is trying to figure out if the book will sell. The content expertise that the professor is so intent upon displaying is, in the editor's view, a given. It need not be displayed, particularly to a person who may be disinterested in the technical aspects of the field and is focused on the bottom line. It is preferable to listen to the editor's read on the market, then pitch your idea briefly or even wait until you have mulled it over a bit more.

Ignorance about the world of publishing—To work with book editors successfully, treat them neither as disciplinary colleagues (most of them aren't) nor as personal friends. Rather, try to appreciate their situation of being held accountable for the success of their book list. Don't expect them to ignore the contract and do you a favor. If there is a form of support you'll need to do the project, get it in writing. On the other hand, don't be so accommodating that you are working for nothing. When websites for textbooks first became all the rage, one of my publishers was anxious to have one and argued that it would help sales. I said, agreeably, "Sure, I can produce the material for a website but only if you do all the technical part. And you'll have to compensate me, because it's not in my contract." Authors who are particularly careful about what they sign in everyday life are sometimes so elated about being published that they don't read their contracts carefully. Then, when publishers make a charge against their royalties for such things as the author's last minute alterations to the final proofs, the indexing, and the photographs, the author is incensed. My first royalty check for a book was a negative number. In other words, after all of these charges were made, I owed them money (fortunately, they just carried it over until the book made some money and I didn't have to write them a check!). Find out what is reasonable in your field by talking with authors who are willing to discuss such matters openly. Compare the contracts offered by different publishers to find your best offer. And, above all, do some homework on the publishing industry before you sign.

Illusions about money—When it comes to books, authors too often rely on what they read in the newspaper about large advances and huge royalty checks paid to authors who sell millions of copies, like John Grisham. Writing for a group of highly specialized professionals in your field is quite another matter. As Luey (1995) explains,

> An author whose book is priced at $40.00 and whose royalty is 10 percent figures, "$4.00 per book, and they're printing 1,500, so I should get $6,000.00." Unfortunately, the royalty may be paid on net receipts (20 to 40 percent less than gross), at least 100 copies will be given away free for reviews and publicity, and not all the other copies will be sold. When the first royalty check arrives and the author gets, say, $1,500— knowing that the first year is probably the best—disappointment sets in. (p. 6)

Where does each dollar go after a book is published? Below is a general breakdown of expenses based upon the retail price of the book:

Printing	10%
Distribution	40-65% (depending on the channel used)
Author Royalty	5-10%
Ongoing Promotion	10%-15%
Overhead and Profit	20-35% (Ortman, 1998)

My doctoral advisor was the author of one of the best-selling research design books, and I assumed that he was making big bucks from his book but he said not. Now I know why. How many total people in America would take an advanced research course? Not many. That makes his book, no matter how popular or wonderful, a small market book. Much of what professionals write for other professionals falls into the small market category. So, even if it were possible to capture the entire market—and it isn't—you still could not make large sums of money.

Writing books for professionals is much more of a service and a labor of love than a get-rich-quick scheme. You don't often see professors retiring early on royalties unless they have written a hugely successful text for an introductory course or a widely read book for general audiences. Why? Because it usually takes large market success to make serious money, which I will arbitrarily define as more than the price of a new economy car, after taxes. Before an editor signs you, he or she has already "run the numbers" to estimate how much your book will cost to manufacture and promote, how many copies would need to be sold in order to make a profit, and anticipated sales for the first year. When you discuss your contract with a publisher, ask how many copies they plan to produce for the first printing. It would not be unusual for it to be less than 5,000 for a small market textbook or 2,500 for a scholarly book. Although editors may tantalize you with a story about their best-selling author in the *AAAA* category who earned a "six-figure royalty check," it is exceedingly rare for that mystifying royalty statement to yield anything beyond a couple of thousand twice a year.

Royalties aside, writing a successful text is an achievement of the first order. Approximately one-third of all new college-level textbook titles published in a given year fail; another third will eventually make enough money to remain in print for about three years, but not warrant a revision; and only the final one-third of college texts will become profitable and will need to be revised regularly to maintain their market shares (Smith, 1997).

My first textbook demanded bushels of time, destroyed reams of paper, and burned out a dot-matrix printer. Still, I am pleased about this book. It has been in print for 10 years—something publishers refer to as its shelf life—and has so far survived to a third edition.

Resentment about editorial changes—Another source of conflict between editors and authors is the editing process. There are some authors who think they are done when the final chapters have been printed off and, from here on, the editorial staff will take over. Nothing could be further from the truth. When their book-length manuscript returns, it frequently looks as though a horde of millipedes with combat boots has marched through it. There will be what is delicately referred to as author queries written in the margins (e.g., "You mention a final solution. This seems slightly redundant and may also offend readers, given Nazi Germany's use of that terminology.") and matters of fact that may send you scurrying back to the library ("The references listed in red are cited in the chapter but do not appear in the your reference list. Please provide. Those without a check mark do not appear in the chapter. Cite or delete.", or "On page 15, you have Smyth, in the references, it is Smythe. Which is it?"). Even if you are the type who is outraged by an error printed in a book, you will be amazed by how many errors can creep into your book despite all of your attention to details.

There may be sections that you inadvertently repeated or places where you need to provide additional material. Sometimes, authors are furious with their changes in their writing. The sentiment goes something like, "How dare they change my words!" but when you sign a book contract, you agree to editing.

THE FUTURE OF BOOK PUBLISHING

In any given year in America, approximately 100,000 books are published, yet only a few hundred make it to the best-seller list (Ortman, 1998). Book publishing is a fiercely competitive market in which only the strong survive. The emergence of the electronic book or e-book will no doubt affect how readers obtain, pay for, and store their personal/professional libraries. The e-book is an electronic device weighing no more than a small dictionary that has a storage capacity equivalent to about 8,000 pages of text.

Suppose, for instance, that a college teacher can't seem to locate a good overall textbook. One alternative is to order several books for the class and use portions of each, a decision that, due to the rising cost of textbooks, is not all that attractive. Instructors confronted with the task of locating the best reading material for students sometimes take the task of compiling a collection of journal articles and book chapters into a course packet sold to students at the local copy center. These packets have drawbacks as well. For the instructor, they are time-consuming to assemble and require releases from copyright holders; for the students, these packets are cumbersome to carry around, costly due to permissions fees, and poorly bound so that they tend to fall apart mid-semester. But if an instructor had the option to use whatever chapters he or she wished from books and students paid to download only what they used into their e-books, it would put a whole new wrinkle on textbooks as we know them. The e-book's appeal is greater still now that readers can highlight and make notes on the text using an electronic stylus without adding to the glut of used books in the process. The e-book is apt to bring the competitive nature of book publishing to an even higher level of intensity and to cause major changes in the book publishing industry. Right now, e-books are limited to best sellers but predictions are (as with other technological advances) e-books will gain popularity, become more affordable, and enjoy wide use.

Whether the book you dream of publishing someday is in traditional paper format or an e-book, this chapter was designed to coach you on how to write a book that will secure a contract and see your book project through to completion.

CONCLUSION

While attending a reception for authors and editors, an author of a book chapter for a book I edited cornered me. She let me know in no uncertain terms that I had no right to suggest that the chapter be condensed. Understand that she had been asked to provide (and I quote from the letter) "a 12-point print, Courier type, double-spaced manuscript with one-inch margins on all sides and an absolute maximum of 20 pages, including references." What she submitted was a 9-point print, single-spaced paper of about 28 pages. That would mean that it was nearly twice as long as it needed to be, after converting it to the desired format. Feeling much like a Saint Bernard dog interacting with a feisty toy Poodle, I stood firm that the chapter was too long. But, the battle had not been won, so she took another run at me, this time letting me know that the huge section I had directed her to cut had been published as a journal article in a prestigious publication. "Congratulations," I said. "That was my point. It didn't belong in your book chapter." Like it or not, editors edit. They have the right to operate on your work or to direct you to alter it to fit the book. You have the right to refuse and pull your work out of production.

Before you write a nonfiction book for fellow professionals, try visiting a major bookseller on the Internet and type in the titles and authors of some of the most respected books in your field, then take a look at the sales rank. Chances are, there will be hundreds of thousands of books more popular than the ones that are instantly familiar to practically everybody in your field. Check also on the availability. Many nonfiction books require a special order or even are out of print—both clear signs that they are far from hot sellers. According to the American Booksellers Association, about 80% of the books are read by 10% of the population. When you add professional credentials to the mix, the market shrinks even further. So nonfiction book publishing in your field, far from being the glamorous national book tour activity we see in the media, is mostly a quiet pursuit made tolerable by the support of competent editorial staff members and the satisfactions of a job well done.

Returning to the question that opened this chapter, could you write a book? Perhaps the best response comes from Issac Asimov (1987) the extraordinarily prolific science author: "So it *can* be done, but not easily, I warn you, not easily" (p. 142).

REFERENCES

AAUP (2000). *The Association of American University Presses directory, 2000-2001.* Chicago: University of Chicago Press.

Abel, R. (1999). The national enquiry into scholarly communication—Twenty years after. *Publishing Research Quarterly,* 15(1), 4-20.

Asimov, I. (1987). *How to enjoy writing.* New York: Walker.

Bowker, R. R. (1999). *American book trade directory.* New Providence, NJ: Author.

Bowker, R. R. (2000). *International literary market place.* New Providence, NJ: Author.

Dillard, A. (1999). *The writing life.* (2d ed.) New York: HarperCollins.

Epstein, J. (2000). *Book business: Publishing: Past, present and future.* New York: W.W. Norton.

Germano, W. P. (2001). *Getting it published: A guide for scholars and anyone serious about serious books.* Chicago: University of Chicago Press.

Harner, J. L. (1996). *MLA directory of scholarly presses in language and literature.* New York: Modern Language Association.

Jassin, L. J., & Schechter, S. C. (1998). *The copyright permission and libel handbook.* New York: John Wiley.

King, S. (2000). *On writing: A memoir of the craft.* New York: Scribner.

Lamb, B. (1997). Booknotes: America's finest authors on reading, writing, and the power of ideas. New York: Times Books/Random House.

Luey, B. (1995). *Handbook for academic authors* (3rd ed.). New York: Cambridge University Press.

Maslow, A. H. (1998). Toward a psychology of being (3rd ed.). New York: John Wiley and Sons.

Ortman, M. (1998). *A simple guide to marketing your book.* Brainerd, MN: Wise Owl Books.

Smith, P. A. (1997). The art and agendas of writing a successful textbook proposal. In J. M. Moxley & T. Taylor (Eds.), *Writing and publishing for academic authors* (2nd ed.) (pp. 91-109). Lanham, MD: Rowman & Littlefield.

Vaughan, S. S. (1985). Letter from the editor. In G. Gross (Ed.), *Editors on editing: An inside view of what editors really do* (pp. 39-53). New York: Harper & Row.

Winokur, J. (Ed.) (1999). *Advice to writers.* New York: Vintage/Random House.

CHAPTER 7

---　❧　---

Learning to Work With Reviewers and Editors

---　❧　---

When you can publish your book online for a mere $120, why would authors subject themselves to the potential ego threat of the peer review process? In the frequently asked questions section of one company web site that promises to publish your work for a fee, they offer what must surely be Nirvana for the frustrated author: unconditional acceptance. Furthermore, they promise not to edit your work in any way. For authors who are still coping with the lingering sting of rejection, this may seem like a solution. Yet during a cursory look at the company's promotional material posted online, I found three glaring spelling and grammatical errors and, presumably, they *did* proofread that copy. Evidently, any language errors that paying customer/authors make would remain in the electronic book in perpetuity. Minor flaws aside, what about the content, the approach, the writing style? If no one reads the manuscript prior to widely disseminating it, the work is likely to have about the same level of literary appeal as a hastily composed e-mail, as well as all the language faux pas.

Thinking as readers for a moment, if we are given the choice between investing our reading time in a book that is obviously flawed and another book on the same topic that is reputedly good, most of us will choose the latter. That is why, when you go to the airport bookstore, you are apt to see selections limited to *The New York Times* bestseller list or Oprah's Book Club. Few readers have the time to sift through every imaginable publication, so they rely on the recommendations of others. Another consideration with paying to publish an electronic book is the limitation of the format. Perhaps it is due to our prior experience with the printed page, but the reading attention span of people who read on screen seldom exceeds the equivalent of a couple of pages of typewritten text. Reading on screen is deceptive. It makes a mere paragraph seem like a full page so that only the most determined reader could read an entire book that way or would go to the expense and trouble of printing it out. And, if nobody is going to read it, why publish your book, electronically or otherwise?

Perhaps you have heard the words "vanity press," used to describe the practice of authors paying someone to "publish" their manuscripts. This can be accomplished by any print shop willing to make copies of a bound book for a price or by paying a fee to have the work posted on the Internet. The goal of vanity press publishing is twofold: first, to generate a product to display on the coffee table (or computer screen); and second, to circumvent rejection or criticism.

What is missing here is an essential dynamic in establishing the credibility of a source: the process of peer review. Without it, one source is no more authoritative than the next. In fact, this is one of the ways in which the Internet has changed the communication environment. Just about anybody can post a website; my nephew had one in kindergarten. In this communication context, the issue is no longer simply locating information, for that is the simplest of tasks requiring the most minimal intelligence. The issue now becomes evaluating the relative merits of myriad sources with respect to accuracy and authoritativeness. That is where editors and reviewers come in.

EDITORS, REVIEWERS, AND THE GATEKEEPER'S ROLE

Whenever accomplished and not-so-accomplished authors congregate, the conversation often turns to complaints about reviewers and editors. Yet, as a writer, you will need to "Be interested in getting your work *im*proved, not *ap*proved" (Trimble, 2000, p. 12). As the saying goes, there is good and bad in everything, and this is no less true of reviewers and editors. The trouble is, that you may not know the difference at first.

Many writers start out treating their writing for publication like a class assignment. They expect reviewers and editors to suggest topics, tell them exactly how to rewrite a flawed manuscript, or offer the equivalent of a gold star. Early in my textbook writing career, I remember chatting with my co-author prior to a conference call with the editor. Our view of the reviews was that we had two "good" ones, one on the fence, and one "bad" one. One reviewer had been completely uncritical in accepting the work; we were counting this one as the best of the reviews. Imagine our surprise when, while talking to our editor, she remarked, "That review was not helpful. We won't use her again." From our editor's perspective, that reviewer had failed to fulfill her role of providing criticism to improve the work. We would not have been awarded a contract if the idea had no merit, so getting "passing" or "failing" grades was not the issue. The goal was to make the book good enough that professors would switch from their current text to ours, and that would require critical feedback from reviewers with different backgrounds and teaching styles. To gain some insight into how reviewers evaluate your work, see Figure 7.1.

These gatekeepers we refer to variously as editors, reviewers, referees, editorial board members, peer reviewers, and copy editors perform several useful functions, including:

- Providing a fresh perspective on the topic

- Reminding the author of how a particular audience might respond to an idea

- Noting holes in the argument

Has the author . . .

- selected a subject that is truly significant and worthwhile and provided a sound rationale for it?

- accounted for the characteristics and interests of the intended audience?

- established the tone most appropriate for the purpose and audience?

- marshaled authoritative evidence from both current and classic sources?

- demonstrated logical thinking and presented a clear argument?

- shored up any gaps in content development and reasoning?

- organized the manuscript effectively?

- established a professional style and tone?

- followed the conventions for documenting sources?

- produced cohesive paragraphs?

- provided transitions from one paragraph and section to the next?

- formatted the document effectively?

- demonstrated familiarity with the publisher's requirements?

Adapted from Moxley (Ed.) (1995). *Publish, don't perish: The scholar's guide to academic writing and publishing* (pp. 20-26). Westport, CT: Greenwood Press.

Figure 7.1 *How to Think Like a Reviewer*

- Suggesting pertinent sources of information of which the author may be unaware

- Recommending ways to make a point clearer and more concise

- Pointing out errors of fact

- Preventing uninformed or misinformed authors from embarrassing themselves

- Identifying mechanical errors in spelling, punctuation, or grammar

- Identifying errors in referencing style (e.g., American Psychological Association)

When I first attempted to write a book, I was devastated by the criticism that came back. I vividly remember sitting in my car reading the reviews in the post office parking lot, unable to wait the 15 minutes it would take to drive home. One reviewer had missed the whole point of the book, or so it seemed, and wanted it to be heavily historical. A second was lukewarm about it. The third saw potential, but recommended major revisions. I was afraid to call the editor, convinced that she would want to abandon the project entirely. Yet, in the midst of all that hard-to-take criticism, one reviewer had written: "This section is strong. Write the entire book in this voice and style." I doubt that this anonymous peer reviewer had any idea how helpful and powerful that comment turned out to be. I had been given permission to be myself as a writer rather than merely reporting on what I had read, a style I had acquired during graduate school. The "best part" section happened to be a story about my niece's response to a picture book read aloud and this reviewer urged me to write my own stories.

Eventually, I mustered up sufficient courage to call the editor. She had not given up on me after all. She, too, gave me permission to write in my own voice; and, oddly enough, my confidence was bolstered because I knew she would never allow me to publish a bad book.

Of course, telling an author who repeatedly gets negative feedback that reviewers and editors perform a useful function is like telling a criminal that police officers are community helpers. Still, the fact remains. Some editors and reviewers are extraordinarily intelligent, possess incredible market savvy, and are especially helpful in improving your work. I laughed out loud when I read Arthur Plotnick's (1982) criteria for selecting an editor: "What kind of person makes a good editor? When hiring new staff, I look for such useful attributes as genius, charisma, adaptability, and disdain for high wages" (p. 1).

What is the editor's skill? My father's craft as an auto technician offers a useful analogy. When I was growing up, my father was a mechanic who worked at a Pontiac garage by day and did repairs and customizing in the evenings and on weekends. By the time I was in college, he was an instructor for Chrysler Corporation who traveled around the globe to train mechanics to do such things as repairing auto air conditioning systems or rebuilding transmissions. As a young adult, I would pull in the driveway and see him, head inclined to the ground, listening to my car. It was not uncommon for his initial greeting to be something like, "It's idling rough. Pop your hood." Good editors are attuned to writing in the way that my father was attuned to a car's operational systems. I can remember people marveling after attending a workshop with former *Phi Delta Kappa* editor Stanley Elam, because he took pages of their work, put them on transparencies, and edited it skillfully on the spot. I'd like to think that after two and a half decades of working on manuscripts and reading literally hundreds each year, I can perform the equivalent of this automotive technician wizardry on writing by figuring out what it needs to run smoothly.

Luey (1995), a university press editor, offers a useful perspective on the role of editors and reviewers in academic publishing: "Their purpose is not merely to screen out bad articles but also to recognize good ones and help move articles from the unacceptable category into the acceptable. . . . Certainly not all criticism is constructive, but much of it is" (p. 18). Often, you will hear published authors talk about the need to develop a thick skin where criticism is concerned. That is because, if every suggestion is treated as a barb, it can derail your work. After about 25 years of writing for publication, I have developed a hide like a rhinoceros when it comes to criticism. So should you.

EDITORS AND REVIEWERS IN ACADEMIC PUBLISHING

When writers hear the word, "editor," they frequently draw upon Hollywood images of posh New York offices and warm, supportive relationships in which the editor "discovers" an author and functions as a powerful mentor for that writer's development. Usually, an editor is more like "a slightly helpful, businesslike acquaintance" and, less often, "a valuable friend or, on rare occasions, a deeply involved collaborator" (Vaughan, 1985, p. 40). As a journalist for *The New York Times* and book author notes,

> I think it depends on the writer what role the editor plays. Obviously I came at the book with a lot of writing experience. I wasn't in any way a novice. But at the same time my editor, I think, played a very important role in helping me with organization. . . . it's very helpful to have someone say, "You know the second half of chapter 5 would really make a perfect first half of chapter 3. . . . " It's only an outsider that can make those recommendations for you. (Friedman cited in Lamb 1997, pp. 288-289)

An editor can be full-time professional employed by a publisher or, as is the case with many academic journals, a field editor. Usually, it is only the widely circulated journals that can afford the services of a full-time editor. For most publications with relatively small circulations, the services of a field editor are sought.

Typically, a field editor is someone like me who already has a full-time job at the university or elsewhere and who does the journal editing as a sideline. A field editor may or may not be compensated. For some professional journals, serving as editor is a short-term volunteer position that is a form of service to the organization. Book editors for large, commercial publishers (such as textbook publishers) tend to be full-time; for small publishers, they are sometimes free-lanced, meaning that they are hired to edit individual books as piecework rather than as permanent staff members. Simply knowing how editors probably function in your field may help you to understand why they will not rewrite for you or engage in heroic efforts to save a manuscript from rejection.

Who are the editors and reviewers for a specific publication? Their names are no secret. Most journal publications list their names prominently in the publication; often this information is printed on the inside of the front cover or on the first page. Usually, the first person to look at your work is the editor. Most journal editors give the work a quick scan prior to sending it out for review by professionals in the field. The work could be rejected immediately if they consider the work to be "illiterate, hopeless, or out of the publisher's range of interest" (Targ, 1985, p. 6). There are also less incriminating reasons for rejection, however. I sometimes reject works that are on topics we have recently covered or because I have such a backlog of manuscripts awaiting publication that it would be almost two years before the piece would appear.

Many new authors are shocked to learn that the people who are editors may not have specialized training in their fields. Editors for large publishing houses are often business people with training in the publishing field or journalism; they may have a background in English literature or might have worked their way up through the ranks by beginning as an editorial assistant. My editor in the field of education later took responsibility for dozens of books on a history list and another of my editors switched from textiles and fabrics to a host of literacy titles. The same may be true of journal editors for large professional organizations. So, how do they know if you know what you are talking about? They depend on reviewers who *are* specialists in your discipline. With the input of reviewers, the editor

> is in a better position to make a decision regarding the disposition of the manuscript than if relying solely on his or her own impressions. No one editor possesses thoroughly comprehensive knowledge about all aspects of one's field, and through the use of peer review, it is hoped that the very best articles will be selected for publication and the less worthy passed over for this honor. (Thyer, 1994, p. 2)

Since reviewers are uncompensated volunteers who usually have other demanding jobs, it is not surprising that they have a reputation for impatience with work that is poorly crafted.

Whatever the particular nature of your relationships with editors and reviewers on various projects, in order to succeed with publishing you will need to learn how to work successfully with them. Doing so will involve, at minimum, two things: a) figuring out what the publication outlets in your field are seeking, and b) delivering it in a timely and well-crafted manner

EARNING APPROVAL FROM EDITORS AND REVIEWERS

When I make a presentation on writing for publication at a conference or in a class, a frequent question is, "What do editors and reviewers really want?" It is without sarcasm that I reply, "Manuscripts they don't have to edit." In truth, I would rather be enjoying time with family and friends than reading the piles of manuscripts that appear in my mailbox every month. I would rather be writing my own books than pointing out errors of logic in someone else's work. And I would rather be scrubbing my 12' X 24' kitchen floor on my hands and knees than correcting someone's invented version of APA style.

Editors and reviewers would just as soon receive work that is virtually ready to print so that all of these time-consuming and annoying processes could be kept to an absolute minimum. They don't enjoy rejecting others' work or delight in marking it up any more than the classroom teacher looks forward to giving poor grades or brandishing a red pen over book bags full of students' papers. The ideal in both cases would be for every writer to get it right the first time. When working with editors, try to "don the crusty attitude of the old-fashioned newsroom: If it doesn't fit, chop it off. If it isn't clear and simple, make it so. If it doesn't make a deadline, it doesn't get in print" (Ieron, 1999, p. 27).

When editors are good, they are very, very good and when they are bad, they are horrid:

> There's nothing better than an editor who intuitively understands what you're suggesting and who responds with encouragement and, above all, enthusiasm. I am sometimes amazed at how little I need to say when I have a good relationship with an editor. . . . I have also had the experience of proposing what I thought was a good story, then watching the blank look of incomprehension on an editor's face . . . if I have to explain . . . I've probably failed. Not being understood is dispiriting and exhausting. I don't know why this is such a widespread problem, but I'm sorry to say that there are many bad editors. (Stewart, 1998, p. 83)

Principle 1: Make your manuscript irresistible to reviewers and editors.

My single best piece of advice to all authors is simply this: *make your manuscript irresistible to reviewers and editors.* In order to accomplish this, do the following

- **Write and think clearly**—As Kilpatrick (1985) notes, "The chief difference between good writing and better writing is the number of imperceptible hesitations the reader experiences as he goes along" (p. 29).

Authors cannot afford to submit works in progress in the vain hope that they will be miraculously accepted. Reviewers expect writing to flow so that they can read it smoothly, without reading it over or puzzling over what the writer intends. A manuscript may challenge editors' and reviewers' assumptions but it should do so with authoritative support and without garbled messages that try the patience of editors and reviewers. The number one thing to which editors and reviewers respond is the quality of the writing and thinking on the printed page.

- **Become familiar with the outlet**—Indications that an author is well acquainted with the journal and its readership will endear the anonymous author to reviewers and editors. If the audience is higher education administrators, then the examples should speak to that group. If a topic has been overworked (or undertreated) in the journal lately, the reviewers know it and expect writers to know it, too. Authors should make it their business to learn some basic information about a publishing outlet before submitting a manuscript to them, such as: the way in which the manuscript is to be formatted; the referencing style used; and the way the author's identifying information is supposed to be supplied.

- **Respect the publisher's role**—Because most reviewers for scholarly journals are published authors themselves, they are well acquainted with the pains and pleasures of writing. When you, as a practicing professional, write nonfiction and ask to have it considered for publication, you are doing four things simultaneously: a) warranting that the work is original, b) presenting yourself as an expert, c) affirming that you believe the work to be publishable, and (when you really think about it), d) inviting criticism. Reviewers and editors are neither secretaries nor public servants. They are required to render a decision of yes, no, or maybe. They are not even obligated, strictly speaking, to say why.

As an author, you try to find suitable homes for your work like so many kittens in a basket; the publishers get to decide whether or not to open their doors and welcome one in. Don't be discouraged if you are not recognized as the leading international expert on a topic. Many editors of publications for practitioners want to include more voices from the field. An excellent resource for educators who want to write and publish is The National Writing Project. I have been a consultant for them for about nine years now; and they sponsor summer institutes for teachers, preschool through college, who want to become better teachers of writing by improving as writers themselves. Their publication, *The Quarterly of the National Writing Project* is replete with examples of articles written by practitioners and good advice on the writer's craft.

Figure 7.2 provides an overview of ways to earn acceptance from editors and reviewers.

What You Say

- Get directly to the point. Assume that most readers will not get past the first page or paragraph if it is boring or confusing.

- Tell or show the readers why they should be interested in your topic/approach. Assume that your audience will include readers who are not as well informed or passionate about your topic as you.

- Make sure that the article delivers what the title and introduction promise. Article titles often need to be rewritten after a manuscript is complete to more accurately describe the finished product.

- Present a sharply focused, reasonably complete, and balanced review of the literature. When writing for practitioners, weave it throughout the manuscript instead of lumping it all together in one section.

- Build to a satisfying conclusion and leave readers with additional food for thought, but do not introduce an issue that was not discussed previously in the manuscript.

How You Say It

- Write sentences that are readable, clear, and concise. Keep jargon to a minimum, remembering that at least a portion of your readership will be novices in the field.

- Scrutinize your paper's logical flow and make sure that it has a clear organizational pattern, indicated by headings and sub-headings.

- Use direct quotations judiciously. Many readers will skip over a long quotation, so it is generally better to shorten or paraphrase and cite the author's name as the source.

- Learn to tell the tiny tale. Intersperse very succinct descriptions of classroom events, children's behavior, teachers' concerns, or families' responses throughout your manuscript to maintain readers' interest.

- Remember the journalist's creed: say what you are going to say, say it, and then restate what you have said, all without sounding redundant.

- Write to communicate ideas rather than to impress and sound scholarly. Use a writer's voice that is something like the dinner conversation you would have with a respected colleague on a topic of real significance.

Figure 7.2 *Ways To Earn Acceptance From Reviewers and Editors*

continued on next page

Figure 7.2   *continued*

What To Do With What You Say

- Proofread carefully. Reviewers and editors who have many manuscripts to choose from may instantly reject a manuscript that
  has numerous errors.

- Use the required referencing style. Most professional publications in education use the current edition of American Psychological Association (APA) style. Purchase the guide and refer to it
  often on all matters of style.

- Conform to the publisher's specific guidelines. Each publication
  usually has published guidelines for authors that can be
  obtained by sending a self-addressed, stamped envelope to the
  editorial offices. Typically, these guidelines ask for such things as
  multiple copies, author's name on cover sheet only (to facilitate
  anonymous peer review), a precisely labeled computer diskette,
  and a self-addressed, stamped envelope.

- Read your paper critically and ask a respected colleague to do
  the same. When you are convinced that the manuscript is ready
  to mail out, put it in a drawer for a week and then reread it
  with a cold, critical eye.

What To Do with What Others Say

- Realize that submitting your manuscript for review invites criticism (Chesebro, 1993). Take reviewers' comments seriously, particularly if more than one reviewer mentions a manuscript flaw
  or if the editor echoes a suggestion in a letter.

- Develop a thick skin about your manuscripts rather than taking
  criticism personally. Approach rewrites as ways to improve an
  already good manuscript and take it "over the top."

- Remember that writing for publication is not merely "try, try
  again." Work to develop your craft as a writer.

Adapted from Sternberg (1993) by Jalongo & McCracken (1997).

Principle 2: Don't waste editors' and reviewers' time.

Like any busy professional, reviewers and editors tend to appreciate people who
make their jobs easier and resent those who make it more difficult. How do
authors waste an editor's time? What follows are the most common ways:

1. *Failing to do the necessary homework*—Just as a jockey who races thorough-
   bred horses would study the course in advance of the big race, authors need

to get familiar with the journal's submission guidelines or book publisher's product line. Most editors lament the fact that many of the manuscripts submitted to them are inappropriate, meaning that they are "wrong numbers." The journal I edit, for example, has the words "early childhood" in the title, yet every year I receive manuscripts dealing with middle school or high school students.

2. *Refusing to revise*—When a publication extends the courtesy of carefully critiquing your manuscript and asking you to resubmit, reciprocity would dictate that you follow through. I know of a faculty member who was indignant that anyone would dare to recommend changes to his work. He sat on the manuscript, an article gleaned from his dissertation, for about two years. It was not until tenure and promotion concerns intensified that he considered making the changes and, by that time, we had published two other articles on the same topic. When we were no longer interested, he was outraged. But a quarterly journal cannot afford to devote too much of its page budget to one topic, and the study was now dated. The window of opportunity had slammed shut.

3. *Protesting fair appraisals of work*—In one particularly memorable case, a Department Editor met someone at a conference and encouraged her to write something for the journal. When it was submitted, both the Department Editor and I invested considerable time in suggesting ways to improve the work. Imagine my amazement when the work was resubmitted in its original form, spelling errors and all! I even gave the author the benefit of the doubt and assumed that she had mistakenly sent the first version while rushing to print it off her disk. I was wrong. She was simply digging in her heels and using passive resistance tactics. She also insisted that she had been "promised" publication when no contract had been sent and her letter (which I copied and sent to her again) had clearly stated, "We are interested in publishing your work *providing that you are willing to make the recommended revisions on the two marked manuscripts that are enclosed."* What a waste of time!

4. *Being impatient*—Most professional journals take about 12 weeks to evaluate your work. This occurs because reviewers need time to get the manuscript, read it, write a review, and send the review in. Then the editor needs to be available to read the reviews, compose a letter, and send it to the author. Travel, holidays, illnesses, exam week, and all other manner of interruptions also enter into the process and can unavoidably delay the process. The worst manuscripts that I receive appear to have been written in haste. As if to underscore the impatience of these authors, they are invariably the ones who call within a few days of mailing the manuscript to find out if their work has been accepted.

I confess to such haste when I first began writing, too. In the mid–1980s I submitted an article entitled, "On the Compatibility of Teaching and Scholarly Writing" to *Scholarly Publishing* and it was provisionally accepted. The editor asked me to balance the piece better. He suggested that, since I had discussed how writing could benefit teaching, I should also discuss how teaching might improve writing. My first reaction was, "Why didn't I think of that!" I was anxious to get another publication before my promotion file was due, so I hurried to produce the additional material that had been requested. Imagine my mortification when the editor's letter mentioned that the new sections "showed greater signs of haste in writing than the original manuscript." Yet I had to admit it was true when I saw his heavy edit of the new copy.

When you consider the issue of wasting reviewers' and editors' time, remember that an editorial staff for a professional association frequently produces a surprising number of publications each year, such as a monthly professional journal, several books per year, and other publications, such as brochures, videos, and the like. Knowing this makes it easy to see why manuscripts needing extensive revision are rejected—there simply is not enough time or personnel to do it, particularly when other, more publishable pieces are waiting in the wings. As one editor put it, "Only someone who has worked in a publishing house can have a sense of how inexorably the manuscripts flood in, from everywhere, as if every household in the world had a typewriter" (Mitchell, 1985, p. 63).

Principle 3: Accept responsibility for finding a suitable outlet.

Just as it is possible for a teacher to teach that same first "survival" year over and over again, learning very little while accumulating additional years of experience, authors can keep writing and fail to improve much. Too many writers approach publication like the state lottery and believe that the secret to success is to keep manuscripts moving through the mail, like so many numbered ping-pong balls being bounced about by jets of air until the lucky one is plucked from its plastic chamber.

There are two problems with this approach. The first is that it completely disregards the peer review process used by scholarly publications as a source of valuable information about your manuscript's quality and contributions to the field. The second flaw in this strategy is that it does not promote professional growth in writers. Rather, it makes the assumption that "the author is always right" and that these imbeciles called reviewers and editors will eventually awaken to this fact, if only an author persists. I actually heard an educator say that whenever a manuscript is rejected, he merely pops it into the next envelope addressed to some other journal. Not only is this approach incredibly inefficient, it is a waste of postage and time.

As mentioned earlier, the typical educational magazine or journal takes about 3 months to review a manuscript and multiple submissions—sending the same article to different journals at the same time—are not acceptable. Such indiscriminate submission of manuscripts is comparable to offering clothing and furniture to several charities, asking all of them to come to your home to pick up the items, and then deciding who actually will get the donation. In both cases, you are being inconsiderate and squandering resources.

Principle 4: Grow up about criticism.

A popular breakfast cereal advertises that it is "kid tested and mother approved." We can buy with greater confidence knowing that, not only will children like to eat this cereal but also that it meets parents' criteria for a nutritious food. Just think how much easier book publisher's lives would be if, for example, all textbook chapters submitted by authors were "student tested and colleague approved!" One way to defuse the explosive potential of criticism from editorial boards is to conduct an in-house edit of any material you write before you submit it. Those who can be of the greatest assistance are intelligent and outspoken people, including members of the following groups:

- Well-read individuals outside your field or who are novices in your field. They can offer a check on clarity.

- Content experts who have in-depth knowledge of your subject. They can offer a check on accuracy.

- Readers of the outlet in which you seek to publish. They are members of the intended audience who can offer an opinion on whether your work is well suited for the particular publication.

- Authors and editors who are sticklers for details and have mastered the style sheet (e.g., American Psychological Association Style) and format of published works.

Occasionally, an author will send me something that has potential but is far too long. When authors (myself included) are directed to cut it down, they often resist. Authors have called me to protest, saying that it is simply impossible and reducing the length would, in the words of one particularly indignant author, "Do violence to the integrity of my work." I think they want me to say, "Oh, well, in your case we will make an exception to our editorial policy. Clearly, your work is so brilliant we should publish it in its entirety." But, I don't. I tell them that it is their prerogative and that they may want to pursue publication in an outlet that will accept a 30 page, double-spaced manuscript. Authors *are* allowed to take their toys and go home.

It seems that every time I do a session on writing for publication at a conference, someone walks up to me and says, "You rejected my manuscript." At first, I was taken aback by this comment because I know that feelings about such things can be pretty raw. But I have learned to respond with, "Oh. What did the letter say?" So far, these authors have admitted that I did try to give them advice about what to do. I had the opportunity to be on a panel of authors and editors who were conducting a session on writing for publication and included on that panel was another editor, now retired. When I introduced him, I said that he had been one of the first editors to reject one of my articles. He looked a little distressed until I added, "And, by the way, you were right! I had a lot to learn about writing and that manuscript should not have been published." This got a chuckle from the audience, who evidently assumed that anyone who writes and publishes has experienced rejection rarely or not at all.

Nobody enjoys seeing that self-addressed, stamped manila envelope come back with a rejection letter inside. Our hearts sink, our stomachs turn. We grow angry at the thought of all the time that we spent on the work, time when we could have been doing something fun and rewarding. We may feel like calling the editor or firing off an e-mail to defend our momentarily damaged self-esteem. My advice is to let yourself be wounded, angry, and sorely disappointed for a short while. Then, get over it! This isn't 1st grade where you are totally reliant on one teacher's approval and cry when your paper fails to earn a sticker. There are hundreds of journals and editors and if your manuscript doesn't fit the one you've selected first, it is hardly the end of your writing career—unless you allow it to be, that is. Still, there is a useful distinction between carefully selecting three appropriate outlets, ranked from highest to lowest, and blanketing the earth with your manuscript.

A highly published and distinguished psychologist characterized the trajectory of rejection this way:

> The rejection of my manuscripts has a sordid aftermath: (a) one day of depression; (b) one day of utter contempt for the editor and accomplices; (c) one day of decrying the conspiracy against letting Truth be published; (d) one day of fretful ideas about changing my profession; (e) one day of re-evaluating the manuscript in view of the editor's comments followed by the conclusion that I was lucky it wasn't accepted! (Underwood, 1957, p. 87)

Figure 7.5 offers some appropriate responses to rejection.

If a journal uses three reviewers and two (or three) mention the same manuscript flaw, then it probably needs attention. Reviewers are not infallible, but their collective judgment is a good indicator of ways to improve a manuscript. Unfortunately, some journals no longer send copies of the reviewers' comments to authors. For a major journal, providing this service could mean the salary for at least one part-time person, plus duplicating costs and postage costs. If the reviews were scathing, some member of the staff would probably take the time to edit them before sharing them with an author. Despite these constraints, most editors will send copies of reviewers' comments at an author's request. A self-addressed, stamped envelope is generally appreciated and helps to speed the process, too.

Inexperienced authors frequently tell me that their work was rejected, yet when they permit me to see the cover letter, it actually invites the author to revise and resubmit. This is *not* a rejection! The door has been left open if authors are willing to do additional work and make certain that they understand what is expected. Figure 7.6 highlights some of the typical suggestions that emerge from the review process and a cover letter for the resubmission that explains how each point of criticism was addressed.

1. **Calm Down**—Set a timer and be hurt or angry for five minutes, then use those strong feelings to fuel your positive response. Resist the temptation to bury your work in that mausoleum of rejected manuscripts, the bottom file drawer. Do not despair.

2. **Make certain that you understand the decision**—Has the editor given you any encouragement to revise and resubmit, or is this an outright rejection? Make certain that you know whether a resubmission will be considered and, if so, if the manuscript has to go through a full review again. If you received a form letter (e.g., "We wish you success in finding a suitable outlet for your work"), then the door is shut. Identify another publication with the same audience.

3. **Become Coldly Analytical**—If the rejection was a form letter ask a trustworthy, successful writer to look at the intended outlet and your manuscript and try to determine what might have gone wrong. If you were lucky enough to get detailed feedback from several reviewers, spread out the reviews and make a chart that summarizes the recommendations. Then make a plan for systematically addressing each one.

4. **Resist the Urge to Call the Editor**—Appeal to the editor only if an error was made (e.g., you received the wrong review). This is not the time to call and argue, become indignant, or beg to have something published. So much time goes into editorial decisions that it is rare to get a reversal.

5. **Rethink the Outlet or Audience**—Submit it to a different, perhaps less competitive journal. If the reason for rejection is that the topic has already been addressed extensively, consider changing your audience. If, for instance, you cannot get an article for elementary educators on cooperative learning published, perhaps you can write an article on the same topic for health and physical education teachers.

Figure 7.5 *Ten Appropriate Responses to Rejection*

continued on next page

Figure 7.5   *continued*

6. **Recycle and Reuse the Work**—If all publication efforts fail, put your work to another use—a conference presentation, a guest lecture in a class, an electronic publication, an ERIC document, an association publication, and so forth. Even if you cannot use the entire work, rip it apart and use it in different places for different purposes.

7. **Expand the Idea**—Perhaps you attempted to write about a broad topic in a short format and that prevented you from being sufficiently thorough. If this is the case, you may want to think about a monograph, a book, or a web site instead of an article.

8. **Reduce the Idea**—If you suspect that your idea was rather mundane and too specific for a national audience, think about a newsletter article instead. Your local project may be of greater interest at the regional or state level, for instance, than it was at the national level.

9. **Revisit the Work Later**—Let it sit for a little while. Read the reviews again. Can you see now what you could not see before? Respond to criticism but don't allow it to shatter your faith in your work. Try to differentiate between unsalvageable writing and writing that was a poor match with the outlet or was badly timed (e.g., on a topic that was the focus of a recent thematic issue).

10. **Find a Collaborator**— Align yourself with others who are engaged in multiple writing projects and who would be willing to invest in a reclamation project with a rejected manuscript. Ask another writer to help you find a home for the manuscript. What may not have worked as a journal article might work very well as a book chapter, and vice versa.

11. **Bury It**—As an absolute last resort, abandon the work in favor of other projects that are more interesting and show greater potential for publication.

Principle 5: Understand the evaluation criteria.

Not far from my home there is an Amish farm where I stop weekly from mid-summer through fall to buy flowers, fruits, and vegetables from people who know how to make them flourish. I have seen drifts of multicolored mums along their lane, purchased pure white cauliflower the size of a soccer ball, and eaten tree-ripened, organic fruit that would undoubtedly fetch four times the price in town. This family knows more than I ever will about growing things; their wisdom on these matters is enviable. We customers must be a source of

---

Recommendation: Resubmit after revision.

Determine the deadline. Find out if the work definitely will be published if you make the changes requested. If you cannot meet the deadline, call right away so that the editor is not counting on your piece for the next issue.

Recommendation: Major revisions are required. Work will be reviewed again.

Determine if the same referees will be reviewing the work. If the referees change, they may disagree with the first review. Find out when the revised manuscript is due. When you submit it, write a detailed letter indicating how you responded to each recommendation.

Recommendation: Shorten the manuscript.

Find out how much you are expected to cut overall. Decide if a particular section might be eliminated and perhaps saved for another article.

Recommendation: Correct stylistic errors.

Make certain that you carefully check the guidelines (e.g., American Psychological Association Style, Modern Language Association Style, etc.). Do not trust your memory or assume that every single error was pointed out for you. Ask a highly knowledgeable person to proof the final draft.

Figure 7.6 *Making the Necessary Revisions*

perpetual amusement to the Amish, particularly the ones who roar up to the roadside stand in shiny SUVs that send the horse manure flying, all the while blabbing on their cell phones. I like to think that the fundamental basis for respect between editors and reviewers is similar to the admiration I have for these farmers. An editor does (or should) know some things about publishing that others do not. Authors, on the other hand, are (or should be) experts on their topic; and they know some things that the editors may not.

Some authors look down on editors and reviewers, characterizing them as biased and opinionated. A participant in one of my writing for publication workshops who obviously had experienced repeated rejection kept trying to get me to say that the journal editor's personal taste was the sole determinant of acceptance or rejection. Yes, taste enters into it. But professional taste in writing that is acquired from constantly working with other people's words is quite different from the capriciousness of personal taste. Choosing wallpaper—something that surely must be the most idiosyncratic task on earth, if the number of wallpaper patterns and books are any indication—is qualitatively different when an interior decorator does it because the decorator has more training, experience, and

March 25, 2001

Ms. Sue Canavan
Editor, Christopher-Gordon Publishers
1502 Providence Highway
Suite #12
Norwood, MA 02062

Dear Sue and Reviewers:

Thank you for your thorough review of the first installment of the book on writing for publication. At the reviewers' suggestion, I have retitled it. It is now called *Writing for Publication: A Practical Guide for Educators.*

Included in the last installment were the Preface and Chapters 1 (myths), 2 (the author), 3 (publishable writing), 4 (strategies), and 7 (editors and reviewers). The Introduction has been rewritten and all of the chapters have been revised in accordance with the specific suggestions of each reviewer. I tightened up the prose, eliminated repetition, and corrected errors that had escaped my notice on the first submission.

After further deliberation, I decided to include the material on transforming conference presentations into publications in Chapter 5 (articles). Also, at one reviewer's recommendation, there is now an appendix in a question and answer format.

There are two chapters that the reviewers have not seen previously:

Chapter 5 Publishing Articles in Your Field
Chapter 6 Writing Books for Fellow Professionals

The Appendices are also included.

I look forward to receiving the reviewers' feedback and will give you a quick turnaround on the corrections so that we can get the book out in time for fall.

Sincerely yours,

Mary Renck Jalongo, Ph.D.

Figure 7.7   *Cover Letter to Accompany a Resubmission*

some insider's knowledge. So, in most cases, I am not willing to concede that a competent editor's appraisal of a manuscript is a whim precariously balanced on an unsubstantiated opinion. Editors are knowledgeable about writing in ways that most authors are not.

To gain a perspective on the editor's dilemma, imagine for a moment that you are at a custom-designed furniture show. Woodworkers throughout the world have handcrafted all of the pieces on display. Many different styles are represented; the only similarity is that all the entries are chairs. Your job is to select the four best from among the two hundred wooden chairs submitted. Think about the process you would use to judge the entries. Now consider this:

- The *quality of the materials* used to build the chair is equivalent to the *content* of the article.

- The *design* of the chair is equivalent to the *conceptualization and originality* of the article.

- The *construction* of the chair (what woodworkers refer to as *joinery*, a word that a professor from Louisiana shared with me and I have loved ever since) is equivalent to the *organization* of the manuscript.

- The *finish* of the wood is comparable to the layers of rewriting and editing that give written work its *style*.

- The *practicality and comfort* of the chair finds its writing corollary in the *usefulness* of the work to readers and the timelessness of its message.

This process of evaluating a manuscript's relative worth is fundamental to peer review. The analogy between rating the chairs and reviewing articles begins to break down, though, because reviewers are selected on the basis of specialized expertise whereas you may not be qualified to evaluate the woodworker's craft.

I had the opportunity to write a set of editorial guidelines for a publication sponsored by Learning Communities Network, a multimillion-dollar project funded by the Rockefeller Foundation to support professional development in several large, urban school districts (for more on this project, see *www.lcn.org*). Figure 7.3 contains the invitation to write and an explanation of the evaluation criteria we used when reviewing manuscripts. We sought accounts of ways in which the project was changing the infrastructure of the schools and contributing to the professional development of everyone associated with the schools—not only professional educators but also staff, parents, and community members.

Principle 6: Volunteer to Become a Reviewer

Instead of railing against incompetent reviewers, consider contributing to your field by becoming a reviewer. Peer review is worth doing for the things you learn about yourself as a writer. It is so much easier to note the warts on someone

On Writing for Narratives

When beginning to write, please keep in mind that we really are looking for *stories*, not articles, editorials or speeches.

Ideally, through the unfolding of your story, you will be seeking to understand your own experiences as a learner and connecting your learning to the learning of children. We do recognize that often what is learned may be painful or unpleasant, and we do wish to honor those stories of learning as well.

In thinking about how to tell your story, consider these questions:

- What do your experiences and your story *mean* for you as a person who has had a hand in educating children?

- What *difference* have these experiences made to you in your learning and work?

- How have you and the people with whom you come into contact *developed* as a result of these experiences?

- How might your story be *helpful* or *illuminating* to others? What benefits might they derive from taking the time to read it?

As you write your story, try to keep in mind the features we consider important to a good narrative:

- Reflection. The purpose of publishing in *Narratives* is to reveal the process of growth and change in you, in your classroom, school, school district or community, and in the children about whose education you write. Stories submitted should delve beneath surface events to show readers the underlying significance and long-term consequences of these events.

- Relevance. Use the *theme* of the particular issue of *Narratives* as a guide in fashioning your story. If your story does not fit well with this particular theme, consider saving it for a future issue of the journal. Suggest an interesting title that underscores the theme.

- Introduction. Your narrative should immediately capture readers' attention and compel them to read on. Summarize the point of the story early on.

- Clarity. Use language that will make your story accessible to a wide range of readers.

- Personal Voice. Write in the first person and in *your* unique voice. Write about your own experiences and how those experiences have affected you and your work to improve schools.

Figure 7.3 *Evaluation Criteria for Narratives*

Figure 7.3 *continued*

- Description. Use specific examples to illustrate key points. Show rather than tell. Give the reader a clear picture of how you are contributing to building a learning community. Share examples of students' comments, drawings and writings if that helps to illustrate your point.

- Style. Employ the techniques of good storytellers—anecdote, dialogue, scene setting, descriptive words that make your story come alive, surprising turns of phrase, a carefully crafted beginning and ending. Use contrast, irony, wit and metaphor, where appropriate. Avoid clichés or technical jargon.

Other Suggestions

Before you submit your story to *Narratives*, consider asking some colleagues who know how to give constructive criticism to read it. Revise your story based on this feedback. Before sending us your final draft, be sure you have followed the manuscript preparation guidelines (see "Submitting" above).

Source: The Learning Communities Network, Inc., Cleveland, Ohio.

else's manuscript that, gradually, you become better at spotting them in your own. You will also encounter brilliant work on occasion and, when you do, you can study how the writer achieved the desired effect. Suppose, for example, that organization is your biggest challenge. Every time you provide a thoughtful response to another's work—whether the manuscript is publishable or not—you can gain additional insight into organizing manuscripts. Reviewing also will enable you to glimpse the world of publishing from the inside out as you work with an editor. When the time between an article being accepted and actually appearing in print is often a year or more, reviewing also offers an "advance look at what may be forthcoming in your field. Moreover, you learn what the characteristics are of manuscripts likely to be accepted by a given journal, and what some of the pitfalls may be. This too is good ... editorial board service accrues good karma, merit if you will" (Thyer, 1994, p. 111).

Reviewers usually are chosen on the basis of criteria such as:

- Commitment to the aims and philosophy of the organization

- Specialized credentials, competence, and reputation in the field

- Demonstrated skill as an author/editor

- Consistency in providing prompt review

- Willingness to provide constructive feedback

As mentioned earlier, reviewers for professional journals are seldom, if ever, paid for their services. Reviewers for commercial or trade publications are usually paid a modest fee, such as $200 to review a book-length manuscript. Other forms of compensation are also used. Actually, my favorite reward for a book review is the one offered by Teachers College Press. They allow reviewers to select 10 books from their catalog; because they publish many excellent books, I relish my book reviewer's version of a gift certificate and shopping spree. Figure 7.4 offers suggestions for fulfilling the reviewer's role.

Editor Beth Luey (1995) offers this bit of advice: "As an academic writer, you are likely to wear the hats of both referee and author during your career. To perform both jobs well, you should try to keep in mind what it is like to be under the other hat" (p. 18). As with writing, the major blunder of reviewing is

---

How to Self-Assess

- Do you get work done and meet deadlines?
- Are you knowledgeable in the field? Do you strive to remain current?
- Are you willing to give of your time and energy, even in the absence of financial incentives?
- Are you able to judge work objectively?
- Are you committed to the goals and audience of the outlet for which you hope to serve as a reviewer?
- Can you identify with authors and provide concrete, helpful suggestions? Will you challenge their thinking and help them to write an even better manuscript?

How to Get Started Reviewing

- Attend meetings of professional organizations where the publications program is discussed.
- Submit your vita and a letter to the editor volunteering to serve as a reviewer.
- Talk to your book sales representative—textbook publishers often pay a small honorarium for reviews.
- Meet book and journal editors at conference exhibits and give them your business card, then follow up with a letter and your resume.
- Scan the conference program for sessions on writing for publication.

Figure 7.4   *Serving as a Reviewer*

Figure 7.4 *continued*

How to Get Fired as a Reviewer

- Lose the manuscript or let it sit on your desk.
- Suggest that the author include something that already appears in the manuscript.
- Criticize the author for making errors, then write a review that contains mistakes.
- Go off on a tangent and write a two-page response to one sentence while ignoring the rest of the manuscript.
- Pass the manuscript on to someone else to review or quote from it prior to publication without permission.
- Write a treatise on how you would have written the article or book.
- Treat anonymous peer review as a way to punish with impunity.

---

a preoccupation with self that blinds you to the needs of the intended audience. As Luey (1995) further cautions

> One question you should not ask yourself is, Is this the way I would have written the article? The least fair, least useful reviews result from asking this question. One reason research is fun and exciting is that no two people approach it in the same way. Perhaps you would have done it differently, and perhaps your way would have been better, but that is not the issue. You have been asked to evaluate an article as written. Do so. (p. 19)

Principle 7: Learn the meaning of deep revision.

There is a major difference between the revision often called for by reviewers and the concept of revision held by those uninitiated into the world of scholarly writing. If you ask junior high school students what it means to revise, they are likely to tell you that it consists of finding mistakes or, better yet, leaving it up to the teacher to find them for you. Likewise, college freshmen are apt to see revision as a quick spell and grammar check on the computer. It is not until many professionals are in graduate school that they begin to see revision for what it is, by definition, to literally see again, to "re-view" the conceptualization of the piece, rather than tinker around.

When I teach writing for publication, doctoral students are encouraged to turn in their papers for feedback as frequently as they wish to me and to their peers. Since part of learning to write for publication is making time for it, I *suggest* due dates for final drafts but do not impose any deadline other than the requirement that everything (a conference proposal that could get on the program, a publishable-quality journal article, a concept for a book prospectus) be turned in the last week of class. Invariably, some students will seek out peers who are notorious for an inability to be critical and do whatever is necessary to keep me from seeing their work—excuses, assurances, and the like. Even if they do ask me to edit, they wait until the last minute so that nothing much can be done about it. Such students' reasoning appears to go something like this: "If I get comments, they might recommend revisions and I'll be obligated to do them; if I really revise, it will force me to make a mess out of the manuscript I have now; if I make a mess, it will take more time than turning it in on the last day; and if I go to all that trouble and it's still not publishable, it hasn't paid off. I'll just work on it now and then and hope it's passable." Of course, the time for the "now and then" just doesn't become available and their work is not nearly as refined as that of the other students who actively sought feedback from peers, the instructor, and other readers. All of this occurs in spite of the fact that I caution students repeatedly about this "too little, too late" phenomenon. They still approach revision like a root canal.

As Miles (1990) points out, real revision "demands that you distance yourself from what you have written so you can see your draft as if for the first time, as your reader will" (p. 268). Interestingly, the flaws that leap out at us from others' work are notoriously hard to see in our own. Arthur Applebee (1986) attributes this difficulty to the fact that "we know so well what we meant to say that it is hard to notice when we have really said something different" (p. 223). Conversely, psychologist and creativity expert Robert Sternberg (1993) attributes our self-editing blind spot to wishful thinking:

> Sometimes when I am writing an article, I notice a sentence or a paragraph that isn't clear. Occasionally, I'm too lazy to change the offending text and I hope no one will notice. I'm particularly likely to hope that people will know what I mean when I'm not sure myself, so that perhaps later they can tell me. Almost without fail, however, readers don't understand what I said any better than I do. (p. 711)

Whatever the source of our difficulty with revision, the best authors get over their fear of making a mess out of a manuscript and force themselves to make extensive use of the cut, paste, and delete keys on their computer keyboards. The worst authors cling to every word. "But I spent all morning writing and, if I take that part out," they think, "I will have produced only about two pages of useable material!" A bad section of writing in a manuscript is like a log in the middle of your living room. If you leave it there, you will have to keep stumbling over it or walking around it. You could wait for it to decompose but it is far more efficient to chop it into firewood or haul it outside as soon as you notice it.

Principle 8: Use editorial feedback to improve the work.

When editors first skim through your article, they tend to seek affirmative answers to three questions related to the accuracy, creativity, and significance of the article. At their simplest, these questions are:

Is it true?

Is it new?

Is it important?

What keeps the editors reading and sifting through scores of manuscripts that are unpublishable is simple: they hope to find "a manuscript that is animated with a life particularly its own" (Mitchell, 1985, p. 63).

If the manuscript makes it through the initial screening, it is then sent to one or more reviewers. In journals with an anonymous peer review system, the name and institutional affiliation of the author is kept confidential. Most publications have specific guidelines for evaluation. The format of feedback on manuscripts varies. Some journals and reviewers use a rating scale, some ask for marked manuscripts to return to authors, some ask for a couple of typewritten paragraphs.

When a manuscript is reviewed, three basic decisions are possible:

1. *Acceptance*—The manuscript requires only minimal revision, changes which can be made during the normal editorial process. This is the response most authors long for because it means that much of their work is done and it will not be necessary to do major rewrites.

2. *Conditional acceptance*—The manuscript has merit but requires more substantial revision. It will be returned to the author and may or may not go through the review process again. The author is expected to read the reviewers' comments carefully and respond appropriately. Sometimes, a marked copy of the manuscript from an especially thorough reviewer is included along with the general comments.

3. *Rejection*—An outright rejection is often signaled by a form letter. Usually the text of the letter says something such as, "We regret to inform you that your manuscript does not meet our current publication needs. . . ." A statement like this is a convenient catchall for major manuscript flaws. The most common problem is that the manuscript is inappropriate for the outlet. It may also be poorly written and conceptualized. The topic may have already received considerable attention in the publication, or the subject may have been trivial from the perspective of the editors and reviewers.

More often than not, if the editor is impressed by a piece, he or she will take the time to comment. This is a "good" rejection letter. I once co-authored a manuscript to *The Library Quarterly* that was not well suited for this research-oriented journal published by the University of Chicago School of Library

Science. The editor understandably rejected it, but he also took the time to suggest that we try *School Library Journal* and the manuscript was published there. Although a glowing letter of acceptance from the editor is any writer's first preference, even rejections can lead to a publication.

Principle 9: Regard reviewers and editors as allies.

Authors often have two opinions about editors: that they are basically adversaries of authors and that they are close friends with a few favored authors, however incompetent. But the editor-author relationship, like any successful interpersonal relationship, is built upon mutual trust and respect. If editors and authors do become friends, this typically happens *after* both are favorably impressed by one another's work, not before. Editors like nothing better than identifying good writers who will be a source of high-quality manuscripts. When the professional relationship between editors and authors is good, an author's name will come up in conversation and the editor will say with obvious pride, "Yes, she's one of our authors." The author, too, will acknowledge an editor's skill. There have been times when I rewrote a sentence or section of a manuscript 15 times and still was not satisfied with it. My editor was able to make it clearer and more concise without altering the meaning. This sort of skill deserves admiration. For authors, the most productive outlook on publishing professionals is a conspiratorial, "We're together in this business of making manuscripts better." The best editors know how to balance priorities and manage people. Like the supervisor of a factory assembly line, the editor is expected to consider the quality of the product and the performance of the workers while remaining accountable to those who hold the purse strings.

When you communicate with editors, strive to be professional and businesslike. The editor of *Teachers College Record*, Gary Natriello (2000), divides the lessons that need to be learned by authors into lessons that were (or should have been learned) throughout life as follows:

- *Lessons Learned in Kindergarten*: politeness counts, persistence pays, listening skills are important, and learn to take criticism well

- *Lessons Learned in Eighth Grade*: follow directions, the basics are important, organization is more important, and share your work

- *Lessons Learned in Graduate School*: match the style of work to the journal, be conservative (editors will be), reviewers disagree, and editors make mistakes (*http://www.tcrecord.org*)

It is popular in academe to discuss abuses of the anonymous peer review system used with professional journals. True, it can be tampered with despite the fact that it is deliberately designed to conceal the writer's identity. Granted, an author's work can be evaluated unfairly. It is also true that what is accepted for publication is not always the highest quality. But these problems tend to take care of themselves over time. If enough authors complain about a particular reviewer the editor will replace him or her or, at the very least, weigh that opinion less heavily. If anonymous peer reviewers are ethical, then they will refuse to review manuscripts when they can figure out who wrote them. If an author's work is evaluated unfairly and is good, it will probably be published elsewhere—assuming that the author persists. And any publication that is full of poor quality manuscripts will eventually be winnowed out by the fierce competition for journal subscriptions.

Personally, I prefer this "free enterprise" system to any other I could concoct. It gives everyone who thinks creatively, communicates clearly, and works diligently an opportunity to participate. After I recover from the sting of a less-than-enthusiastic review, I usually understand—sometimes even appreciate—the reviewer's comments. Learn to get on with the task of improving your manuscript. Peer review is no mystery. It's simply the process of selecting the best possible articles for a particular audience and publication at a particular time.

When a manuscript is sent out to several reviewers, the author's lament is that these referees disagreed. This isn't all that surprising. Each of us has different training, background, experiences, and admitted biases that are brought to bear on a work. Just as a doctoral student will submit a chapter to a dissertation committee and get some similar comments and some that are unique to each reader, an author whose work is subjected to peer review *should* expect differences of opinion. Put another way, if everyone came up with exactly the same response, why send it to more than one reviewer in the first place?

A respected colleague from the English Department asked me to look at the mixed reviews of her manuscript, an act that surely must be the essence of trust. One reviewer had hated it and made a few snide remarks that hurt her feelings, one was on the fence, and the third recommended publication. The editor had asked the author to revise and resubmit. What to do? I read the reviews dispassionately, and this was my assessment:

- Reviewer 1 missed the whole point, critiqued it from the perspective of a research article (it wasn't), and found it deficient. It seemed like this Reviewer 1 was misled by the title and was exceedingly harsh.

- Reviewer 2 was a bit confused but could see the merit of the overall work. Reviewer 2 was not forthcoming with much concrete advice on how to improve the work, however.

- Reviewer 3 had warmed to the topic so much that he or she was willing to overlook the flaws.

- The editor must have liked it, at least, or she would not have left the door open and asked the writer to come back.

My sense was that the purpose of the piece had not been made sufficiently clear early on and that the title failed to adequately describe what was included in the piece. Making these fairly minor changes might have kept Reviewer 1 from going into a tirade. I suspected that it would have gotten Reviewer 2 off the fence as well. Reviewer 3 had already gotten the point. A few months after that analysis, I was working in the yard when a florist's truck pulled into the driveway. It was a beautiful arrangement from my friend from the English Department. She had been successful in publishing her manuscript in a scholarly journal. In the past, whenever her work did not earn positive reviews across referees, she had been so discouraged that she totally abandoned the idea of attempting to publish it.

No one is immune to the ego-deflating effect of negative comments about a rejected manuscript. As one author I know confessed, "When I get a good review, I don't work for the rest of the day. When I get a bad one, I can't work for the rest of the week." It is also possible for your work to be rejected even after you have revised it. Before you revise, find out if the same referees will be critiquing your work the second time around. If the reviewers change, it might mean that you revise it in accordance with what the first set of reviewers recommended only to find that a new group of reviewers disagree with the original recommendations.

If you are serious about publishing your work, someday (if it has not already happened), you will go to your mailbox and find an acceptance letter. Although it is fine to rejoice, it is not yet time to breathe a sigh of relief. Actually, there may be much more work to be done, depending upon how careful you were about getting everything in apple-pie order from the start. If you were careless with your reference list, you will go to your mailbox perhaps six months to a year later and find a large envelope and a manuscript with numerous author queries. Author queries consist of annoying little details of life, such as:

- The Thomas reference is 2000 in the text and 2001 in the reference list. Which is correct?

- The page number for this quotation is missing.

- APA style requires inclusive page numbers for chapters in edited books. Please provide.

The first time that I published an article, there were so many questions and notes on the manuscript that I thought I must have submitted an earlier draft by mistake (I hadn't). The first stage of proofs (those that are marked directly on my typed copy) arrived during finals week and was due within 72 hours. I almost cried when I realized how much work it would take, in those days before scholarly resources were on line, to track down some of the sources and correct some of the errors. Depending upon the process that your particular publisher uses, you will reach a stage when you are notified that it is your final opportunity to make changes. After that, the work is ready to be typeset and mistakes are irretrievable.

CONCLUSION

Following the nine basic principles discussed in this chapter has the potential to significantly increase your success rate in having your manuscripts accepted for publication. When I first began submitting articles to journals, almost nothing was accepted. My husband kept assuring me that, someday, instead of me begging to be published, editors would be coaxing me to write for them. Nowadays very little of what I write is rejected, and my husband was right—editors do invite me to write. Writing for various outlets, profiting from criticism, and taking on new writing challenges enables you to acquire a much clearer sense of what editors and reviewers want. Gradually, the fog of self-doubt will lift, fear of criticism will begin to dissipate, and a much higher percentage of your work will be favorably reviewed. After this occurs, your motivation to write will increase exponentially. You may even find yourself so intrigued by the world of publishing that you agree to join the ranks of reviewers or serve on an editorial board. You might even come to enjoy that gatekeeper role that you feared or wondered about before.

REFERENCES

Chesebro, J. W. (1993). How to get published. *Communication Quarterly, 41*(4), 373–382.

Fox, M. F. (1985). *Scholarly writing and publishing.* Boulder, CO: Westview.

Ieron, J. (1999). Edit yourself before someone else does it for you. In S. T. Osborn (Ed.), *A complete guide to writing for publication* (pp. 25-32). Bloomington, MN: Bethany Press International.

Jalongo, M. R., & McCracken, J. B. (1997*). Writing about teaching and learning: A guide for aspiring and experienced authors.* Olney, MD: Association for Childhood Education International.

Kilpatrick, J. J. (1985). *The writer's art.* New York: Andrews & McMeel.

Lamb, B. (1997). *Booknotes: America's finest authors on reading, writing, and the power of ideas.* New York: Times Books/Random House.

Luey, B. (1995). *Handbook for academic authors* (3rd ed.). New York: Cambridge University Press.

Miles, T. H. (1990). *Critical thinking and writing for science and technology.* Philadelphia: Harcourt Brace College and School Division.

Mitchell, B. (1985). The manuscript. In G. Gross (Ed.), *Editors on editing: An inside view of what editors really do* (pp. 63-67). New York: Harper & Row.

Moxley, J. (Ed.) (1995). *Publish, don't perish: The scholar's guide to academic writing and publishing* (pp. 20-26). Westport, CT: Greenwood Press.

Natriello, G. (2000). *Lessons for young scholars seeking to publish*. Available online http://tcrecord.tc.columbia.edu/

Plotnick, A. (2000). *The elements of editing*. Upper Saddle River, NJ: Pearson Higher Education.

Sternberg, R. J. (1993). For the article writer. . . . How to win acceptances by psychology journals: 21 tips for better writing. *American Journal on Mental Retardation, 97*(6), 709-712.

Steward, J. B. (1998). *Follow the story: How to write successful nonfiction*. New York: Tarcher/Simon & Schuster.

Targ, W. (1985). What is an editor? In G. Gross (Ed.), *Editors on editing: An inside view of what editors really do* (pp. 4-31). New York: Harper & Row.

Thyer, B. A. (1994). *Successful publishing in scholarly journals*. Thousand Oaks, CA: Sage.

Trimble, J. R. (2000). *Writing with style*. Upper Saddle River, NJ: Prentice Hall.

Underwood, B. J. (1957). *Psychological research*. New York: Appleton Century-Crofts.

Vaughan, S. S. (1985). Letter from the editor. In G. Gross (Ed.), *Editors on editing: An inside view of what editors really do* (pp. 39-53). New York: Harper & Row.

A Final Word

❦

---

*T*hroughout my early struggles to become a published author, we would go on semester break or spring break at the university and, invariably, that would be the very time when I was expecting reviews of an article to come in. It would be so disappointing to drive into school to find nothing of importance in the mailbox that, over the years, I explained the difference between "good" mail and routine correspondence to the Departmental secretary. That way, she could notify me if any had arrived. Good mail consisted of first-class envelopes on high-quality stationery with a publisher's return address. My name had to be typed—no mass-generated labels were allowed. After years of trying, more good mail came my way.

Several years ago, I received just such a letter on embossed stationery from the Rockefeller Foundation. At first, I wondered if it was a high-budget request for a donation; but, when I opened the envelope, it was good mail after all. The letter began by talking about a book I had co-authored in 1995 for Jossey-Bass, *Teachers' Stories: From Personal Narrative to Professional Insight* and inviting me to join a very distinguished Editorial Board who would be responsible for producing a publication entitled *Narratives*. I eagerly agreed, honored to be in such good company; and, during the telephone call that followed the Editor, Melissa Groo, said that she had read the teachers' stories book and "resonated" with our work.

As a writer, I think this is the best you can achieve—readers who respond with mind and heart to the integrity of what you have published. Aiming for that instead of foolish dreams about bulging bank accounts and superstar status, offers the best hope of experiencing writing's satisfactions.

As a writer of nonfiction, you'll need to heed the namesake of the leading award for nonfiction in America, The Pulitzer Prize. Joseph Pulitzer advised writers to, "Put it before them briefly so they will read it, clearly so they will appreciate it, picturesquely so they remember it, and, above all, accurately so they will be guided by its light" (www.bemorecreative.com/org/9217.htm). When you produce nonfiction, you are, by definition, obligated to write about what is real, live, true, and honest. That genuineness is not limited to accuracy in facts and figures, however. It should also apply to the examples and anecdotes you choose to make your point; above all, your writing should ring true.

If you want to go beyond writing, even beyond managing to break into print, and become an author who is avidly read, then strive for words that are saturated with meaning and aim for the uncontrived. This is what will distinguish your manuscript from the many others that are submitted. Speaking both as an editor and as a reader, I appreciate those moments when authors draw me in and make me believe. In order to attain this, you'll need to be yourself as a writer and speak in your own voice about what truly matters.

When you really think about it, editors and reviewers, despite their reputations, are not necessarily the toughest readers or critics. At least some of these gatekeepers are compensated for their work and, even if they are not, they have agreed up front to read with some measure of forbearance. Your ultimate audience will be those who have no such obligations. Their only rewards for reading occur when you engender enthusiasm for the topic, expand their understandings, challenge them to change, or evoke an emotional response. Writing nonfiction is not simply reporting the facts anymore than a book review is just a summary. Without your voice, your perspective, and carefully selected details, nonfiction is powerless to create impact. What follows is a story about one frustrated author who came to realize this.

Once, when conducting a faculty professional development session, I asked all 40 or so participants to write a single paragraph on a topic of their choice. I read them that night. The next morning, the paragraphs were returned with comments and this announcement, "I have good news. Everyone in this room has the ability, based on these samples, to write an article for publication." They chuckled, but I was serious.

Included in this group of faculty was a historian who challenged my claim that his work was publishable. He had been pestering the editor of a regional publication with the story of a local sports team. I read the article (which had been rejected several times, even after revision) and, although I could see why the story was remarkable and of regional interest, the writer had not succeeded in writing it in a compelling way that would cause the editor's heart to beat a bit faster. Even for factual, historical pieces, that pulse-quickening part is too often overlooked. If the editor had taken the trouble to read and reread it, he must have seen that potential too. I did a heavy edit of the story, assured him that it was publishable, and flew back home.

Several months later, I received a large envelope in the mail from an unfamiliar publication. Inside was a letter from the editor about that sports team article, along with a free copy of the publication in which it had appeared. The editor thanked me for bringing the story to fruition and, presumably, for relieving him of a determined author with a flawed manuscript. The editor also expressed collegial admiration for my ability to tease out the essential elements of the story and to transform it from a dry account of a long-dead sports team into a fascinating piece with relevance for today's readership. I still have that letter and the one that followed, this time, from a joyful author/historian.

The message here is one that is of profound importance for authors. Think of your writing as telling a story. Even a research report, scholarly and erudite as it may be, may be thought of as the story behind the study. Think of the authors who delight and surprise instead of those who want to baffle us with convoluted sentences or confound us with their knowledge of obscure terminology. If you do, eventually you will begin to understand the attractions, not only of managing to get something published, but also of writing with power. And, once you have experienced the satisfactions of genuine communication through writing, you will make what may now seem unimaginable sacrifices to living the writing life.

Believe me, the writing life can take a hold of you and become downright addictive. As I finish this book, I have four others that will be due to their respective publishers before next summer. I know that work will never get done without a monumental effort, yet I persist. The drive to write can be so compelling that it will override your good sense and the wisdom of your body. My spine is rotated from inestimable hours of crouching over computers and papers. A laptop won't solve the problem (even though I've purchased one) because I cannot seem to adjust to the smaller keyboard, the touchpad, or get the screen positioned in a way that I can see with bifocals—at least not without having the laptop slide away. I've marked several websites that cater to bad backs on the Internet and am anxiously awaiting the arrival of a special table used by the bedridden that supposedly lets you type while flat on your back. My office seating, which began as a metal folding chair purchased at a garage sale, has become a ridiculously expensive chair designed by a person who had unsuccessful back surgery. Last year I resorted to a space pen that has a pressurized cartridge. It allows me to write in any position when reviewing articles and responding to students' papers. Evidently, I'm not the only one who is writing crazy. One of my co-authors developed such a case of carpal tunnel syndrome from writing that she could barely attend to her basic needs. So why put yourself through all of this physical torture, not to mention the mental part?

I suspect that, after years of trying, you become convinced that, finally, you can, with tremendous effort, write in ways that reach and touch an audience. When this happens, writing becomes a basic need rather than a casual interest; it will propel you as surely as a nesting instinct when making a home or hunger and thirst after a hard day of physical labor. Yet unlike these other basic needs, your need to write is never fully sated because writing is a perplexing, challenging, and continually changing desire. What was once good enough no longer suffices. You know at the outset that you can never completely master the craft, yet you keep on trying because even an approximation of mastery gets the endorphins going.

Some years ago, I had the opportunity to work with a group of professors from the former USSR in St. Petersburg, Russia. The goal of these sessions was to introduce faculty who had been living in a closed society with very traditional methods of college instruction to consider alternatives to lecture. We sought to encourage them to try more interactive teaching methods with their college students/pre-service teachers. Our team of presenters attempted to practice what we preached; and, rather than lecturing about learning activities, we modeled these methods, discussed adaptations, and allowed our international colleagues to experience strategies such as role playing, cooperative learning, and so forth throughout the seminar. I treasure still the evaluation of one participant who wrote, in large script, "I will dare more."

May this book urge you to venture forth into the world of publishing, manuscript in hand, determined to dare more.

APPENDICES

❦

Additional Resources for Authors and Writing Teachers

❦

Appendix A

❦

Words Used to Describe
Effective Writing

❦

Brainstorm a list of attributes of effective writing. Then compare your list to these descriptors gleaned from various sources.

WORDS USED TO DESCRIBE GOOD WRITING

accessible style

appropriateness

authoritative

breadth

brevity

brilliance

candor

clarity

cohesiveness

conciseness

creative

credibility

ease

economy of words

effective use of analogy

effective use of metaphors and similes

emphasis

evocative in sound

freshness

genuine

honesty	powerful	surprisingness
humor	precision	suspense
illuminating	proportion	thoroughness
lack of sentimentality	resourcefulness	tone and style
lightness	rhythmic	unpretentiousness
memorability	richness	use of analogies
originality	sensitivity	vigor
parsimonious	sensuousness	vitality
perceptivity and insight	simplicity	vividness

Sources: Adapted from Macrorie, 1984; Persig, 1974; Trimble, 2000.

Appendix B / Chapter 1

❧

Publish or Perish?
Some Challenges to the Concept

❧

Before you buy into this tired, old phrase, consider these opposing views from noted authors.

Kenneth Eble (1983):

> Across a university, faculty perform about as well or as badly as teach-
> ers as they do as writers. Most—not all—faculty members can write
> a reasonably serviceable prose adequate to communication within the
> peculiarities of their disciplines. Not one in ten of that number has
> any distinctive style even as measured against what the discipline
> regards as writing well. Not one in fifty has a distinguished writing
> style as measured against effective prose over its long history as a car-
> rier of thought and inciter of emotion. The proportions are probably
> not far different as regards teachers. Most college faculty members have
> enough of personality and character, skills, and technique to teach at
> a level their departments and disciplines find tolerable. A greatly
> reduced number can be singled out as possessing a distinguished style
> as measured by their colleagues. And fewer still will have a style that
> measures up against more demanding comparisons. (p. 15)

L. Lewis (1977):

> The slogan, "publish or perish" is more often than not used in a pejo-
> rative way to suggest the inauspicious attention on campus of self-
> centered, over-achieving exhibitionists who promiscuously produce
> insignificance at the expense of careful attention to teaching. More-
> over, this to some, seductive image of the quill-driving professoriate
> may be largely motivated by jealousy against those who may in effect
> be rate-busters. There seems to be a great need to disdain ordinary,
> that is, not groundbreaking, publication, as if it reflected greater incom-
> petence than no publication at all. But whatever the intention of this
> backbiting, it is a clear assault on quality, and often a concealed devo-
> tion to mediocrity in the name of a commitment to students and
> teaching. (pp. 177-178)

J. H. Hexter (1968):

> For most scholars their teaching-by-writing and classroom teaching
> stand in symbiotic relation: each profits and grows in excellence from
> the practice of the other. (pp. 75-76)

THE RELATIONSHIP BETWEEN RESEARCH AND TEACHING

In a review of the literature, Hattie and Marsh (1997) discuss three models that
have been used to explore the relationship between teaching and research: a) *negative relationship models* (e.g., time devoted to one detracts from the other, research
is a solitary pursuit while teaching is communal, research and teaching are rewarded
by different systems); b) *positive relationship models* (e.g., research is a prior condition for good teaching, both teaching and research require commitment as evidenced by perseverance, dedication, hard work and creativity as evidenced in
imagination, originality, inventiveness); c) *zero relationship models* (e.g., research and
teaching are different enterprises with little in common, personality attributes of
teachers and researchers are distinctive, and sources of financial support for teaching
and research are independent). They conclude: "A meta-analysis of 58 studies
demonstrates that the relationship is zero" (p. 507).

> The strongest policy claim that derives from this meta-analysis is that
> universities need to set as a mission goal the improvement of the nexus
> between research and teaching. The goal should not be to publish or
> perish, or teach or impeach, but to beseech you to both publish and
> teach effectively. The aim is to increase the circumstances in which
> teaching and research have occasion to meet, and to provide rewards

not only for better teaching or for better research but for demon-
strations of the integration of teaching and research. . . . Thus, insti
tutions need to reward creativity, commitment, investigativeness, and
critical analysis in teaching and research and particularly value these
attributes when they occur in both teaching and research (Hattie &
Marsh, 1997, pp. 533-534).

*Now think about the teachers you have admired most during your postsecondary edu-
cation. How many of them contributed to their respective fields through writing? Now
think about those who have bitterly complained about pressure to publish. How would
you rate them as instructors? Do your anecdotal impressions support the argument that
those who write somehow neglect their teaching?*

REFERENCES

Eble, K. E. (1983). *The aims of college teaching.* San Francisco: Jossey-Bass.

Hattie, J., & Marsh, H. W. (1997). The relationship between research and teaching: A meta-
analysis. *Review of Educational Research, 66*(4), 507-542.

Hexter, J. H. (1968). Publish or perish: A defense. *The Public Interest, 17*(69), 60-77.

Lewis, L. (1977). Writers of the academy unite. *The American Sociologist, 12,* 176-181.

APPENDIX C / CHAPTER 2

❧

Taking Care of Yourself as a Writer

❧

Patricia A. Crawford

Trish Crawford is a former master's student, now a professor at the University of Central Florida and an established author. Here are her observations on the challenges of writing and how she has learned to cope. Which of these strategies seems most useful for you?

SOUP'S ON: WRITING AND THE CARE OF THE SOUL
Patricia A. Crawford

On a recent trip to a local bookstore, I was overcome by chicken soup, not the hearty broth by which my mother still swears, but rather chicken soup of a textual kind. Located directly at the intersection of "self help" and "inspiration," were two huge tables, brimming with scores of books and spanning nearly a dozen titles in the popular *Chicken Soup for the Soul* series, pioneered by Jack Canfield and Mark Victor Hansen. The scope of the series now extends beyond that which was ever anticipated. One can find a "chicken soup" book designed for almost any person in any situation. From pet lovers to parents, and children to teenagers, there is a form of literary chicken soup for everyone.

The *Chicken Soup* authors have developed a series of anthologies designed to help readers feel better about what they do and who they are. No matter that some of the stories have been heard before, or that they often have seemingly unrealistic endings. The books continue to sell off the shelves. Perhaps readers love the short, poignant stories because they consist of the human stuff to which we can all relate. They remind us that others have walked similar paths as our own, and help us to know that we are not alone in our journeys.

Given that the chicken soup stories are only a small portion of the "make-you-feel-good-and-get-you-through-the-clutch" market, it seems evident that no mater what our walk of life, there are many of us who recognize the need for support, long for a bit of encouragement, and seek to develop a few good coping strategies for dealing with all that life offers. Because we know ourselves as people, we seek the nourishment and nurturing that soup (albeit literary, emotional, or authentic broth) offers.

WRITERS AS SOUP ADDICTS

If anyone should be in the market for a chicken soup type of remedy, it would be the academic writer. Publication requirements, along with the desire to share specialized knowledge, cause us to put ourselves on the line in a unique way. In addition to addressing the needs of potential readers, the academic writer must cope with the demands of in-house promotion and tenure committees, as well as those of external editors. These, combined with the internal desire to publish high quality, meaningful material, can exert a great deal of pressure on aspiring authors. They must learn to deal with conflicting and sometimes high-stakes demands, cope with the agony of rejection, and develop a perspective that allows them to move their writing in a positive direction, even in the face of negative feedback.

The immense time and effort demanded by quality writing, combined with the harsh world of rejections and negative responses, can take a toll on an aspiring writer. For many, writing success becomes entwined with issues related to self-esteem and professional image. Thus, it is a good idea to keep a steady supply of "soup" on hand; that is, writers need to have concrete strategies for finding encouragement and developing coping skills in the writing world. In short, they need to know how to protect and nourish their writing souls. Here are a few suggestions for nurturing the writing selves of new and aspiring authors.

Accept rejection, but resist dejection

Rejection slips are not hard to come by in the world of academic writing. New writers (as well as many seasoned ones) tend to take these notices personally, reading the "rejection" as being aimed either at themselves or their writing ability.

Often, nothing could be further from the truth. Rejections come about for many reasons, most of them impersonal in nature. For example, a rejection may result from issues of timeliness. Perhaps, the editor recently accepted several other manuscripts on a similar topic. Or, it is possible that rejection relates simply to an issue of audience. The manuscript topic may be fascinating, the research meticulous, and the manuscript well written. However, editors are not just looking for good writing, they are looking for good matches between the contents of manuscripts and the journal's readership. Authors can avoid both of these types of problems by carefully analyzing their intended outlet. More importantly, new writers can look at this type of reasoning and recognize that there are many factors involved in the editorial process; many of which are completely out of the author's control. By depersonalizing the editorial decision, writers can protect themselves by assuring that rejection does not lead to dejection.

Calculate the risks, vary the stakes

Most writers would love to have their first submission published in the top research journal in their field. While this goal is not necessarily impossible, it also is not very realistic. One strategy for helping writers to find success, while at the same time coping with the possibility of rejection, is to choose projects of graduated risk. For example, a writer might balance a submission to a high level journal with a very low publication rate, with another submission to a state journal in which acceptance is more likely. Similarly, a submission of a long, time consuming article might be balanced with that of a short, relatively simple book review. By including smaller projects and incorporating outlets that are likely to bring success into their writing agendas, new writers will begin to develop a sense of self-confidence and nurture their writing selves with the knowledge that they are bona fide published authors. This sense of confidence will enable them to take greater risks in other projects. At the same time, writing for less competitive markets will help aspiring authors build a solid publications record and, in turn, gain credibility in their professional field.

Multiple projects, keep hope alive

A rejection can be especially hard to bear, and a request to "revise and resubmit" can seem daunting, if a writer has invested all of his or her energy and hopes into that particular piece of writing. New writers can experience a sense akin to devastation when their one and only submission, endowed with all of their hopes for publication, is not received as warmly as they had expected.

Therefore, it is advisable to have multiple manuscripts out for review at the same time. Then, if one piece is rejected, the author still has the hope that another will be accepted. By having multiple pieces under review, authors protect the hearts and hopes of their writing selves.

Swallow, don't wallow

When it comes to responding to a negative editorial decision, authors often have few choices. Sometimes there is nothing left to do but swallow hard and accept the notice of rejection. However, academic writers can save themselves a good deal of anxiety and maintain the pace of their writing agendas by having a concrete plan of action to follow in these situations. The goal is to avoid the "tortured-writer-wallowing-in-pain" stage and move quickly on to the next option in the publication process. For example, a writer might resolve to meet any notice of rejection by turning the piece around and sending it to another outlet within one week of receiving the notice. Aspiring authors can make the turn around easier by taking practical steps such as having alternative outlets in mind for each piece, and by keeping postal supplies on hand. Similarly, a writer might make it a goal to meet any request to revise and resubmit by reworking the piece within one month of receiving the request. And, of course, authors should always plan to greet notices of acceptance with some form of celebration. Publication is typically the fruit of much labor and dedication—it is worth celebrating.

IS IT SOUP YET?

Surely this list is not exhaustive; there are many other things that authors can do to take care of their writing selves, as they embark on the publication process. Although it is not necessary that aspiring authors follow these specific suggestions, it is vitally important that they identify and develop both the strategies and habits of mind that will assist them in dealing with the many challenges that academic writing offers. Essentially, some ingredients are offered here, but each writer must develop a personal recipe for soup; one that will bring a little comfort, keep the work on track, and even provide a bit of nurturing for the writing soul. The goal is to keep hope and vision alive, and to keep the writing simmering.

Writer's Block

PATRICIA A. CRAWFORD

Writer's block,
What a shock!
What to do?
Wish I knew.

Wordless page,
Filled with rage!
Elusive word.
How absurd.

Passing time,
Empty mind.
No time to kill,
Feeling ill.

Page so white,
Dreadful blight.
Heavy hearted,
Must get started.

Try again,
Paper and pen.
Less distraught,
Here comes a thought!

Black on white,
Precious sight.
Fingers drumming,
Words are coming.

Writer's block,
Needs mental talk.
Muddle through,
Just words and you.

ADDITIONAL RESOURCES ON WRITER'S BLOCK

Rodier, A. (2000). A cure for writer's block: Writing for real audiences. *The Quarterly of the National Writing Project, 22*(2), 16–18.

Rose, M. (1985). Complexity, rigor, evolving method, and the puzzle of writer's block: Thoughts on composing process research. In M. Rose (Ed.), *When a writer can't write: Studies in writer's block and other composing problems* (pp. 227-260). New York: Guilford.

Sommers, N. (1997). Revision strategies of student writers and experienced adult writers. In V. Villanueva (Ed.), *Cross-talk in comp theory: A reader* (pp. 43-54). Urbana, IL: National Council of Teachers of English.

Appendix D / Chapter 3

❧

Basic Principles of Nonsexist Language

❧

How have you handled these issues in your writing? Here are the basic guidelines used by most publishers.

Dealing Skillfully with His/Her—Use the plural whenever possible (e.g., "Teachers need to be writers themselves in order to teach writing effectively." rather than "A teacher needs to be a writer himself or herself . . .") Be careful about subject/pronoun agreement when you choose to use plurals. It is incorrect to say "The child learns to write when they . . ." because the subject (child) is singular and the pronoun is plural (they). Another option is to address the reader directly—"You need to be a writer yourself in order to teach writing effectively."

Balance Gender Representation—Analyze how many examples of males and females are presented. Be alert also to stereotypes (e.g., writing an article in which all of the examples of socially unacceptable behavior in adolescents are males).

Use Parallel Forms—Do not refer to a male author with a doctorate in your manuscript as "John Doe, Ph.D., an expert on . . ." and a female professor with a doctorate as "Jane Doe." This parallel forms caveat also applies when referring to classes of people. Instead of man and wife, for instance, write husband and wife.

Avoid the generic "man"—Avoid implying that all members of a group are assumed to be male when they are not (e.g., use work force instead of man-power, company representatives instead of spokesmen, staffed instead of manned, chair or chairperson rather than chairman).

ADDITIONAL RESOURCES

Miller, C., & Swift, K. (2001). *The handbook of nonsexist writing*. New York: HarperCollins.

National Council of Teachers of English (1985). *Guidelines for nonsexist use of language in NCTE publications*. Urbana, IL: Author

Appendix E / Chapter 4

❧

Writing the Nonfiction Journal Article: An Instance of Problem Solving

---
❧

In a study of counselors who were also published authors, respondents were asked to identify the most daunting tasks (La Forge & Coelho, 1998). These challenges were clustered into four categories, as follows:

1. **Manuscript Submission**
   - Responding to reviewers' critiques
   - Waiting for editor's response
   - Selecting an appropriate outlet
   - Lacking knowledge of submission procedures

2. **Manuscript Conceptualization/Organization Concerns**
   - Organizing and manuscript formatting concerns
   - Limiting article length, being succinct
   - Using appropriate style—APA, Chicago, MLA, etc.
   - Editing/revision concerns

3. **Resource Barriers**
   • Organizing use of time
   • Lacking mentorship
   • Poor academic writing skills
   • Failure to seek colleagues for feedback

4. **Personal Apprehensions**
   • Insecurity
   • Fear of rejection
   • Lack of statistical skills
   • Motivation or procrastination

In fact, composition theorists Flower and Hayes (1997) regard writing as a cognitive problem solving task. Cognitive psychologist Pressley (1995) has identified the following steps in the process, which I elaborate on here.

Step 1: Explore the nature of the writing task.

Questions: *What is the rhetorical task? What is the purpose of this manuscript? What effect do I seek to achieve?*

Strategy: The Topic/Fact/Pronouncement Distinction. Differentiate between a topic (food allergies in children), a statement of fact (being uninformed or misinformed about a child's food allergies can be dangerous), and a pronouncement. (Overlooking a child's food allergies can jeopardize a child's health and a teacher's career. In this article, I will argue that teachers not only need to stay abreast of general facts about various types of food allergies but also need to be well informed about the individual children in their care so that they can work with families to avoid a tragedy.)

Step 2: Make a plan.

Question: *Where do I begin?*

Strategy: The Top-Ranked Resources. According to one survey, the most important written resources for article writers were: 1) computer databases, 2) the *APA Publication Manual*, 3) the journal or target journal and 4) the library. The top four human resources were: 1) colleagues, 2) co-authors, 3) reviewer comments, and 4) editorial assistance (La Forge & Coelho, 1998). Use all eight of these sources *before* you submit your work to a journal. Make writing appointments with yourself on your calendar and post a realistic timeline for completion of the work in your work area.

Step 3: Generate your ideas.

Question: *What are some of the examples that I am dying to use? Brainstorm a few.*

Strategy: The Interesting Incident or Comment. You are the expert now. Don't be afraid to use your personal experience. When an infant care program supervisor described an article about managing the behavior of toddlers, she said her concern was that expectations for toddlers tended to be unrealistic and that a child development professor had described toddlers as "really, just babies who can walk." This statement was authoritative and captivated her, yet she had not put it in the manuscript. I urged her to do so.

Step 4: Organize your ideas.

Question: *Now that I have located all of this material, how do I impose order on all of this chaos?*

Strategy: The Graphic Organizer. Instead of wallowing in words, use a schematic of your ideas. Several sources offer a sophisticated look at the graphic organizer (Buzan & Buzan, 1996; Hyerle, 1996; Rico, 1999).

Step 5: Know the needs of your readers.

Questions: *How can I identify with and be helpful to my readers? Is my audience likely to be . . . deeply or only mildly interested? Familiar/unfamiliar with authoritative sources in the field? Committed/uncommitted to a viewpoint? Likely or unlikely to find your stance threatening or demanding of considerable change in thought or action? Formally or informally associated with groups or organizations that are involved in some way with the idea or issues?* (Ewing, 1974)

Strategy: The Grocery Store Errand. Do this exercise. Suppose that you were sending someone to the grocery store to buy something for you. How would your explanations change for: 1) a young child, 2) a visitor from another country who has never visited a supermarket, and 3) a person who is familiar with the store and shops there frequently? This will give you a glimpse of how much your writing style needs to change.

Although different audiences place different demands on the writer, successful writing still has to satisfy four audiences within that group:

1) The *professors* who ask "What?"—They are seeking mastery and competence that allows them to perform new skills, so *engage them with facts, figures, and authoritative support.*

2) The *friends* who ask "So what?"—They are seeking personal involvement and interaction with other participants, so *attend to their feelings by using emotionally compelling examples and anecdotes as appropriate.*

3) The *scientists* who ask "Why?"—They are seeking understanding and the opportunity to reason about the information, so *reflect critically on the issues in your work to pique their interest.*

4) The *inventors* who ask "What if?"—They want to create, adapt and reorganize information, so *give them something fresh and original to ponder.* (adapted from Garmston, 1997).

Step 6. Transform writer-based prose into reader-based prose.

Questions: *Which specific articles were the most useful to me in my review of the literature? How can I make my article more like the helpful ones and less like the ones that had little or no value?*

Strategy: The Simulated Publication. First, let your manuscript get cold. Open a copy of the journal in which you seek to be published. Write the title and your name on a post-it note and see how it looks in the table of contents. Does it fit? Now insert your manuscript into the center of the publication and read it as if it were part of the volume. Skim through several other articles in the journal. Does it fit?

Step 7: Review your goals.

Questions: *Are there discrepancies between my purpose (stated in Step 1) and the manuscript? Are the goals of this writing project consistent with the content, style, and format of the piece? Is the manuscript so good that I can hardly believe that I wrote it?*

Strategy: The Manuscript Audit. Study your manuscript. Compare the title with the thesis. Does it match? Compare the pronouncement paragraph with the headings for the main sections of the paper. Is there a one-to-one correspondence? Analyze the introduction and conclusion. Is there a sense that they provide mirror images of the essence of your work?

REFERENCES

Buzan, T., & Buzan, B. (1996). *The mind map book: How to use radiant thinking to maximize your brain's untapped potential.* New York: Dutton.

Ewing, D. (1974). *Writing for results.* New York: John Wiley.

Flower, L., & Hayes, J. R. (1997). A cognitive process theory of writing. In V. Villanueva (Ed.), *Cross-talk in comp theory: A reader* (pp. 251-276). Urbana, IL: National Council of Teachers of English.

Garmston, R. J. (1997). *The presenter's fieldbook: A practical guide.* Norwood, MA: Christopher-Gordon.

Hyerle, D. (1996). *Visual tools for constructing knowledge.* Alexandria, VA: Association for Supervision and Curriculum Development.

La Forge, J., & Coelho, R. J. (1998). Writing for publication: Advice from authors. *Journal of Applied Rehabilitation Counseling, 29*(2), 35-39.

Pressley, M. (1995). *Advanced educational psychology for educators, researchers, and policy makers*. New York: HarperCollins.

Rico, G. (1999). *Writing the natural way: Turn the task of writing into the joy of writing*. New York: Putnam.

APPENDIX F / CHAPTER 5

❦

From First Draft to Article Draft

❦

The following is an example of a co-authored manuscript. Note that the portions in boldface were my suggestions/contributions while the rest of the work was from Charlotte Krall's initial attempt to draft a journal article. As you read, pay attention to the following features:

- How Charlotte Krall produced an article that only she could write, based on her experience and in her own voice.

- How the boldfaced items (my contributions) helped to shape this manuscript into a more publishable piece.

This is a draft. The final, edited version was published in *Childhood Education*.

CREATING A CARING COMMUNITY IN CLASSROOMS: ADVICE FROM AN INTERVENTION SPECIALIST

Charlotte M. Krall, M.A. and Mary Renck Jalongo, Ph.D.

For nine years, I have been an intervention specialist for elementary school children. **This means that I have worked with groups of children and individual students to help them develop social skills such as resolving conflicts, coping with powerful emotions, enhancing self-esteem and learning ways to prevent drug and alcohol abuse.** While discussing these and other sensitive topics, children often confide in me **and the concerns that weigh heavily on their minds have been imprinted on my own.** Here are some of the things children have shared.

"My brother ran away. Well, really he died . . . he killed himself." (Kindergarten boy)

"My stepdad bothers me when I come home from school before my mom gets there. Can I stay after school this week?" (1st grade girl)

"I worry about getting good grades cause my dad says I have to get good grades to get into Notre Dame College where he went." (1st grade boy)

"I'm worried about my mom, she smokes marijuana." (3rd grade girl)

"When my dad's on drugs he does scary things. Yesterday he smashed my mom's head against the garage wall and it was bleeding." (3rd grade boy)

"My mom has no hair. She gets chemo. She has cancer." (4th grade boy)

"My mom and dad joined a motorcycle club . . . and they don't believe in drugs. They haven't been drunk for 4 weeks." (5th grade girl)

"Yes, I want to talk about something, but my dad said I can't talk about it. (5th grade boy—His father filed a custody suit against his wife.)

These heartfelt words from children remind us that there are numerous stressors that may impair children's ability to concentrate on schoolwork. We assume that children have the "usual" school pressures of academic achievement, peer acceptance, and rule adherence. We assure ourselves that home is home and school is school, yet children bring home to school as easily as they tote their backpacks and lunches. **Many teachers argue that they are not responsible for solving children's home problems, protesting that they cannot "make everything better" and that is certainly true.** But teachers do more than impart information, they also enhance motivation and promote positive self esteem (Weinreb, 1997). **Interestingly, a national survey identified teachers' ability to motivate children to learn as the characteristic most prized by parents while teachers' respectful care and concern for the child was the characteristic most prized by children (Boyer, 1995).**

Teachers and other adults have the responsibility to create a classroom atmosphere conducive to learning. If students cannot ignore their home situations and concentrate in school, then teachers cannot afford to ignore students' home lives either. This does not mean that teachers need to probe the details of every incident. Rather, they can create a learning community where students feel comfortable enough to express their concerns, worries, fears or problems when and if they choose. **A recent review of research suggests that such opportunities for children to talk with caring, concerned teachers are particularly important (Kontos & Wilcox-Herzog, 1997).**

In order to learn, children need to be able to relax enough to cope simultaneously with the demands of school and home. **Like a game of tag where a child can call out, "Safe!" school should be a safe haven—both psychologically and emotionally. Otherwise, fear can destroy intelligence (Ayers, 1995). Teachers can use their professional power to create a safe, just, inclusive, communicative, welcoming and caring classroom community, one that promotes development of the whole child.**

BUILDING MUTUAL TRUST AND RESPECT

Another dimension of my professional role is working with practicing teachers through in-service programs. In that capacity I have had the opportunity to work with teachers who are seeking to replenish their efficacy beliefs by restoring their confidence that they truly can make a difference in children's lives. When I ask teachers, "What characteristics do teachers need in order to establish good relationships with students and have a successful classroom where children share their feelings, life events, and learn to cope with stressors?" I get responses such as:

"respect for students"

"good personality"

"discipline . . . consistent discipline"

"a sense of humor"

"be a friend"

"demand respect from students"

"be flexible . . . not just flexible, but real flexible"

"laugh a lot with them and at yourself."

Similarly, when I have asked children, "What makes a good teacher, one you can trust?" some of their responses have been:

"cares that you learn"

"nice, funny, makes learning fun"

"your friend"

"is his own self and not mean"

"doesn't always say no"

"likes me"

These responses reflect children's personal opinions about what kind of teacher enables them to take risks that are an inevitable part of learning, the risks that teach them not only content and skills, but also how to act and interact in a social context.

BECOMING MORE CARING, COMPETENT TEACHERS

After spending thousands of hours teaching, observing, and listening to teachers and children in and out of classrooms, I have formulated my own response to questions about the traits that enable educators to establish a caring community in their classrooms. Included among these characteristics and skills are:

1. Be Honest . . . Build Mutual Trust

(*5ᵗʰ grade girl*) *"I won't trust a man counselor. It has to be a lady. I told Mr. B. my story. He promised it was 'just between him and me.' Then he went and told my parents and my teacher. I was so mad. I just cried."*

Children need to know where they stand. They need to understand the rules and anticipate reasonable consequences for transgressing those rules. "The single most important ingredient in a nurturing relationship is honesty" (Briggs, 1975, p. 75). Being honest and building trust does not mean the teacher of the child must "tell all" at all times. Both may choose to keep certain feelings and events to themselves. Even when all of the information is not shared, a person certainly can recognize the intensity of the emotions and can respect the time needed to work things out. Part of that mutual trust and respect is accepting the child's right and desire to be left alone.

Rather than saying "nothing is wrong" when asked, a child can be taught to use "I statements." These statements allow the child to tell what he or she is feeling and why, for instance, "I am angry, but I don't want to talk about it right now." Or "I am angry. You told someone what I told you, so I can't trust you." When a child shares a feeling, that child has a right to be heard with understanding. If children know that adults strive to understand them, then they feel safe to talk. **Yet teachers often act out of their own discomfort with sensitive issues and often choose to say nothing or to make some off-handed remark like:** "Your mom probably didn't mean what she said" or "We don't talk about those kinds of things in school." When children are not taken seriously or a teacher discounts their feelings, they learn to reject feelings or hold them inside. It is important to listen to children and respond honestly to their concerns.

Caring teachers let children know that talking things over with an adult often makes powerful emotions more manageable

2. **Cultivate Communication Skills . . . Be a Role Model**
   (3rd grade boy) "A good teacher reads stories and plays "Seven-up" with his class. And plays sports together. He gives good examples for things kids are learning. Teachers talk to their students about problems."

   It is important to be nonjudgmental and respect each child's right to privacy and self-preservation when developing classroom communication skills. Each day, ask yourself, "How would I feel if my actions were broadcast for others to evaluate?" Consider placing an illustration of a video camera on the wall in the back of your classroom as a reminder to self-monitor your classroom behavior. Even if you know how you should respond to children, your picture of a video camera will remind you to respect your students the way you would like to be respected and treated.

   As you interact with students, state your expectations clearly and react to how a child behaves rather than resorting to negative labeling. For example, say, "I don't want to hear loud voices in this room!" Instead of saying, "Some of you have been so noisy that you are all going to lose five minutes of recess." Say, "I want you to concentrate harder on memorizing your spelling," rather than "You are so lazy!" "Negative judgments make you a negative mirror for children" (Briggs, 1975, p.6), while positive encouragement is more likely to inspire children to behave in socially acceptable ways. By promoting positive self-image and appropriate behavior, the child feels more comfortable taking the risks associated with learning something new and learns to develop communication skills.

   Body language and a tone of voice are particularly powerful means of communication. Even when verbal communication is a barrier, most children will respond more appropriately to a comforting look and a soft voice rather than using a glare and a lecture voice, particularly those who are accustomed to the latter. Perhaps most important is that observant children will be more apt to learn from your example and model your behavior.

3. **Adjust the Schedule . . . Be Flexible**
   (2nd grade teacher) "Not now, it's time for math . . . we'll get to that later." (But later never arrives).

   Effective teachers constantly reflect upon their approach, observe whether students are learning or not, and then adjust their practices accordingly (Charney, 1992). They tend to be more flexible and pause to provide opportunities for teachable and creative moments rather than adhering to a fixed inflexible curriculum. If the class is anxious and expresses tension about standardized testing, for example, a teacher may adjust the curriculum so there is time to read a book such as *First Grade Takes a Test* (Cohen, 1980) to help reduce test anxiety. Likewise, take time out to learn some before-the-test exercises or relaxation techniques, like stretching, deep breathing or alternately shrugging/relaxing shoulders. Developing a practice session on positive self-talk and pep talks (Kaufman & Raphael, 1990) may also give children extra encouragement to be persistent and keep on trying. When a situation arises where a child shows signs of unbearable or unmanageable frustration such as crying, screaming, trying to run away or just giving up, be prepared to make schedule adjustments that will help that child regain control. This approach will also allow the rest of the class to relax and reflect for a moment on kindness and patience before continuing the academic lesson.

4. Alter Perspective . . . Be Empathetic

(4ᵗʰ grade boy) "Now I see it. You did it different. I understand it!"

One of the joys of teaching is "seeing the light bulbs go on" and noticing the accompanying flash of insight that leads to understanding. Each child follows a different path and timetable to get to that "aha!" stage; each approaches an experience with a different perspective and experiential background that may cause miscommunication and misunderstandings.

When the teacher's interpretation of a situation is treated as the only right one, it sets up barriers and discounts the child's perspective. **Teachers who foster dynamic classroom interactions acknowledge a child's perspective before offering other options or solutions (Wheeler, 1994). Thus, part of being a careful teacher in the true sense of the word— full of care—is taking a child's eye view of situation and adapting strategies to facilitate that child's needs.**

What we see, what we experience, and what we are told (Munson, 1991) comprise our belief systems and affect our perspectives. The best way to discover what a child is thinking or struggling with is to ask and then really listen with eyes connecting, ears hearing, and brain concentrating. When the teacher models good listening skills, children get a powerful message about listening to one another and learn that good listeners get involved intellectually and emotionally in the messages they hear (Jalongo, 1995). Such active involvement leads to fewer miscommunications and misunderstandings. Give children the opportunity to listen empathetically to their classmates and be certain to exemplify such behaviors yourself.

5. Be Human . . . Promote Humor

(5ᵗʰ grade boy) "Jason penciled a mustache on a piece of tape and put it over his upper lip. The small group laughed. Angie begged, 'Wear it to class, Jason, we could all use a good laugh. No one's laughed all day!' Everyone chimed in, 'Yes!' 'No way,' Jason replied, 'Ms. T. would kill me.'"

Caring teachers pay attention to beginnings, endings, and transitions. **They draw the children gently into the school day and help ease** them back out, ready to re-enter the world outside or, as Selma Wasserman (1990) describes it, "breathing out" and "breathing in." Humanness, kindness, and humor help children enter the classroom community and bring satisfying conclusion to the school day. When teachers stop thinking of themselves as teachers who cover content and start thinking of themselves as human beings who facilitate learning, they bring a sense of caring into the classroom. If teachers dare to go one step further and let the children know they don 't know everything, they begin to learn with and from their students. The genuine teacher is often a subtle teacher, a quiet backseat driver, allowing the student to be in the driver's seat moving forward with gentle and consistent encouragement from behind the scenes.

We now know that emotions play a far greater role in learning than was previously assumed (Goleman, 1996). Laughter stimulates the body's level of endorphins, thereby diminishing stress and even pain (Sylwester, 1995). Helping a student to see the lighter side and laugh can relieve some of the stresses, prevent a problem, and build community in the classroom. Teaching should never be humorless out of fear of losing control over children's high spirits. Comics, jokes, silly sayings, rhymes, humorous stories, and just plain giggling have a purpose in the curriculum (Shade, 1995). When children feel good physically and mentally, they can enjoy being themselves and, with their needs met, children are more inclined to help others.

6. Promote A Positive Self-Image . . . Be Kind

Following a lesson on changing negative self talk to positive, a young child approached me in the hall, smiled, held up an imaginary mirror to her face, and said "Hi, Mrs. K. . . . I like myself just the way I am." I smiled. She continued, "See, I remember to tell myself positive stuff everyday . . . well, almost every day."

Students' and teachers' positive self-talk is restorative—it builds us up and structures our character (Helmsetter, 1986). Provide time for students to practice positive affirmations and self-messages. Place positive poems around the room and create activities that allow children to be kind and to give compliments to each other. Give children the opportunity and responsibility to contribute a thought for the day and post the messages they gather somewhere in the classroom throughout the school year.

Adding positive messages around the room helps children to reinforce the habit of giving positive messages to themselves and others. Days may go by when children receive no positive comments or compliments. If they are taught to give compliments and use positive language with others they also learn to give compliments to themselves, thereby realizing some of the personal rewards of kindness.

Talk Box: Provide a classroom mail box and a supply of paper notes placed in a strategic place. Students can anonymously suggest topics they would like to discuss together or they can use the box to communicate with the teacher individually about an issue of concern.

Talk Time: The teacher would preview the notes ahead of time and establish a daily sharing/discussion time. The class has the opportunity to discuss topics together. If a student wants to talk to the teacher privately, an appointment can be set up.

Journaling: Use dialogue journals to interact with your students on a daily or weekly basis. Communicate with individual students in notebooks, on special note pads, in computer files, or on cassette tapes.

Classroom Library: Read and discuss fiction and nonfiction books that cover a variety of sensitive topics of concern to children. Be certain to use open-ended questions during these discussions and to follow the children's lead.

"I Can": Decorate an oatmeal box or snack food can that contains statements of things that children would like to be able to do (e.g., "I can do long division"). Children select one "I Can" to work on for the week and report on their progress. "We can" statements may be selected for the entire class as well, such as "We can make the playground safer."

Help Wanted/Help Offered Board: Each child identifies a task he or she has mastered and can teach to someone else as well as a task that has proved to be too difficult. Children use the board like want ads to gain and lend support to classmates.

Giant Eye Glasses Illustration: Invite the children to create the wildest looking "eyeglasses" they can think of. Put their creative eyeglasses up on the classroom walls to remind everyone that perspectives vary and that the number of people in the classroom may equal the number of perspectives in the class at any one time.

Ladder to Success: Create a ladder illustration so that children can monitor their own progress toward a goal. Children paste strips of paper describing each step in their progress.

Humor Box or Corner: Engage the children in designing and stocking a box or corner of the room that holds joke books, funny pictures, humorous poems, silly sayings, riddles, records and tapes, puppets and props to incorporate humor and fun into the day.

Smile Folder: Children decorate a folder and use it to keep notes from teachers and friends, positive poems, affirmations, correspondence, drawings, comics, work samples, awards, or other items that make them smile. The folders provide a lift on a gray day.

Figure 1   *Classroom Strategies to Communicate Caring*

Figure 1 *continued*

"Thought for the Day" Bulletin Board: Supply students with books, magazines, and newspapers. Give them opportunities to work in pairs or small groups to find sayings or short poems to add to the bulletin board. Give students an opportunity to create their own positive statements, sayings, or slogans.

Success Sharing: To promote active listening, invite children to work in pairs pair and take turns listening to each other share a significant accomplishment. The ask the listeners to report to the class in a creative way.

Treasured Object: Invite children to bring an object to school that has special significance for them. Display the items on a table and have each child write a card describing what the object is, how they acquired it, and why it has special meaning for them. The rest of the class then makes positive comments about how the treasured object reflects some important personal attribute of the owner.

---

7. **Look beyond the classroom walls . . . Establish Interpersonal Relationships.**
   In order for teachers to share kindness, have positive attitudes and function with enthusiasm, creativity and excitement, they must communicate effectively with other staff members (Munson, 1991). **Seek out co-workers who share enthusiasm and who constantly work on ways to become better at teaching (Ayers, 1995). If teachers work with colleagues to share successes, take delight in children's words and deeds, and rely on colleagues as sounding boards who help to resolve problems,** they generally feel better about themselves and what they are accomplishing in their classrooms and schools. A positive approach increases enthusiasm among other teachers that the staff can build on to gain positive momentum school wide. **True colleagues accept responsibility for their own actions while feeling and sharing a sense of responsibility for their co-workers.**

8. **Monitor Personal/Professional Growth . . . Make a Plan**
   A good place to start upgrading your classroom community is to identify personal attitudes and behaviors you would like to change or improve. Keep a maintenance checklist in your planning book and review it weekly (Figure 2). **Surround yourself with responsible colleagues, not those who are merely affable, but those who will dare to point out that you need to rethink an attitude or a behavior.** Strive to create an environment where humor, honesty, caring, respect, flexibility, humanness, empathetic listening, nonjudgmental attitudes, enthusiastic learning and classroom

Do I . . .

___ Clearly define acceptable classroom behavior?

___ Model the behaviors and attitudes I hope to elicit from students?

___ Pay attention to and quickly address individual student behavior problems?

___ Accept myself and be myself?

___ Generally expect responsible behavior?

___ Use reflective listening when a child shares personal information?

___ Use "I" statements when there is a problem?

___ Exhibit and cultivate my sense of humor often and appropriately?

___ Provide stress relievers in my curriculum throughout the day?

___ Spend more time encouraging students than correcting them?

___ Maintain and promote a "you can do it" attitude?

___ Communicate acceptance to my students?

___ Encourage consideration, kindness and patience?

___ Respect my students' opinions?

___ Adjust my perspective often as appropriate?

___ Notice my students growing comfortable enough to try new things?

___ Respect the privacy and confidentiality of my students?

___ Encourage positive talk from colleagues, particularly in the teachers' lounge?

___ Get excited about learning and new projects?

___ Set reasonable expectations for myself?

___ Have reasonable expectations for each individual student?

___ Function as a staunch advocate for my students, just as I would for a child from my own family?

———————— ❧ ————————

(Tuck this checklist in your daily planner to review occasionally for a maintenance check. Work each day on one you'd like to improve. It's often easier to make a new habit than to break an old habit.

Figure 2 *Teacher Self-Monitoring Checklist*

interactions thrive on the positive energy in the room. This energy begins when you believe in your students and in yourself.

Teaching demands thoughtfulness, so take a few moments for reflection (Ayers, 1995). After all of your students have left the classroom community for the day, sit in a child's seat toward the back of the empty classroom. Close your eyes and visualize yourself at work. For a few moments take yourself back to your childhood and regress back to the age of your students. **Perhaps you will conclude, as Karen Gallas (1994) did, that**

> what I needed as a child in school was a teacher who wanted
> to hear my voice, my ideas, the words that were always pre-
> sent but never spoken; a teacher who would have given me
> the support and safety and a space in which to project that
> voice . . . a teacher who would have valued my voice because
> it was mine, not because it provided the right answer. (p. 14)

Open your eyes as that child and visualize yourself as the teacher in the front of the room. Look around the room, listen to your voice, watch your actions and ask yourself, "Would I like to be a student in my classroom? Why or why not?" **Then reinvent and invest yourself in a plan that would build that richly imagined classroom, the one that you had hoped for as a student and dream of as a teacher.**

CONCLUSION

Recently some college sophomores contributed to a bulletin board on metaphors for teaching. Their contributions reflected the idealism of their age; there were metaphors such as "teacher as nourishment" in which teachers nurtured learning, "teacher as potter" in which teachers shaped children's futures, and "teacher as navigator" in which teachers guided children toward success. Part of remaining vital and committed as a teacher is staying in touch with those feelings that led you to pursue the career in the first place. Nobody goes into teaching thinking, "I will grow indifferent toward children, cynical toward the profession, and eventually become the type of teacher I now criticize."

As you work toward the goal of creating a caring community in your classroom, keep the overarching purpose of education uppermost in your mind. Teachers begin teaching and children begin school with wonder, excitement, curiosity, and a large measure of concern about whether or not they will succeed and be treated fairly. Both teachers and children need to be heard, respected, appreciated; to grow in confidence, competence, and commitment. When teachers retire and students graduate, both adults and children should be able to look back over their careers and conclude that their fundamental needs were met.

REFERENCES

Agne, K. J. (1994). Relationships between teacher belief systems: Teacher effectiveness. *Journal of Research and Development in Education, 27*(3), 141-52.

Ayers, W. (Ed.) (1995). *To become a teacher: Making a difference in children's lives.* New York: Teachers College Press.

Boyer, E. L. (1995). Princeton, NJ: Carnegie Foundation for the Advancement of Teaching.

Briggs, D. C. (1975). *Your child's self-esteem.* New York: Doubleday.

Charney, R. S. (1992). *Teaching young children to care: Management in the responsive classroom.* Greenfield, MA: Northeast Foundation for Children.

Cohen, M. (1980). *First grade takes a test.* New York: Bantam Doubleday.

Gallas, K. (1994). *The languages of learning: How children talk, write, dance, draw and sing their understanding of the world.* New York: Teachers College Press.

Goleman, D. (1996). *Emotional intelligence.* New York: Bantam.

Gordon-Browne, A. M., & Williams-Browne, K. (1995). *Beginnings and beyond* (4th ed.). Albany, NY: Delmar.

Helmsetter, S. (1986). *What to say when you talk to yourself.* Scottsdale, AZ: Grindle.

Hewitt, D. (1995). *So this is normal too? Teachers and parents working out developmental issues in young children.* St. Paul, MN: Redleaf Press.

Jalongo, M. R. (1995). Promoting active listening in the classroom. *Childhood Education, 72*(1), 13-18.

Kaufman, G. & Raphael, L. (1990). *Stick up for yourself.* Minneapolis, MN: Free Spirit Publishing.

Kontos, S., & Wilcox-Herzog, A. (1997). Teachers' interactions with children: Why are they so important? *Young Children, 52*(2), 4-12.

Munson, P. J. (1991). *Winning teachers teaching winners.* San Francisco, CA: ETR Associates.

Shade, P. A. (1995). License to laugh: Humor in the classroom. Englewood, CO: Teacher Ideas Press.

Sylwester, R. (1995). *A celebration of neurons: An educator's guide to the human brain.* Alexandria, VA: Association for Supervision and Curriculum Development.

Tobin, L. (1991). *What do you do with a child like this? Inside the lives of troubled children.* Duluth, MN: Whole Person Associates.

Wassermann, S. (1990). *Serious players in the primary classroom: Empowering children through active learning experiences.* New York: Teachers College Press.

Weinreb, M. L. (1997). Be a resiliency mentor: You may be a lifesaver for a high-risk child. *Young Children, 52*(2), 14–19.

Wheeler, E. (1994). *Peer conflicts in the classroom*. Urbana, IL: Clearinghouse on Elementary and Early Childhood Education. (ERIC Digest No. EDO-PS-94-13)

RECOMMENDED RESOURCES FOR MORE CARING, REFLECTIVE TEACHING

Brogue, E.G. (1991). *Journey of the heart: The call to teaching*. Bloomington, IN: Phi Delta Kappa.

Brophy, J. (1996). *Teaching problem students*. New York: Guilford.

Clark, C. M. (1995). *Thoughtful teaching*. New York: Teachers College Press.

Curtis, D., & Carter, M. (1996). *Reflecting children's lives: A handbook for planning child-centered curriculum*. St. Paul, MN: Redleaf Press.

Developmental Study Center (1997). *Blueprints for a collaborative classroom*. Oakland, CA: Author.

Erwin, E. J. (1996). *Putting children first: Visions for a brighter future for young children and their families*. Baltimore, MD: Paul H. Brookes.

Gallas, K. (1994). *The languages of learning: How children talk, write, dance, and sing their understanding of the world*. New York: Teachers College Press.

Hall, N. S., & Rhomberg, V. (1995). *The affective curriculum: Teaching the anti-bias approach to young children*. Scarborough, Ontario: International Thomson Publishing (ITP).

Jalongo, M. R., & Isenberg, J. P. (1995). *Teachers' stories: From personal narrative to professional insight*. San Francisco, CA: Jossey Bass.

Karns, M. (1994). *How to create positive relationships with students: A handbook of group activities and teaching strategies*. Champaign, IL: Research Press.

Kohn, A. (1996). *Beyond discipline: From compliance to community*. Alexandria, VA: Association for Supervision and Curriculum Development.

Lickona, T. (1992). *Educating for character: How our schools can teach respect and responsibility*. New York: Bantam.

Meier, D. R. (1997). *Learning in small moments: Life in an urban classroom*. New York: Teachers College Press.

Power, B. M., & Hubbard, R. S. (1996). *Oops! What we learn when our teaching fails*. York, ME: Stenhouse.

Rodd, J. (1996). *Understanding young children's behavior*. New York: Teachers College Press.

Saifer, S. (1990). *Practical solutions to practically every problem: The early childhood teacher's manual*. St. Paul, MN: Redleaf Press.

Smith, C. (1993). *The peaceful classroom: 162 easy activities to teach preschoolers compassion and cooperation*. Mt. Rainier, MD: Gryphon House.

Soronson, R., & Scott, J. (1997). *Teaching and joy*. Alexandria, VA: Association for Supervision and Curriculum Development.

Strachota, B. (1996). *On their side: Helping children take charge of their learning*. Greenfield, MA: Northeast Foundation for Children.

Tobin, L. (1991). *What do you do with a child like this? Inside the lives of troubled children*. Duluth, MN: Whole Person Associates.

Waterland, L. (1996). *The bridge to school: Entering a new world*. York, ME: Stenhouse.

Appendix G / Chapter 6

❧

The Nonfiction Book Production Process

❧

BOOK PROJECT PLANNING PHASE

Select a Publisher. Identify 2 or 3 publishing houses that would be a good fit for your idea and approach. Conduct a thorough search of books on the topic and make a chart that compares/contrasts existing works with your own.

Briefly discuss the idea with editors until you find one or more that is warmly receptive. Obtain the publisher's guidelines for a book prospectus.

Prepare a Prospectus. Develop a proposal, outline, and sample chapters. Keep in mind that a book prospectus is a piece of persuasive writing, designed to convince a publisher that the book will sell. Include your curriculum vita. Submit the prospectus and wait for the reviews of your proposal. Analyze them thoroughly and systematically prior to discussing the project with your editor. Keep careful notes of this discussion.

BOOK DEVELOPMENT PHASE

Refine Your Ideas. Remember that your goal is wide acceptance of your book. Address all objections or criticisms in some way, even those with which you may disagree. Strive to make your book even stronger than it was originally by capitalizing on strengths and minimizing flaws.

Request Permissions. You must request written permission for material that you wish to use in the book—unpublished work, photographs (if available), and, of course, copyrighted material beyond fair use. Keep a log of when the request was submitted, how much it will cost, and the credit line to be used. Make multiple copies of everything because you will need to submit the entire file with your completed book.

Produce the Remainder of the Book. Develop a plan for addressing the revision work and a timeline for generating the remaining chapters. Display deadlines prominently at your workspace and keep your editor apprised of your progress. Send the revised manuscript to your editor and await a response. Respond as necessary to any additional editing.

BOOK PRODUCTION PHASE

Submit the Entire Manuscript. Produce the complete, typed version of your entire book. Most publishers have a checklist that is used to make certain that everything necessary for book production is included in this package. Such things as the dedication, acknowledgements, permissions log, and all of the marketing/ advertising information typically are submitted at this time. Decide who is doing the index. If the publisher does it, it will be charged against royalties.

Correct/Revise the Manuscript. Brace yourself for the copy edit phase in which all of those little details and time consuming errors will be pointed out. Persist until the manuscript is as flawless as you can make it, even though you are exhausted. Remember that this is your last chance to make changes before the publisher charges you.

Proofread the Entire Manuscript. Take your time and proofread *everything*—even those things that you would normally overlook when reading a book, such as running heads and page numbers. Do not skip over tables, figures, charts, or graphs—errors can be introduced in the transition from your typed copy to the typeset copy. Try to break the proofreading into several shorter sessions instead of doing it all at once to avoid lapses in attention. If possible, get someone else with a critical eye to proofread too. At this point, only absolute errors of fact can be corrected.

Celebrate the completion of your book. Wait for it to appear in print and see it neatly typeset. Watch for the royalty statements to see how it does. Hope that it survives in a cruel marketplace.

ADDITIONAL RESOURCES

Germano, W. (2001). *Getting it published: A guide for scholars and anyone else serious about serious books.* Chicago: University of Chicago Press.

Appendix H / Chapter 7

❧

What Do Editors Want? What Do Editors Routinely Reject?

❧

Editors want the same thing that they imagine their readership wants, namely: 1) to acquire knowledge, 2) to amass experiences, 3) to read about themselves, 4) to be up on the latest, and 5) to be prepared for the future (Applebaum & Evans, 1982).

"I want to see ground uncovered, not just covered. I accept pieces that are thoughtful, that encourage the audience to think more deeply about a topic, to take a second look. . . . They should be fresh in the sense that they give us new eyes to see with and new ideas to think with" (J. Harste quoted in *Writing for Language Arts*, 1997, p. 274).

"Authors can advocate 'old' ideas as long as they do it in a wide-awake way, arguing for their value by showing how these 'old' ideas really fit in with recent research or perhaps how they contradict certain more recent research or theory that they find to be wrong" (C. Edelsky quoted in *Writing for Language Arts*, 1997, p. 274).

"to appeal to the reader's interest does not mean to salute their every prejudice. No editor should make that mistake. . . . But the challenge should be to their (the readers') beliefs, not to their patience" (Plotnick, 1982, p. 26).

WHAT DO EDITORS ROUTINELY REJECT?

Read the following introductory paragraph as an illustration of what to avoid—verbosity and pomposity, emotionally charged words, convoluted sentences, muddy logic, awkward constructions, and punctuation errors. In addition to all of these writing flaws, the manuscript was entirely inappropriate for the intended journal's audience. This author was writing about sports programs for children, such as little league. Here is how the author began:

> By painful experience we have learned that rational educational approaches do not suffice to solve the problems of our youth sport programs. Painful and penetrating sports medicine research and keen psychological work have revealed tragic implications for youth sports, producing, on the one hand experiences which have liberated youth from the tedium of the classroom, making childhood richer and fuller. Yet, on the other hand, such has introduced a grave restlessness into childhood, making youth a slave to the athletic establishment. However, most catastrophic of all, is the created means for the mass destruction of integrative academic and fruitful opportunities of childhood and youth. This, indeed is a tragedy of overwhelming poignancy a secular, distorted perspective during the developmental years of childhood and adolescence.

To earn acceptance from editors, make your writing less like this.

REFERENCES

Applebaum, J., & Evans, N. (1982). *How to get happily published*. New York: Plume/American Library.

Writing for Language Arts: Editor, Editorial Review Board, and Editorial Staff (1997). *Language Arts*, 74(4), 273-278.

Plotnick, A. (1982). *The elements of editing: A modern guide for editors and journalists*. New York: Macmillan.

APPENDIX I

❦

Common Questions About Writing

❦

"How can I tell if I have talent as a writer?"

Many writers are stalled even before they begin; they are too preoccupied with worrying about wasting their time to get much writing accomplished. Yet writing talent can only be uncovered through writing. When you write,

> You'll discover what your strengths and weaknesses are as a writer. You'll learn through hands-on experience what comes easily to you and what gives you the most trouble. And you'll find out what genres, styles, subjects and parts of the writing process give you the most pleasure. Don't try to come to any conclusions too soon. Just keep writing, and observe. The answers will emerge on their own. (Edelstein, 1999, p. 12)

"How do you make the time?"

Kenneth Atchity reminds us of the authors whose output has been astonishing, such as Ray Bradbury, Neil Simon, Joyce Carol Oates, and John Gardner. He then explains that these works were accomplished because these authors:

"Weren't deflected from their priorities by activities of lesser importance. The work continues, even though everything else may have to give. . . . When people ask them, 'Where do you find the time?' they wonder, 'Where do you lose it?'" (Winokur, 1999, p. 47)

Think about where your time might be wasted. Many accomplished writers, for example, find small talk aversive. They want to talk about big ideas or share interesting stories rather than discuss the weather, the local news, or sporting events at length. They are not familiar with every popular television show and do not turn the set on first thing in the morning and last thing at night. They do not invest more time than is absolutely necessary in routine tasks. Rather, they zealously guard their time—particularly that period of the day when their minds are at their productive peak. They hack out blocks of unscheduled time, even if it means acquiring a reputation for being ever-so-slightly antisocial. Writers schedule writing time because,

> How we spend our days, of course, is how we spend our lives. What we do with this hour, and that one, is what we are doing. A schedule defends from chaos and whim. It is a net for catching days. It is a scaffolding on which a worker can stand and labor with both hands at sections of time. A schedule is a mock-up of reason and order—willed, faked, and so brought into being; it is a peace and a haven set into the wreck of time; it is a lifeboat on which you find yourself, decades later, still living. (Dillard, 1998, p. 14)

"How do authors get the self-discipline?"

When it comes to producing an unsolicited manuscript, no editor is waiting impatiently at the mailbox for your envelope to arrive. You can go throughout your workday and, chances are, unless you are a college professor, your writing can be placed low on the "to do" list without incident. Believing in your topic and yourself is a start at discipline. Later, the discipline can emanate from the knowledge that you have experienced some success with writing. Diane Ackerman, author of the book and PBS series, *A History of the Senses*, observes, "There are yards of writers under the age of thirty but not many who stay the course. The ones who do aren't necessarily the most gifted but those who can focus well, discipline themselves, persevere through hard times, and spring back after rejections that would cripple others" (Winokur, 1999, p. 26).

"How do you begin putting words on the page?"

The most frustrated writers are those who treat writing like an invasion of bedbugs: they flail around and fear the bites. Learn to quiet your mind in the same way that you deliberately make your body still (Brande, 1981). Many successful authors approach the task of writing in a meditative state, even if they don't label it as such. They have trained themselves to "work on in full calmness and serenity, as regularly and concentratedly as possible" (Ueland, 1987, p. 22). Figure out what conditions tend to put you in a relaxed, yet alert frame of mind. Write then.

"What is the best way to identify a topic?"

Choose a topic that ignites a passionate curiosity. Historian David McCullough advises that you'll know you have found your subject matter for a project when you are in a kind of love affair with your topic such that "it reaches out and takes you; it lights the imagination" (Lamb, 1997, p. 55). There are times when you may not exactly love the topic, such as when writing about child abuse or censorship, but still it must have the power to draw you in. A good topic is as nagging as a chipped tooth: it is an incessant distraction, you cannot resist examining it repeatedly, and you will not rest until its mysteries are revealed. Paul West (interviewed by Adams, 1998) puts it this way: "You write about the thing that sank its teeth into you and wouldn't let go" (p. 212).

Above all, don't work on a topic and focus that fails to capture your interest. Graduate students often resurrect papers that they have written at someone else's behest and try to make them into publishable pieces. The trouble with this is that, as Stewart (1998) points out, "your lack of enthusiasm, I can almost guarantee, will be painfully apparent in your finished work. Writing is never entirely painless, but satisfying one's curiosity should certainly be one of its great pleasures" (p. 86).

"When is it okay to use 'I'?"

Most of us have been trained to avoid using the first person pronoun in our writing. In secondary school, our teachers discouraged us from using "I" because it often was the easy way out. A book review became "I didn't like it" or a research paper deteriorated into unsubstantiated opinion "I think . . ." Later, during professional training, we were urged to humbly cite the big name sources rather than venture an opinion ourselves. Writing about yourself in an unabashed way can smack of self-promotion or become self-indulgent. Besides, when you use "I," that aura of objectivity begins to dissipate and the word "I" forces you to take personal responsibility for what you have written.

For all of these reasons, "I" is often avoided in academic and professional writing where the writer is expected to provide "just the facts" and function as an impartial expert. But conventional wisdom about the first person can be taken to extremes and result in affectations—the royal "we" in the field of English ("We see in Faulkner's work . . .), the passive construction ("Initial efforts have been made to . . . "), the disembodied writer ("One must ask oneself . . . "), or the faceless persona ("The researcher determined that . . . ").

A sociologist had this to say about her struggle to connect with published research:

> I was still finding myself feeling disconnected and excluded from some of the texts I was asked to read. I puzzled over jargony and pretentious scholarly articles, filled with lifeless, boring prose where people were replaced by abstract categories and faceless group identities, by symbols and numbers, and where actions happened miraculously, without anyone taking responsibility for them. I wanted to read about real human beings. . . . I asked myself then—and continue to ask . . . where are the people in some of this academic babble? (Casanave, 1997 p. 193)

> I don't mean to say that I expect authors to narrate personal experiences and feelings in everything they write. Even without a first person confessional from them, I believe I can experience an author, and certain histories, intentions, and passions that emanate from them in well-written prose. (Casanave, 1997, p. 197)

When writing for professional audiences, avoid "I" when it is not suitable or necessary. Suppose you were asked to write a position statement for a professional organization. In that case, you are a spokesperson for the group and "I" would be inappropriate. On the other hand, when you want to give an example and it is not important for readers to know that it is your experience, you could write, "A professor . . . " or, if you want to identify yourself as part of a group, you might write, "As educators, we . . . " William Zinsser (1998) points out that "Even when 'I' isn't permitted, it's still possible to convey a sense of I-ness. . . . Good writers are visible just behind their words. If you aren't allowed to use 'I,' at least think 'I' while you write. . . . It will warm up your impersonal style" (p. 22). You may have noticed that some of the "big fish" in your field use "I" more liberally without invoking criticism. I suspect this is because they have paid their dues and are established as authorities; now they can relax the unwritten rules a bit. So, particularly for the new writer in the professional literature, use "I" rather sparingly, reserving it for instances where it is essential to establishing credibility (e.g., "I have been a practicing psychologist who works with adolescents for the past 13 years.").

"I've been rejected many times. Should I give up?"

Rejection is an inescapable part of writing, particularly at first. It should not be taken as an indication that you are unsuited to the writing life. I like Dorothea Brande's (1981) advice to aspiring writers. She suggests two exercises: first, to deliberately write in that twilight zone between wakefulness and sleep (although she insists on early morning, it might be evening for you) and second, to make a writing appointment with yourself that will not be cancelled except in a real emergency. If you cannot do these two things, find something else to do. Where rejections are concerned, perhaps the best attitude is expressed by Samuel Beckett: "Ever tried? Ever failed? No matter. Try again. Fail again. Fail better" (Winokur, 1999, p. 52).

"What is the best way to find a focus?"

It is a common misconception that you need to have your thesis clearly formulated before you begin, but that is not always the case. Often the material suggests a focus to you as you write. Gail Godwin explains how writing "one true thing" can help through the following passage (somewhat autobiographical), from her novel. The character is a college student who is frustrated by her efforts to write a college term paper:

> She began to panic, as she used to, long ago, whenever she had to write a book report for school. One night she had worked herself into hysterics because she couldn't get the first sentence of her book report. Daddy had taken her downstairs to his study and sat her down on his leather sofa with a soft, sharp pencil and one of his brand-new legal pads. "Now all you have to do is write me down one true thing about that book," Daddy said. "Just write down one true thing about that book."(National Book Award Authors, 1995, p. 6)

"Writers always recommend that you read. That makes sense. But what, exactly, should you be reading?"

Stephen King (2000) suggests that you read a full range of material:

> So we read to experience the mediocre and the downright rotten; such experience helps us to recognize those things when they begin to creep into our own work, and to steer clear of them. We also read in order to measure ourselves against the good and the great, to get a sense of all that can be done. And we read in order to experience different styles. . . . The more you read, the less apt you are to make a fool of yourself with your pen or word processor. (p. 147, 150)

Equally important is *how* you read:

> A civilian reads for entertainment, information, solace. A writer reads for all these, and for craft and technique and tricks of the trade. A writer reads critically, noting what works and what doesn't, silently cheering the arabesques and booing the clunkers, quibbling about the choice of a word here and the use of a semicolon there, always judging. . . . a writer is always watching, even when he's reading. (Winokur, 1999, p. ix).

"How teachable is writing?"

That depends on how you define writing. If you mean to ask, "Can you take an ordinary person and train him or her to be a poet laureate?" my answer would be no. I believe that type of writing to be inspired and doubt that even the best of teachers could elicit writing performance at that level. I have a former writing student who won *The Atlantic Monthly's* award for the best student writer, but I take no credit for it. On the other hand, if you mean to ask, "Can a competent professional with keen insight and graduate school-level writing skills be taught to write informative and thought-provoking prose for fellow professionals?" then my answer would be, "Yes, providing that she or he has the motivation to take on the task and the persistence to work at it over a period of time until something like a pattern of success has been built."

Mostly, what writing teachers do is serve as readers who hold up a mirror and say, as John Casey puts it, "Here is what all those marks on a page meant to me." (National Book Award Authors, 1995, p. 61).

The good news is that writing style tends to be fairly malleable. Just as a western drawl or southern accent is affected if a speaker spends long periods of time back east, writing style is shaped by what we read. If you doubt that this is the case, read several books with a very distinctive style, such as books written by newspaper journalists. Then write something. If you are like most people, your writing sample will show traces of what you have been reading lately. You need not enroll in a credit-bearing course to get better as a writer. Models and mirrors may be sufficient.

"I've heard that editors frequently prefer the shorter, more concise pieces. Why?"

As Casey notes, "I can't explain why shortness is a good thing. I can only think of how many gallons of maple sap it takes to make one gallon of maple syrup— forty. Maple sap tastes like water—very good water, but water. Maple syrup is a miracle" (National Book Award Authors, 1995, p. 68). Editors will take the miracle over the water every time.

One way to be concise is to choose details that speak volumes. Stephen King's (2000) brief description of his brother's approach to Science Fair projects, for example, tells us quite a bit about Dave in short order:

> My big brother wasn't the sort of boy to content himself drawing frog diagrams on construction paper or making The House of the Future out of plastic Tyco bricks and painted red toilet-tissue rolls; Dave aimed for the stars. His project that year was Dave's Super Duper Electromagnet. My brother had great affection for things which were super duper and things which began with his own name. . . . (p. 32)

"I can't seem to tell how my writing is going while I am doing it. Can you help?"

At first, this is one of the greatest challenges the writer confronts. How can you tell when you are following a productive lead versus going off track, for instance? I tend to experiment with different versions of a piece and leave them on my computer until I decide which path is most fruitful. About this, Edelstein (1999) says: "Writing is usually a matter of feeling your way, line by line and page by page. Much of the time, you simply won't know whether something will work until after you've written it" (p. 54).

Some writers are appalled by such answers—"You mean I might take the time to write something and not even use it?" Yet, think about how a choreographer, a gymnast, or a figure skater arrives at a program. They try out many moves and combinations, then select the best. What makes you think you should work any less hard at the computer? What makes you think you should have any more certainty about how to proceed?

"I am frankly surprised by all this talk of audience. It seems that, as a professional, you are obligated to be an expert and impart information, not try to be entertaining."

Consider the situation of Ron Chernow, who decided to write a popular book on the history of banking in America. When he shared his idea with others at a party, they treated him as if he had lost his mind. In preparation for the task, he read about 200 books on banking history, "most of them written in deadly, leaden prose" (National Book Award Authors, 1995, p. 180). Should he contribute to what he described as dusty heaps in the most mildew-ridden and least used corners of libraries, or should he strive to write something someone might want to read? His response was a best seller and award-winner, *The House of Morgan*. As far as concerns about audience go, Chernow remarked, "I didn't assume that my readers would be kindly or tolerant souls. I pictured them as humorless sadists with short attention spans, who would keep glancing at their watches. . . . So I had to work the whole bag of writer tricks: I crooned, hoofed, juggled, swallowed fire, balanced boxes, spun saucers, did cartwheels—anything to keep the restive crowd under the Big Top" (National Book Award Authors, 1995, p.180). The result was no lightweight book, literally or figuratively.

Writing for an audience does not mean that you pander to the lowest tastes or resort to scandal sheet style. It means that you care enough to resist donning the mantle of scholarship as an excuse for dull prose. Contrary to what you have heard or what poorly written textbooks may have implied, it doesn't take ponderous prose to be "serious." Remember that your purpose in writing, even when you are writing as an expert on a nonfiction topic, is not to show off but to share your ideas in a spirit of generosity (Ueland, 1987).

"What differentiates ordinary writing from writing with style?"

Think about how you might write an essay in which you complain about the problems associated with travel. Now read how E. Annie Proulx captures the hazards of travel with wry wit.

> Travel, any kind of travel, is an unnerving experience. Drive and there are the serial killer highways, the chance of running out of gas at midnight in Idaho, sticking in mud wallows, dodging tornadoes or outrunning blizzards, eating cruel food in Mud Butte or Biloxi. Fly, and it is paralysis in boa-constrictor seats, headache from oxygen deprivation, the salmonella sandwich, babble of a seatmate who has just started a religious cult and needs followers, ice on the wings, lost luggage. (National Book Award Authors, 1995, p. 105)

Effective writing, academic or otherwise, has a certain unpredictability and element of surprise. To write with style, first be "a good date for your reader" (K. Vonnegut, quoted in Safire & Safir, 1994, p. 64); create something of interest and value (Robinson, in National Book Award Authors, 1995); get below the surface, which is really the writer's job (McCullough, in Lamb, 1997, p. 55); and never write a bad sentence, if you can help it (Begley, in National Book Award Authors, 1995). Novelist Kurt Vonnegut (1994) offers this final bit of advice about style: "Find a subject you care about and which you in your heart feel others should care about. It is this genuine caring, and not your games with language, which will be the most compelling and seductive element in your style" (p. 240).

How important is the title?

Sometimes you will know the title before you write the manuscript and other times you will be nearly finished and in search of a title. Don't obsess about the perfect title, just give it a working title and write on. Even if you have a great title, something can be lost in the translation. M. E. Kerr (1998) reports than when the title of John Steinbeck's great novel, *The Grapes of Wrath*, was translated into Japanese it became *The Angry Raisins*!

Generally speaking, a good title in nonfiction 1) is concise and understandable, 2) piques the reader's curiosity, 3) sets appropriate expectations for the content, 4) attracts the intended members of the audience, and 5) hints at the scope of the work and the point of view (Provost, 1985). Stop-and-read-this titles often capture the essential tensions surrounding a topic rather than being "all about ____".

"I've heard the advice to 'show, rather than tell the reader,' but I'm still not clear on what that means."

Suppose that someone asked you to summarize your early life experience. Most inexperienced authors would feel obligated to begin with birth and write a chronological account of their lives, based on some timeline of events. But would that approach give readers the emotional essence of the experience? Would it be the purest way to tell the story? Here is how Bob Shacochis *shows* the reader what it meant to him to have Lithuanian heritage:

> My story is very much the story of twentieth-century America, a story of immigration, of Ellis Island, of ethnic disadvantage, of having no alternative but to hammer a new world and a new life into existence; a story of upward mobility, of each generation sacrificing itself to provide a springboard for the next. The emblems of my tribe are pinochle and kielbasa and pickled mushrooms; old ladies with babushkas wrapped tight around their skulls, a cross of ashes smeared on their dry foreheads; the cidery, cabbage-and-coal smell of the Baltics; the sound of a language that was not English; the disillusioning climb away from poverty; outsiders grasping for the mainstream; children being educated irreversibly out of reach, beyond the world of their parents. (National Book Award Authors, 1995, p. 123)

These two sentences not only strike me as emotionally honest and poignant, they are also evocative. I find myself immersed in thoughts about my ethnic roots and reflecting on other writers' accounts of the consequences of embracing American culture.

"Is there a way to work more efficiently?"

Learn to write in your head. Writing in your head is like mental mathematical computations—it does not consist of writing each symbol down, it consists of working out a problem. Gary Provost (1985) offers this advice on writing more efficiently by writing in your head:

> Clear up the inconsistencies while you are brushing your teeth. Get your thoughts organized while you're driving to work. Think of a slant during lunch. And most important, come up with a beginning, a lead, so that you won't end up staring at your typewriter as if you had just arrived from another galaxy. If you have spent time writing in your head, you'll have a head start. The writing will come easier, and you'll finish sooner. (p. 14)

"It must get somewhat easier to write, otherwise, how would some authors become so prolific?"

I had a friend who became a marathon runner. At first, she ran around the track, gradually increasing the number of laps. Next, she ran a mile. Eventually, she ran in marathons. Writers are comparable to athletes in training. At first, it may seem torturous to spend an hour composing but, with practice and encouragement, you'll learn to tolerate longer stints of writing. No matter how well conditioned you may be, you will always break a sweat. A trained writer has built up the endurance take on more demanding writing tasks and complete them. But whether you are a marathon writer or a marathon runner, the measure of your success is doing more, not doing less. Another distinction between the more and less experienced is the determination and confidence to go the distance.

"How do you know when your topic and focus are right?"

Don't sabotage your writing efforts by getting too serious too soon. Many inexperienced authors are like people desperate to get married—they want to skip over the wooing and extract a commitment almost immediately. The consequences are much the same: for the person in search of a mate, possible spouses are frightened away; for the writer, a topic and focus that aren't the perfect match are doggedly pursued. Learn to play the field where writing is concerned. Entertain many suitors before you settle on one, and don't be afraid to break off the relationship with your topic if it ultimately disappoints you.

"If writing for publication does not prove to be lucrative, why bother?"

Think about the things that you have written already. How did the act of writing shape your ideas? Gail Godwin (National Book Award Authors, 1995) reminds us that we arrive at realizations in the midst of struggles with writing, digress into reveries sparked by the topic, and acquire a keener vision built from personal observations, rather than secondhand ones.

Creative work is worthwhile because it is good for your mind in the same way that being healthy is good for your body. As Ueland (1987) notes, "With every sentence you write, you have learned something. It has done you good. It has stretched your understanding. I know that. Even if I knew for certain that I would never have anything published again, and would never make another cent from it, I would keep on writing" (p. 16). Jane Bernstein (1998) is candid about the attraction of writing for those of us who never have a best seller: "The rewards: no fame, not much in the way of recognition, but the immense satisfaction of a single reader who says, 'You found the words for me.' Or, 'This is my life, too.'"(p. 219).

Which of these responses validated what you already knew? Which were surprising? Why?

REFERENCES

Adams, B. (1998). A stylist's delight: A conversation with Paul West. In L. Gutkind (Ed.), *The essayist at work: Profiles of creative nonfiction writers* (pp. 199-213). Portsmouth, NH: Heinemann.

Bernstein, J. (1998). How and why. In L. Gutkind (Ed.), *The essayist at work: Profiles of creative nonfiction writers* (pp. 214-219). Portsmouth, NH: Heinemann.

Brande, D. (1981/1934). *Becoming a writer.* New York: Tarcher/Putnam.

Casanave, C. P. (1997). Body-mergings: Searching for connections with academic discourse. In C. P. Casanave & S. R. Schecter (Eds), *On becoming a language educator: Personal essays on professional development* (pp. 187-200). Mahwah, NJ: Lawrence Erlbaum Associates.

Dillard, A. (1998). Schedules. In L. Gutkind, (Ed.), *The essayist at work: Profiles of creative nonfiction writers* (pp. 14-22). Portsmouth, NH: Heinemann.

Edelstein, S. (1999). *100 things every writer needs to know.* New York: Perigree.

Kerr, M. E. (1998). *Blood on the forehead: What I know about writing.* New York: Harper-Collins.

King, S. (2000). *On writing: A memoir of the craft.* New York: Scribner.

Lamb, B. (1997) *Booknotes.* New York: Times.

National Book Award Authors (1995). *The writing life.* New York: Random House.

Provost, G. (1985). *100 ways to improve your writing.* New York: Mentor/New American Library.

Safire, W., & Safir, L. (Eds.) (1994). *Good advice on writing.* New York: Simon & Schuster.

Stewart, J. B. (1998). *Follow the story: How to write successful nonfiction.* New York: Touchstone/ Simon & Schuster.

Ueland, B. (1987/1938). *If you want to write: A book about art, independence and spirit.* St. Paul, MN: Graywolf Press.

Winokur, J. (1999). *Advice to writers.* New York: Vintage Books.

Zinsser, W. (1998). *On writing well* (6th ed.). New York: HarperPerennial.

Index

About the Author

Mary Renck Jalongo is the author or co-author of 18 books with major publishers, including Prentice Hall, Allyn & Bacon, Jossey-Bass, and Teachers College Press. Her work is targeted to many different audiences, including elementary school students who refer to *The World Book Encyclopedia*; preservice teachers who are studying about children's creativity (*Creative Expression and Play in Early Childhood*, now going into its fourth edition); and advanced college students enrolled in research methods courses (*Annual Editions 2000-2001: Research Methods*, Dushkin/McGraw-Hill, 2000).

Mary Renck Jalogo is also a contributor to professional journals, including such publications as *Childhood Education*, *Educational Leadership*, *The Reading Teacher*, *The Educational Forum*, and *Young Children*. Some of these articles have been recognized through national awards, including two EDPRESS Association awards for "Outstanding Feature Article," and a "Best Essay" award from the American Association for Higher Education. Also, as the editor-in-chief of *Early Childhood Education Journal*, published by Kluwer Academic Press, she writes four editorials per year and edits the manuscripts of scholar/authors in education, psychology, social work, and health care from around the world.

Dr. Jalongo lends her support to other writers by teaching a doctoral seminar on writing for publication, collaborating with graduate and undergraduate students on writing projects, and serving as a reviewer for colleagues' work at Indiana University of Pennsylvania, where she is a professor. Additionally, Mary Renck Jalongo is a frequent presenter at national and international conferences on the topic of writing for publication.

DATE